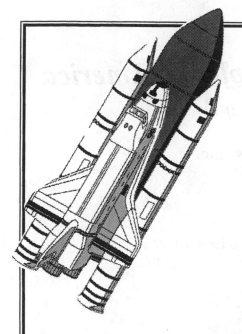

The People, Places and Principles of AMERICA

The Defending of America

Volume IV of IV
Chapters 10-12

The People, Places and Principles of America
(with reading enhancement)

Published by
Paradigm Alternative Centers, Inc.
Dublin, Texas U.S.A.

All rights reserved.
Contact Paradigm about other courses in
English, Science and Social Studies for grades 8-10.
Training in the Paradigm philosophy
and method is also available.

For information contact:
Paradigm Alternative Centers, Inc.
P.O. Box 200, Dublin, Texas 76446
www.pacworks.com
learn@pacworks.com

PAC
™

ISBN: 1-928629-03-2
Volume: IV of IV

This text is a part of an entire family of books for American History & Reading Enhancement; The four texts are:
The Discovering (item: 62900), *The Designing* (item: 62901), *The Defining* (item: 62902), *The Defending* (item: 62903);
four corresponding booklets: *Activities, Quizzes and Tests* (items: 62904, 62905, 62906, 62907);
and one booklet: *Answer Keys* (item: 62908).

PROFESSIONAL CREDITS

The Defending of America
Volume IV of IV

Publisher and Managing Editor
Ronald Johnson, Ph.D.

Production
H. Michael Young, Manager

Page Composition
Randy Burch
Hugh Johnson

Activities and Tests
Wilson Gauntt
Nancy Johnson, Editor
Ginger Johnson
Sarah Johnson
Crystal Wade

Graphics
Randy Burch
Connie Watson
Shara Wright
H. Michael Young

Quality Assurance
Nanci Budge
Carolyn Hood
Nancy Johnson
Sarah Johnson
Lisa Weber
Nora Young

Writing Team Coordinator
Lena Nelson Dooley

Writers

Janet Barr	Linda Edwards	Paul Thrower
Myretta Bell	Tim Haynes	Oleta M. Thrower
Carol Bennett	Virginia Haynes	Laura Winter
Nancy B. Carr	Nancy Johnson	Mark Winter

AUTHENTICITY

The People, Places and Principles of America is a product of Paradigm Alternative Centers, Inc., Dublin, Texas, U.S.A. A team of 28 researchers, writers, artists and editors produced the four volume course of American History in a three-and-a-half year period. Careful attention was devoted to addressing the essential academic elements expected of a high school course in American History. Research for this course revealed an astounding amount of references to Judeo-Christian terms used by America's Founding Fathers. Original documents indicate that the majority of men and women involved in establishing America were indeed very religious people. The publisher has attempted to be accurate and fair by including ample references to the religious beliefs of the Founding Fathers, but has omitted a great many more references in order to assure that the material complies with criteria regarding religion in public schools. Dates, names, events and places were confirmed primarily through *What Happened When* by Gorton Carruth, (Signet, 1989 New York, New York) and *America's God and Country* by William J. Federer (FAME Publishing, Inc., 1994 Coppell, Texas) as well as primary source documents. Events of recent years were substantiated through a variety of contemporary periodicals and books.

Stylebook, A Usage Guide for Writers and Editors (U.S. News & World Report 1997) was used as the official policy for grammar, punctuation and appropriate use of terms for ethnic, political and religious groups.

Life Principles were collected from numerous sources. Effort was made to locate authorship for principles identified by the term anonymous. Proper credit will be assigned in subsequent editions if the editor receives authenticating notification in writing. Art consists of work-for-hire pieces, works of antiquity and public domain clip art made available by commercial suppliers.

VOLUME FOUR
Table of Contents

Chapter Eleven 85

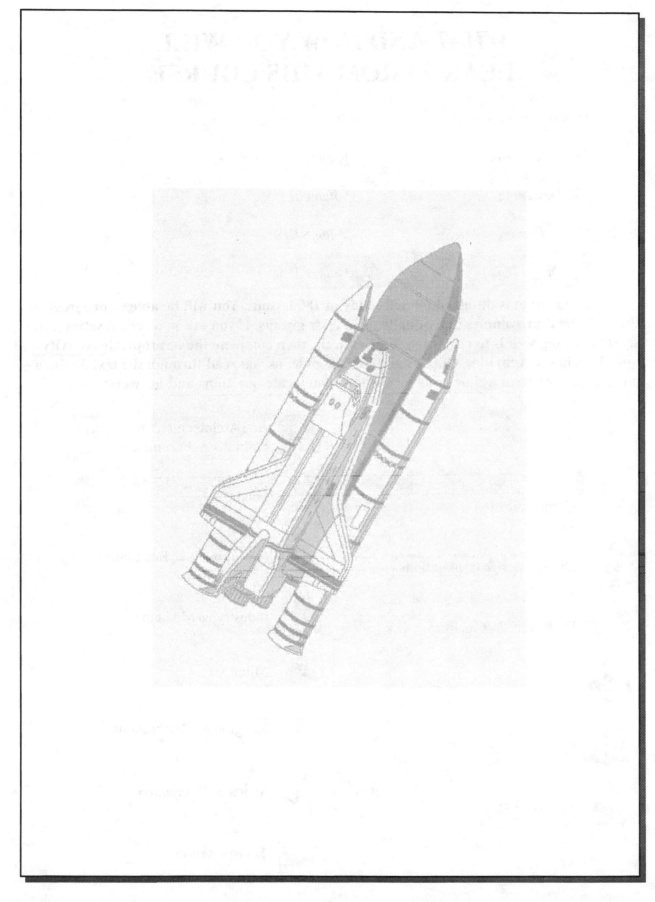

WHAT AND *HOW* YOU WILL LEARN FROM THIS COURSE

This study of *America* is presented in four volumes.

The Discovering   *Volume I*

The Designing   *Volume II*

The Defining   *Volume III*

The Defending   *Volume IV*

The format is designed for self-study of 180 lessons. You will be able to progress through the four volumes individually or in class groups. If you are in a school setting, the secret to doing well is to read each topic entirely, then complete the appropriate Activity questions in the Activities, Quizzes and Tests booklet as you read through the text again, a paragraph or two at a time. Topic icons help you locate questions and answers:

 Agriculture

 Art, Architecture, Fashions & Furniture

 Communication

 Food

 Discoveries & Explorations

 Government & Economics

 Dominant Personalities

 Industry & Medicine

 Education & Literature

 Military

 Light & Energy

 Religion & Celebrations

 Family & Home

 Sports & Recreation

 Transportation

Each Volume (or unit) is divided into three chapters. Each chapter is further divided into three sections of five topics each: (Volume I; Chapter 1; Section 1; Topics 1-5). The course is designed in a "textazine" (texbook/magazine) format so you will enjoy your study of America. Topics are written in vignette style (short stories) that can usually be read in a few minutes. You are encouraged to read each topic completely, then respond to the activity questions which are packaged in the booklet: *Activities, Quizzes and Tests*. You may answer the questions directly on each activity page, or answer the questions on a separate sheet of notebook paper. Your teacher will inform you of local school policy.

Answers to activity questions are contained in a booklet labeled: *Answer Keys*. The keys are divided by chapter and section number. Your teacher will inform you about policies for grading activity questions.

A section quiz is assigned by your teacher at the end of every 5 topics. Your teacher will issue each chapter test after you complete all 15 topics (after the third quiz). The chapter test is compiled from the three quizzes. Students who score 85% or higher on the three section quizzes may not have to take the chapter test.

A mid-course exam (Volumes I and II) and a final exam (Volumes III and IV) are available in *Activities, Quizzes and Tests*.

The entire course consists of 230 assignments: 180 lessons, 36 quizzes, 12 chapter tests, 1 mid course and 1 final exam. Students who want to complete the course in one school year will work six lessons (activities) plus one quiz each week.

Activity questions identified with an underline (example: **25**.) will appear on quizzes and tests. Activity questions and skills identified with an *asterisk* (example: ***25**.) are essential academic elements or skills which may appear on state exams.

Life principles, time lines, quotes and historical selections will be included on quizzes and chapter tests. When you turn in your activity questions, you may be required to quote the life principles or historical selections to your teacher.

Vocabulary words are identified at the beginning of each topic and are noted in bold, italics type within the text. You will be required to know vocabulary words.

The last few sentences in each vignette are in bold letters and are designed to give you an introduction and smooth transition to the next subject.

Ask your teacher about the *Academic Contract*, *Academic Objective Chart* and *Transcript Planner* included at the back of the Answer Key Booklet. These forms are provided to help you plan your daily work.

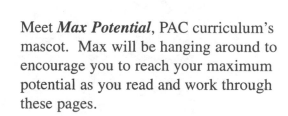

Meet ***Max Potential***, PAC curriculum's mascot. Max will be hanging around to encourage you to reach your maximum potential as you read and work through these pages.

The Defending of America

Teddy Roosevelt's charge up San Juan Hill, Santiago de Cuba in 1898, demonstrated the manner in which America would defend freedom during the 20th Century. "The war to end all wars" between 1917 and 1918 (WWI) did not accomplish that objective. Out of the ash heaps of Germany rose the Third Reich of Hitler. The Nazi military force marched across Europe while Japanese bombers obliterated the U.S. Navy and Air Force in the Phillippines and Hawaii. America was drawn into WWII and successfully defended freedom worldwide against the awfulness of Fascism and Nazism. Then from 1950 into the 21st century, American military personnel were called upon to defend freedom against Communism and dictators in Asia, Central America, the Middle East, Europe and North Africa. Citizens in medicine and industry applied their efforts to defend America against disease and economic depression.

Cannons and missiles were not the only weapons used to defend American freedom. Other patriots used radio, television, books, marches and assembly halls to oppose people, ideologies or actions which attempted to chip away at America's core values and principles. Volume IV puts into focus the scope of America's defenders.

The Defending of America
1917-1947

The People, Places and Principles of America

Chapter 10

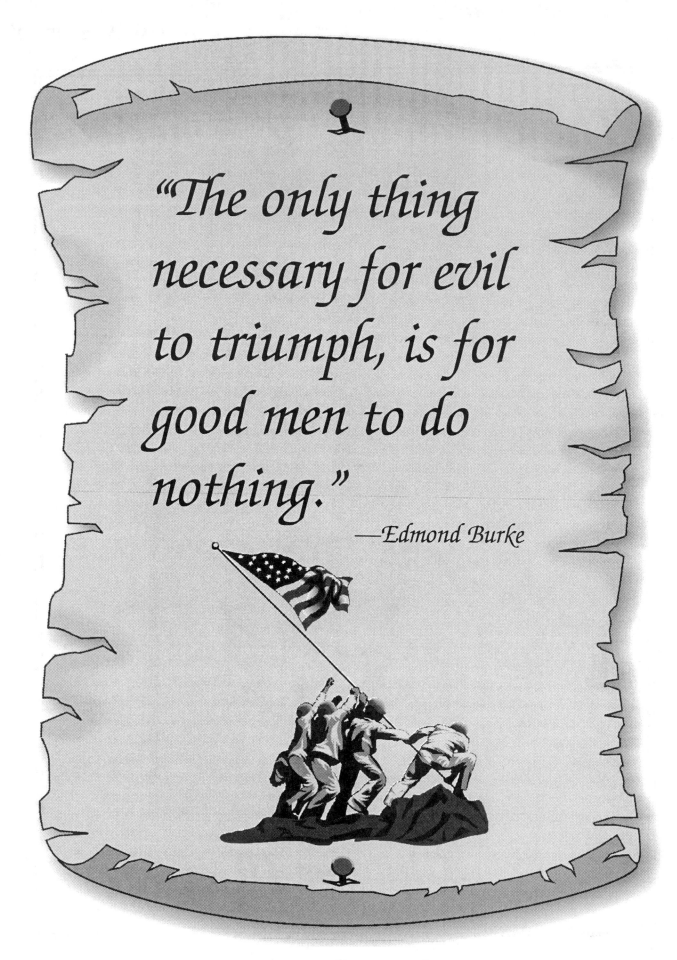

"The only thing necessary for evil to triumph, is for good men to do nothing."

—Edmond Burke

CHAPTER 10
TABLE OF CONTENTS

Chapter 10
Time Line 1917-1947

*Use this time line for referencing important
dates throughout the chapter.*

1917 *Bolshevik Revolution in Russia*

1918 *World War I ended*

1919 *Cummins Engine Company Founded*

1920 *First Successful Radio Station*

1926 *Richard Byrd Flew over the North Pole*

1927 *Mount Rushmore Dedicated;
Lindbergh Flew Spirit of St. Louis*

1928 *Kellogg-Briand Pact*

1930-1933 *Worst time of the
Great Depression*

1930s *Monopoly Board Game
Invented*

1932 *Empire State Building
Finished*

1935 *Social Security Act*

1947 *First Black Professional
Baseball Player
(Jackie Robinson)*

The Defending of America

Topic 1
Family
& Home

Chapter 10

Section One
Topics 1-5

THE PEOPLING OF AMERICA

By the early 1900s, the United States had become a genuine melting pot of *nationalities*. The freedoms enjoyed by U.S. citizens were desired by people around the world. Coming to America was the hope of downtrodden people. America meant not only freedom, but also opportunity to begin a new life. Many people gave up everything to experience America's opportunities. America represented all the hopes and dreams of distressed people all around the world. The Statue of Liberty in New York Harbor reflects the American attitude of friendship toward downtrodden *exiles* from war-torn nations. "The New *Colossus*" by Emma Lazarus is a poem which conveys the reason thousands of immigrants have sought citizenship in the United States of America since the statue was dedicated in 1886.

As steamships barreled into New York Harbor after weeks at sea, the thousands of hopeful immigrants who stood speechless on the ships' decks, were fascinated by an impressive figure rising above the harbor mist. A giant woman, the Statue of Liberty, *beckoned* "*Welcome*" to exhausted immigrants seeking better lives.

The Statue of Liberty was a gift from the people of France to the United States in recognition of the friendship established between the two countries during the American War for Independence. Designed by sculptor Frederic Bartholdi, the statue was commissioned to commemorate the centennial of the American Declaration of Independence. Officially named "Liberty Enlightening the World," the statue is lovingly known as "Lady Liberty." Rising higher than 305 feet from the ground to the tip of her uplifted torch, the Statue of Liberty is an awesome sight to behold upon arrival in America. In the crook of her left arm, "Lady Liberty" holds a book of law inscribed with the date of the United States' Independence, July 4, 1776. The seven spokes in her crown represent the seven continents of the world. To many of the immigrants traveling to America, the

VOCABULARY

Nationalities: belonging to a particular nation by origin, birth or naturalization
Exiles: those forced to leave their native countries
Colossus: something big or important
Beckoned: invited or attracted
Culmination: the final point, the end
Regimen: a system or course of action
Simultaneously: at the same time
Polygamist: someone who has more than one spouse at a time

Statue of Liberty was more than just a monument. "Lady Liberty" was a living symbol of freedom and inspired hope to the frightened, weary travelers.

The sight of the Statue of Liberty elicited a multitude of emotions from the immigrants who passed into New York Harbor. The impressive monument that symbolized freedom marked the *culmination* of a journey often years in the making. Immigrants saw the Statue of Liberty and thanked God. They had finally arrived after much hard work, sacrifice and danger. Perhaps the weary travelers thought about their sacrifices to come to America—money raised for passage . . . businesses sold, households shut down . . . meager life savings spent in hopes of joining husbands, wives and children. Many family members had not seen their relatives for years.

While many languages were spoken on each ship's deck, one word was understood by all: *America!* Soon most of those scared and excited passengers would begin a new life in a young country, in America, the land of their dreams. But their dreams could not become reality until they passed through Ellis Island, otherwise known as the Isle of Hopes, the Isle of Tears.

Almost daily since 1892, multitudes from Russia, Poland, Germany, the Middle East, Asia and many other countries made America their home. America's new residents represented a cross-section of almost every race, age, color, creed, religion and walk of life, such as: Julia Greenberg, who came from Russia in 1903 at age six . . . Manny Steen, who sailed from Ireland at age 19 . . . Axel Ohrn, a 13-year-old immigrant who left Sweden in 1925. More than one million such children, teenagers and adults came seeking refuge in America, often fleeing war, famine, poverty and political or religious persecution. When various nationalities from different backgrounds came together in one place, Ellis Island became a huge melting pot of diverse languages, ideologies and cultures. Most immigrants came to America for a better life, but ended up making America a better place.

The few immigrants traveling as first-or second-class passengers were allowed to disembark at Battery Park in New York City. However, most men, women and children had to pass through the immigration process at Ellis Island. On this tiny island (located just one mile south of Manhattan, New York) dreams were realized or destroyed.

Questioning, document checking and a thorough medical exam awaited immigrants at the 27½ acre Ellis Island complex. Most of those who passed through the island were admitted into the United States, but about 2 percent (or 1,000 individuals per year on average), were rejected for a variety of reasons: papers not in order, illness, or because they did not have the $25 required to prove financial security. Waiting could be the most agonizing part of the process for all who approached their turn, even though thousands of immigrants successfully progressed through the system.

A New York journalist equated an immigrant's arrival on Ellis Island to *"the final day of judgment, when we have to prove our fitness to enter Heaven."*

Barbara Barondess, a Russian Jewish immigrant in 1921, described the uncertainty and fear faced by people longing to become Americans: *"The time I spent on Ellis Island seemed like the longest waiting period for me because of the **regimen** . . . They weren't unkind, but you had no communication with the people who took care of you . . . and you had no communication with the other people that were there because everyone was so full of their own fright."*

Ellis Island

Ellis Island was designed to receive two shiploads of foreign passengers **simultaneously**. After disembarking, immigrants crowded into a large hall in a maze of lines to begin the questioning process. The main processing center at Ellis Island could handle 5,000 people each day. At the height of immigration, twice that many immigrants were processed. Those immigrants who passed the initial screening were separated into groups according to their destinations: New York City or elsewhere.

Depending on the decade and the political climate of America toward immigration, the line of questioning included the following: name, age, gender, marital status, occupation, nationality, last residence, destination. Questions pelted frightened immigrants: *"Can you read and write? Did you pay your own passage? Do you already have a job in the United States? Have you ever been in a poorhouse? Any deformities or serious illnesses? Are you a **polygamist**?"*

Medical examinations were a particularly unsettling aspect of the immigration process. One of the most common reasons for rejection was *trachoma*, a contagious disease of the eye that could cause blindness if left untreated. While most immigrants processed through Ellis Island in a matter of hours, some would be detained for days or weeks while papers were corrected or a family member recovered from an illness. Detainees slept in dormitories and ate in a large dining hall, anxiously awaiting approval to enter the United States.

Once allowed into the country, new Americans reunited with family members, joyfully embracing each other on American soil. Estelle Belford, who immigrated from Romania in 1905 when she was only five years old, recalled when her mother and father were reunited in New York: *"I remember my father putting his arms around my mother and the two of them standing a while and crying. And my father said to my mother, 'You're in America now and you have nothing to be afraid of. Nothing at all.'"*

Once approved for entry into America, immigrants rode a ferry into Battery Park on the Manhattan shoreline. The majority of immigrants stayed in New York City. Others traveled elsewhere to join friends and family who had already arrived. Sections of U.S. cities became communities for immigrants. In bigger cities like New York City and Boston, ethnic neighborhoods sprang up marked by distinct sights and smells of their inhabitants. Neighborhood names like "Little Italy" and "Chinatown" are still common.

Most immigrants worked very hard. Even though strenuous 12 hour days were common, immigrants felt they were better off in the United States than in their homelands. In America, immigrants could take advantage of many privileges and opportunities that were forbidden in other countries—privileges such as children receiving free education, industrious men or women opening businesses, and saving money to buy homes. Family units were strong, with children, parents and grandparents often living together, supporting each other as they established homes in the New World.

Immigrants receiving tickets

Restored in the 1980s, the buildings now house the Ellis Island Immigration Museum. The only transportation to the island is by ferryboat. Stepping onto Ellis Island is like stepping back in time. With the Statue of Liberty looming nearby, visitors can sense the excitement, fear and hope of men and women as they became new Americans willing to give everything to live in the "Land of Liberty."

People coming to America in the early 1900s did not realize that their new home was also on the brink of World War I. The next vignette will tell how the United States became involved in the world war that started in Europe.

VOCABULARY

Heritage: family traditions and lifestyles passed down from generations
Wretched: miserable, very unhappy, terribly poor

Adjusting to life in America, with a new language and strange customs to learn, was difficult, especially during the first few years. But even in awkward social and economic circumstances, immigrants developed strong patriotic loyalties toward their new homeland and were proud of their jobs and simple use of the English language.

Six decades of immigration through Ellis Island can truly be called "the peopling of America." Almost 40 percent of Americans today can trace their *heritage* to the twelve million people who passed through that tiny island. When immigration laws changed in 1954, the doors closed on Ellis Island.

"Those who turn back never reach the summit."
—H. Jackson Brown, Jr.

Life Principle

Memory Work

"The New Colossus"

Not like the brazen giant of Greek fame,
With conquering limbs astride from land to land;
Here at our sea-washed, sunset gates shall stand
A mighty woman with a torch, whose flame
Is the imprisoned lightning, and her name
Mother of Exiles. From her beacon-hand
Glows world-wide welcome; her mild eyes command
The air-bridged harbor that twin cities frame.
"Keep ancient lands, you stories pomp!" Cries she
With silent lips. **"Give me your tired, your poor,**
Your huddled masses yearning to breathe free,
The *wretched* refuse of your teeming shore.
Send these, the homeless, tempest-tost to me,
I lift my lamp beside the golden door!"

—By Emma Lazarus

**For a bonus of 10 points on the section
quiz, quote the bolded section of
"The New Colossus" to your teacher.**

9

The Defending of America

Topic 2
Military

Chapter 10

WORLD
WAR I

Section One
Topics 1-5

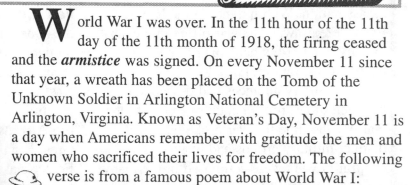

World War I was over. In the 11th hour of the 11th day of the 11th month of 1918, the firing ceased and the ***armistice*** was signed. On every November 11 since that year, a wreath has been placed on the Tomb of the Unknown Soldier in Arlington National Cemetery in Arlington, Virginia. Known as Veteran's Day, November 11 is a day when Americans remember with gratitude the men and women who sacrificed their lives for freedom. The following verse is from a famous poem about World War I:

> *In Flanders fields the poppies blow*
> *Between the crosses, row on row,*
> *That mark our place; and in the sky*
> *The larks, still bravely singing, fly*
> *Scarce heard amid the guns below.*
> —John McCrae

Flanders is a region in Belgium where some battles of World War I were fought. The crosses mark the graves of fallen soldiers.

Most Americans of that time did not know why the Europeans were fighting, and the causes are still not well understood today. Several centuries of various empires ***vying*** for control of Europe had engaged in wars that left Europe with strange national boundaries. After these wars national boundaries were drawn according to preferences by rulers rather than according to national loyalties of resident people. In 1914 some parts of Germany consisted of French-speaking people. Some Italians were part of Austria-Hungary. Other national groups were entirely absorbed by other countries: the Czechs and Slovaks became part of Austria-Hungary; the Poles, Finns and others were absorbed by Russia; Bulgarians were dominated by the Ottoman-Turk Empire which is now Turkey. Additionally, various countries, especially Germany, desired to control more land in Europe and more colonial resources and markets outside of Europe. In 1914, Europe was a powder keg waiting to explode.

VOCABULARY

Armistice: an agreement to stop fighting; a truce
Vying: competing
Catalyst: an event or person that causes change
Neutrality: belonging to neither side
Paradox: a statement that contradicts itself
Sentiment: public opinion
Atrocity: act of vicious cruelty
Appalled: filled with horror or dismay
Contraband: smuggled goods designed to assist the enemy

The *catalyst* that lit the fuse of the European powder keg was the shooting of the Archduke Francis Ferdinand, heir to the throne of Austria-Hungary, in Sarajevo, Bosnia, on June 28, 1914. The small country of Serbia wanted to possess parts of Bosnia and Herzegovina in order to gain an outlet to the sea. Because Bosnia and Herzegovina were parts of Austria-Hungary, the Austrian-Hungarian people accused Serbia of the assassination. Within a month the battle lines were drawn. The war officially began on July 28, 1914, when Austria-Hungary declared war on Serbia.

Military alliances had developed between the European countries prior to the war. By the time the war broke out, two distinct military groups had formed. The Central Powers were composed of Germany, the Ottoman-Turk Empire and Austria-Hungary. The Allied Powers were composed primarily of Great Britain, France, Russia, Belgium and Serbia. Japan also joined the Allied Powers, hoping to win some German-controlled regions of China and the Pacific. Italy joined the Allied Powers in 1915, and Portugal and Romania joined in 1916. In all, 24 nations, including the United States in 1917, entered the war on the side of the Allied Powers. Other western hemisphere nations joined the Allies after the United States' entry.

For the first three years of war, the United States managed to keep a position of *neutrality*. President Woodrow Wilson asked the American people to be neutral in both thought and deed. Most Americans tended to be pro-Ally because they believed Germany was wrong for using the war as an excuse to control more land. The United States was pro-Ally also because of our close ties to Great Britain and our appreciation for France's assistance in our past wars. The largest group of immigrants in America, however, was German, and these German-Americans expressed support for the Central Powers. But, the rest of the nation was united in support of Allied forces.

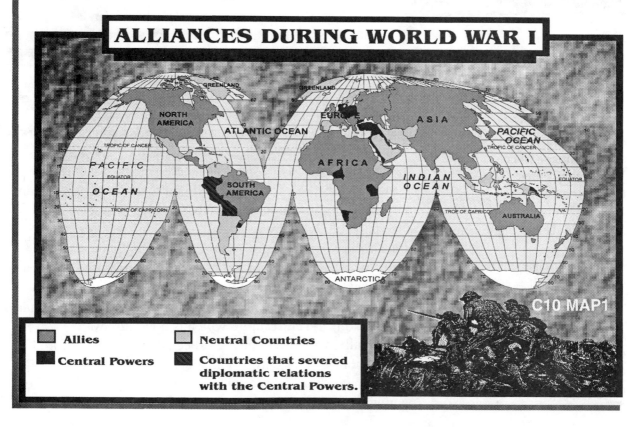

ALLIANCES DURING WORLD WAR I

Allies

Central Powers

Neutral Countries

Countries that severed diplomatic relations with the Central Powers.

C10 MAP1

America was in the midst of hard financial times, but despite economic circumstances, U.S. businesses were able to accumulate investment capital. The Allied Powers borrowed money from American banks and bought ammunition from American industries. When the Germans protested that America was violating a neutral position, the State Department told the Germans that they could purchase ammunition from America too, if the Germans would come get the weapons. The *paradox* was the British blockade effectively preventing the Germans from doing so.

American *sentiment* was increasingly in favor of the Allied Powers. In order to acquire a pathway to France, Germany steam rolled over neutral Belgium. Reports of German cruelties against Belgian citizens spread across America. Even though some of the alleged cruelties were not verified, Americans understood that the Belgians suffered tremendously because war by its very nature is cruel, even in defense of freedom.

Another *atrocity* the Germans committed was the execution of Edith Cavell. Miss Cavell was an English nurse who stayed behind German lines to help injured Allied soldiers and then to assist in their escape. Although Cavell's death before a firing squad was a legal act in wartime, it *appalled* the civilized world that Germany would shoot a female nurse.

International laws governed the treatment of neutral vessels in occupied waters. Cargo ships that were discovered near war zones expected to be checked by Allies and German warships to identify war materials. Merchant ships not found carrying *contraband* cargos were supposed to be released. However, the British seized neutral ships, claiming that the supplies on board might be used to equip German troops. Also, German submarines sank neutral ships without warning. Because passenger ships sometimes carried contraband and were targeted for bombing, Germany published notices in newspapers warning Americans not to travel on British or any other Allied ships.

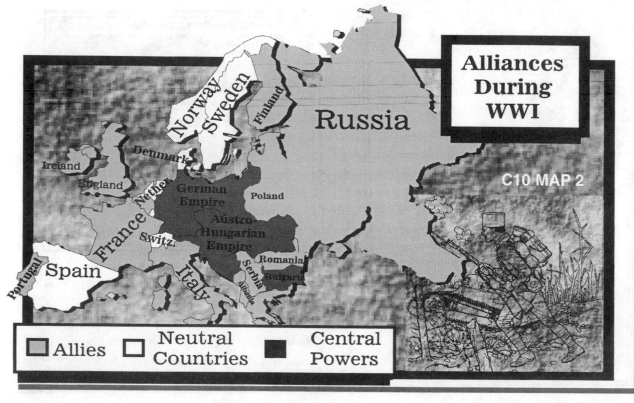

Alliances During WWI

C10 MAP 2

Allies   Neutral Countries   Central Powers

In 1915, Germans sank a British passenger ship called the *Lusitania*. One hundred twenty-eight Americans were on board, but even such a horrible attack did not persuade President Wilson to declare war on Germany. German submarine warfare continued to escalate. Hundreds of ships were sunk by German submarines known as *U-boats*.

Then, in January of 1917, a message, known as the Zimmermann Note, was intercepted. This note indicated that Germany was seeking an alliance with Mexico in case America entered the war. Germany secretly promised that if Mexico would help defeat America, Mexico would receive portions of the land the United States had bought from Mexico after the Mexican War of 1846—California, Arizona, New Mexico and Texas. President Wilson asked Congress to declare war because, *"the world must be made safe for democracy."*

America was ill-prepared to fight a war. A *draft* was instituted, which called for all males between the ages of 21 and 30 to register with the government for possible service in the Army or Navy. "Uncle Sam" appeared on patriotic posters, pointing his finger and declaring, *"I want YOU!"* Uncle Sam had long been a symbolic representative of the American government. The image of Uncle Sam inspired patriotism, loyalty and the desire to defend one's country.

With the help of Uncle Sam, hundreds of young men signed up for the armed services, and the draft for U.S. soldiers was a rousing success.

President Wilson was granted spending power by Congress, enabling the president to establish numerous organizations to manage war operations. The War Industries Board was designed to control war production. The Shipping Board built ships. The Food Administration promoted ways to conserve food. The Fuel Administration curbed use of fuels so that gasoline could be sent to the Army. The War Trade Board managed imports and exports of products. American business flourished, and the American people *rallied* enthusiastically to help protect democracy. General John J. Pershing was named commander of the American forces.

General Pershing

General Pershing Meeting Leaders

General Pershing's intelligent leadership effectively turned the tide of battle in favor of Allied forces.

World War I was fought on three *fronts*. The Western Front stretched across Belgium, between Germany and France. The

---

VOCABULARY

Rallied: came together for a common cause
Fronts: battle areas in warfare
Stalemate: a situation in which neither side makes progress
Cockpit: where a pilot sits in a plane
Impasse: a deadlock; no way out of a situation

Eastern Front divided Russia from Austria-Hungary. The Southern Front extended East to West between Austria-Hungary and Italy.

Technology had changed the methods of war. Submarines were used at sea. On land, water-cooled machine guns made traditional charges across open fields impossible. Armored tanks and mobile field artillery enabled Allied commanders to strike enemy forces quickly and decisively.

Trench warfare developed in fields along the lines of each front. Trenches were dug deep enough for men to stand in, connected to other parallel trenches where a second or third line of men would stand ready to join in the battle. Some hand dug trenches were as long as 600 miles, and were connected to each other by ditches and

Trench Warfare

tunnels that enabled supplies and men to be moved to the battle front. Rain, rats and dysentery combined with cannon shells—making conditions in the trenches harsh for Allied and Central armies.

Between the Allied and Central trenches were rows of barbed wire meant to slow down attempted attacks by invading enemy forces. Tanks were developed by the British to break the **stalemate** of trench warfare. The Germans attacked Allied trenches with deadly chlorine gas and grenades.

For the first time in history, opposing forces fought in the air. Open *cockpit* biplanes were equipped with machine guns which enabled pilots to shoot enemy planes out of the sky. Pilots who shot down five or more enemy planes were called "Aces."

Some men struggled with personal and religious beliefs regarding war. These men of integrity were called *conscientious objectors* because they objected to fighting with deadly weapons. One such man was Alvin York, a deeply religious man born in the hills of Tennessee. The family pastor encouraged Alvin to go to war to oppose evil. The young conscientious objector read his Bible on a lonely mountain to make a decision about participation in the war. When Alvin came upon the passage of Scripture that read, *"Render unto Caesar that which is Caesar's, and unto God that which is God's,"* Alvin York decided that defending the country was under the category of "rendering unto Caesar" (obeying the government).

Not only did Alvin York join the Army, the young man from Tennessee dedicated his entire energy toward his duty. York was an expert marksman; he shot more than 20 Germans in one battle. York also captured a German officer, forcing the officer to command his troops to surrender. Then York began marching his prisoners toward U.S. lines. He forced the prisoners to tell other Germans along the way to surrender. Alvin York reached Allied lines with a total of 132 prisoners. Sergeant York was awarded the Congressional Medal of Honor and was hailed as a national hero in a parade in New York City. York's bravery and fortitude illustrated how much difference one man could make.

The war had been somewhat of an **impasse** for the Allied Powers before the entry of American forces. With the addition of U.S. soldiers and military strategy, the Allied Powers forced the Germans to bring an end to World War I on November 11, 1918.

President Wilson presented a plan for peace, called the *Fourteen Points*. It was rejected by the Allied Powers, and, instead, the *Treaty of Versailles* was drawn up and signed. Germany had to admit guilt in causing the war and was forced to pay a huge sum of money as payment for damages. World War I also marked the end of the monarchy form of government. A *monarch* is one ruler (such as a king or queen) who possesses absolute authority over all national matters. The monarchy system of government was replaced with a republican form of government in Austria, Germany, Hungary and other European countries.

The Treaty of Versailles included a provision for formation of the *League of Nations*, at the insistence of President Wilson. However, the United States Congress neither joined the League of Nations, nor was the Treaty ratified by Congress. Senators and Congressmen believed the League of Nations and Treaty of Versailles forced Americans to give up too many freedoms. America did, however, enter separate peace treaties with Germany, Austria and Hungary.

The bloody overthrow of the Russian Czar in 1917 was another tragic consequence of World War I. Bolsheviks, under the ruthless leadership of Leon Trotsky and Vladimir Lenin, killed the czar and established the first communist government in the world. By the end of World War I, the Communists had murdered thousands upon thousands of Russian doctors, teachers, businessman, farmers, officials and clergy. Churches were converted into warehouses. Farmers were forced to give their land to the communist government which converted the farms to collectives where slave labor produced agriculture products. Anyone who opposed Trotsky or Lenin was shot or hanged. After taking over Russia, the Communists laid detailed plans for infiltrating and subduing all other world governments.

Ironically, the war boosted the American economy. In the midst of hard times, the country pulled together to meet the hardships of war. The next vignette explains how the needs of the war were met by America's farmers.

Life Principle

"America is great because America is good, and if America ever ceases to be good, America will cease to be great."

—Alex De Tocqueville

The Defending of America

Topic 3
Agriculture

Chapter 10

Section One
Topics 1-5

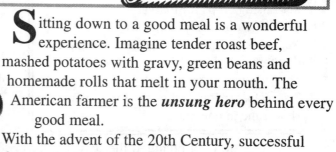

FARMERS, WAR AND GOVERNMENT

Sitting down to a good meal is a wonderful experience. Imagine tender roast beef, mashed potatoes with gravy, green beans and homemade rolls that melt in your mouth. The American farmer is the ***unsung hero*** behind every good meal.

With the advent of the 20th Century, successful farmers had to be wise businessmen. A farmer's challenge was to find a profitable way of feeding a nation. The Industrial Revolution enabled farmers to produce more goods with less physical labor. ***Entrepreneurs*** had provided better crops, better tools and better farming methods. A combination of technology, research and wise use of privately owned farm land enabled America to become the world leader in production of agriculture products.

In 1862, the Department of Agriculture was formed to provide government assistance to farmers. The department provided research reports on animal and plant diseases, soil composition, destructive insects and new plant varieties for differing soils. The Agriculture Department also operated experimental farms where new ideas were tested.

In 1862, Congress passed the Morrill Act, which granted U.S. states large tracts of public land for colleges that taught agriculture and mechanical arts. Agriculture was changing, and young farmers needed training in new methods of efficient farming. Studying agriculture in college equipped future farmers with more efficient skills and knowledge about plants and animals.

Empowered by the Smith-Lever Act of 1914, the Department of Agriculture assisted local farmers by assigning county agents to live in farming communities. County agriculture agents gave farmers access to research information that helped solve agricultural problems.

VOCABULARY

Unsung hero: a hero who gets no credit or recognition
Entrepreneurs: people who invest their own money and time to start and operate a new business
Empowered: possessing legal power
Urban: in a city
Rural: in the country
Disheartening: discouraging, disappointing
Staple: main ones, most important ones

World War I changed the way Americans lived. Soldiers who fought overseas and women who worked in **urban** facilities developed a taste for urban lifestyles. **Rural** life seemed dull compared to the lure of big cities where young men and women found more adequate education, recreation and medical facilities. Young people abandoned family farms to seek adventure and job opportunities in cities. Farmers were ridiculed and called *hayseeds*. Something was needed to lend respectability to farming as a profession and to encourage American young people to stay on the farms.

The Smith-Hughes Act of 1917 gave high schools federal money to teach agriculture and home economics. 4-H Clubs were organized in rural areas. The 4-H Club's name came from the club's pledge: *I pledge My Head to clearer thinking, My Heart to greater loyalty, My Hands to larger service, and My Health to better living for my club, my community, and my country.* Club members were taught agricultural techniques and encouraged to undertake projects to show at county fairs. Students competed for prizes for the best garden produce or farm animals. Promoting agriculture as a patriotic profession, 4-H Clubs still flourish in rural America, with a recent upsurge in suburban and even urban areas.

The death of so many American sons, fathers and brothers caused World War I to be a **disheartening** blow for the country, but farmers took deep sighs and went on. Ironically, the same war that devastated so many families caused farmers to prosper. Farmers were in demand to feed the nation, as well as American troops and allies overseas. The Federal Farm Loan Act of 1916 had made financial credit available to farmers at low interest rates, and The Warehouse Act of 1916 authorized loans on **staple** crops like wheat and corn. Rising to the occasion, American farmers put their tractors to work and provided crops and cattle for food and leather for boots, rifle straps and belts.

President Woodrow Wilson named an American mining engineer, Herbert Hoover, as the administrator of the Food Administration. Mr. Hoover was a Quaker by faith, and a well-known **humanitarian**. When Germany steamrolled through the tiny country of Belgium earlier in the war, Mr. Hoover was called upon to help feed that starving nation. He successfully put Belgium

4-H Children

18

back on track and earned the nickname of "Miracle Man." The goal of the newly formed Food Administration was to increase food production, reduce food waste and encourage the public to substitute plentiful foods for scarce ones.

Mr. Hoover was an excellent organizer who coined the slogan, *"Food Will Win the War—Don't Waste It."* He **blitzed** the country with slogans like: *"Use all leftovers"* and *"Full garbage pails mean empty dinner pails."* Hoover encouraged people to practice *"the patriotism of the lean garbage can."* Hoover's program inspired the American people, who followed the administrator's requests voluntarily, even inventing recipes that omitted hard-to-find ingredients. Wheatless Mondays and Wednesdays, meatless Tuesdays, and porkless Thursdays and Saturdays were all regular weekly standards during World War I.

Perspiring patriots planted *Victory Gardens* in their back yards or on vacant lots. Farm products increased by 25%, and the United States shipped food to hungry Allied forces. Hoover encouraged wheat growers to participate by guaranteeing each 1917 crop a purchase price of $2.20 per bushel.

The end of the war also ended the farmer's prosperity. Small wheat growers suffered when machinery reduced the need for extensive cheap manual labor. Tractors and improved knowledge of agriculture enabled farmers to produce far more per acre than ever before. These advances were wonderful during the war, but in peace time, exports decreased and no market was available for excess crops. The war had created market demands which diminished after peace was established.

Again the federal government stepped in to control America's farm economy. The Agricultural Adjustment Act of 1933 was designed to raise farm prices by controlling production. The government would pay farmers a bonus not to cultivate some of their acreage. The idea was that if farms produced less, prices would go up and the farmer could balance his costs.

Other parts of the law were designed to boost the farmer's sagging economy. Loans were granted to help farmers store extra produce so they could withhold products from the market until prices were better, then release those same products at higher profits. Farmers were allowed to refinance their mortgages at low interest rates to keep from losing their farms. A federal electrification program brought electricity to isolated farms.

A Second Agricultural Adjustment Act of 1938 encouraged farmers to plant soil-conserving crops on extra land, or to let land lay dormant. Emphasis was on conservation. If a farmer followed restrictions on excessive planting, the farmer was paid a bonus called *parity*. The Agricultural Adjustment Act provided farmers with sufficient profit to remain operative, but simultaneously made farmers dependent on government subsidies.

Farmers also faced a severe blow from nature. Late in 1933, a long drought devastated the Great Plains states of North and South Dakota, Nebraska, Kansas, Oklahoma and parts of northern Texas. Furious winds followed the drought, ripping topsoil from thirsty ground. The farmer watched helplessly as his hard-earned farm *literally* blew away. Dust storms were

Government Official with Child

sometimes so dense that farmers could not see across their grassless yards. The Great Plains area became known as the *Dust Bowl*, and that terrible time in history became known as the Great Depression. The entire country was in difficult financial circumstances.

Farmers by the tens of thousands abandoned their ruined land and became *refugees*. They traveled to California, hoping to find affordable, farmable land. In the meantime, they had nowhere to live and they had no way to make a living. Suffering *dire* poverty, displaced farm families huddled in makeshift camps, often sleeping in their broken-down cars and trucks. Homeless farmers called *transients* were sometimes treated unkindly by communities along the way. John Steinbeck captured the mood of America and experiences of transients in two books, *Tobacco Road* and *Grapes of Wrath,* which later became award-winning films.

John Steinbeck

Once again, the U.S. government tried to assist exhausted, starving farmers and their children. In 1935, President Franklin Roosevelt set up a Resettlement Administration to help farmers move from the poor land to better land. Men and boys in the Civilian Conservation Corps planted millions of trees in the Dust Bowl to act as windbreaks so the land could be recovered.

Those were hard years for our nation's farmers. Farming was forever changed by events which surrounded World War I. Technology replaced horses and men. Research improved crop yields, and government involvement established a relationship between privately owned farms and the federal government. After World War I, America's farmers were free to live on or move off their farms, but the choice of which crop to raise, sell or plow became a matter of government concern.

The next vignette will tell about food products that were not produced on rural farms.

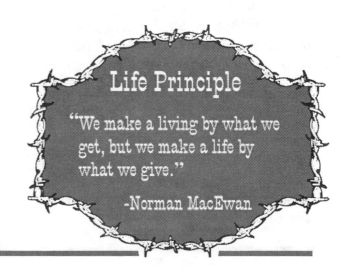

Life Principle

"We make a living by what we get, but we make a life by what we give."

-Norman MacEwan

The Defending of America

Topic 4
Food

Chapter 10

Section One
Topics 1-5

BEN NELSON: HATCHING A WEALTH OF FISH

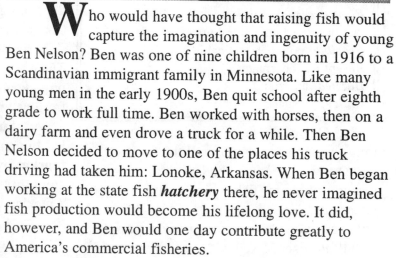

Who would have thought that raising fish would capture the imagination and ingenuity of young Ben Nelson? Ben was one of nine children born in 1916 to a Scandinavian immigrant family in Minnesota. Like many young men in the early 1900s, Ben quit school after eighth grade to work full time. Ben worked with horses, then on a dairy farm and even drove a truck for a while. Then Ben Nelson decided to move to one of the places his truck driving had taken him: Lonoke, Arkansas. When Ben began working at the state fish *hatchery* there, he never imagined fish production would become his lifelong love. It did, however, and Ben would one day contribute greatly to America's commercial fisheries.

Fish has been on American dinner tables since the First Thanksgiving back in 1621. Rich in protein, numerous species of fish are harvested continually from this nation's oceans, rivers, lakes, ponds and fish farms. Fish are fried, broiled, baked, steamed and *poached* in a variety of delicious ways.

Oceans are America's largest source of fish. While fish farms produce the smallest portion of our nation's fish supply, they are still important providers of catfish, crayfish, oysters, salmon and trout.

At Lonoke's fish hatchery, Ben Nelson put his creative mind to work, becoming interested in the scientific side of raising fish. Ben began finding ways to improve fish production. Successful attempts at improving *propagation* of channel catfish earned Ben Nelson recognition across the state.

In 1953, the owner of a commercial trout farm in Rogers, Arkansas, hired Nelson to build a catfish hatchery. At that time, farm raising of channel catfish for use in restaurants was still in its infancy. Ben became a hatchery expert, developing new methods of increasing production to make raising catfish profitable.

VOCABULARY

Hatchery: a place where eggs are hatched under artificial conditions
Poached: cooked in hot liquid just below boiling point
Propagation: to reproduce or breed
Gestation: the time necessary for embryos to develop; pregnancy
Serum: any watery animal fluid

One of the most unique improvements Nelson offered the fishery industry was a new method of shortening the *gestation* time for fish. Using individual aquariums, Nelson injected female catfish with *serum* made from the *pituitary gland* of buffalo fish. Mixed with penicillin to prevent infection, the serum caused female catfish to lay their eggs quickly. After the males fertilized the eggs, the fish were removed from the aquariums and returned to separate ponds at the hatchery.

Nelson invented a type of *incubator* for fish eggs. In nature, a male catfish hovers over the nest after the eggs have been fertilized. Using fins to move the water back and forth, the male catfish keeps *sediment* from settling on the eggs and killing them. Nelson's incubator moved the water, keeping sediment off the catfish eggs automatically. Eggs were put in baskets made of fine wire. In the fish building of the hatchery, the whole *apparatus* was submerged in one of twenty concrete tanks of water. Once the eggs hatched, the tiny fish (called fry) swam out of the basket holes.

Ben Nelson gladly shared his knowledge and innovations. Nelson's generosity and helpful nature were rewarded with financial prosperity, not only for him but for other catfish farmers who implemented Nelson's ideas.

Nelson produced a new species of albino catfish called Golden Channel Catfish. Since Nelson was the only one who owned these new catfish, he was able to sell them at a good profit. Production of Golden Channel Catfish enabled Nelson to enjoy financial security for the rest of his life. Thanks to Ben Nelson, grocery stores provide an abundant, year-round supply of freshwater catfish.

America's love for protein-rich fish led to a creative breakthrough in the food market by Clarence Birdseye who built a company which brought frozen fish to the American dinner table.

I n 1917, Clarence Birdseye worked for Fowler Fisheries Company, which processed and sold fish out of Bay Shore, Long Island. As Clarence processed frozen fish, he recalled how fresh the fish caught off Labrador's banks tasted when it was thawed to eat. Birdseye believed the fish tasted better because it was frozen almost immediately.

MOM OKAYS FLAKED & FROZEN FOOD

Birdseye's Food Processor

The fish could be frozen for months at a time and still taste as fresh as when it was originally caught. Birdseye discovered that freezing fish quickly prevented formation of large ice crystals that caused thawed fish to be mushy.

22

That first-hand experience with *flash-freezing*, combined with his work in the fish distribution business, inspired Birdseye to experiment with freezing processes. Clarence wanted to develop a freezing method that was both economically *feasible* and also safe for consumers.

In 1923, Birdseye established General Seafood Company in Albany, New York, freezing and selling thousands of pounds of fish. His initial freezing process involved electric fans, ice cakes and salt brine. Although his company was very successful, Birdseye was not satisfied that his fish was of the best possible quality.

In 1927, Clarence Birdseye developed a continuous freezing process, in which whole fish or packages of fillets were sprayed with a forty-degree-below-zero salt brine solution. This system allowed for the economical large-scale production of frozen fish and launched America's frozen food industry.

Thanks to Birdseye, the frozen food process enabled Americans to buy a variety of frozen foods—peas, peaches, cherries, fish, beef, in their grocer's freezer section. By 1940, 15,000 grocery stores proudly offered freezer cabinets, and frozen food sales topped $150 million. The first full-color frozen food advertisement ran in *Life Magazine* that same year.

By World War II, the frozen food market was particularly popular (due in part to the need to ship canned foods overseas to feed American soldiers). Families on the home front relied on frozen food, which up to that time had remained little more than a luxury. Grocery stores doubled their freezer space. Americans who sampled frozen foods, developed an appetite for fresh frozen products. Consequently, the frozen food business boomed.

By 1946, concentrated frozen orange juice, inspired by Gail Borden's success with condensed milk, was in full production. In ten years, Americans were consuming 68 million gallons of orange juice annually.

Today, next to the glass of orange juice, a bowl of cereal holds a standard place on the nation's breakfast table. Americans became fond of breakfast cereals after refrigerators enabled homemakers to serve cold milk over cereal. Hot, soupy cereals such as oatmeal, mush and gruel were standard breakfast food before 1930. When "ready-to-eat" cold cereals hit the market in the early 1900s, Americans gave a big "thumbs-down" reaction.

But each night after work and school, Americans from coast to coast crowded around talking boxes called radios. This newest source of entertainment and news also provided a ready audience for advertising cold cereal. Radio advertisements played a big role in making cereal a popular breakfast food. Children took to heart endorsements from radio celebrities such as the Lone Ranger and his Indian sidekick, Tonto, along with

Fishery

Tom Mix and Jack Armstrong. These and other radio heroes made cereals household words among America's youngsters. By the 1930s, cereal boxes were given a favorable *reception* on America's breakfast tables.

Manufacturing and advertising can claim partial credit for the growth of America's cereal industry. Cereals made from grains like wheat, corn, oats and bran are shaped into flakes, circles, stars, nuggets, puffs, biscuits and even little tiny slices of toast. For decades, these cereals in every imaginable shape, color and flavor have *dazzled* the taste buds of American consumers. Today, mass advertising and marketing techniques *entice* buyers to spend millions of dollars on packaged breakfast cereals.

Boxed cereals and frozen foods represent only a portion of the convenience food industry in this country. American life became more complex during the 20th century, and so did the demand for better and more efficient ways to provide food and beverages. Entrepreneurs like Nelson and Birdseye saw market needs and provided products which consumers were willing and eager to buy.

After World War I, many changes were taking place in U.S. government economic policies, but as we will learn next, all changes were not pleasant.

LIFE PRINCIPLE

"A wise man will make more opportunities than he finds."
- Francis Bacon

The Defending of America

Topic 5
Government & Economics

Chapter 10

BIG GOVERNMENT AND FREE ENTERPRISE CLASH

Section One
Topics 1-5

Washington D.C.

VOCABULARY

Ostensibly: apparently, seeming to
Noble: honorable, good
Despots: evil tyrants, vicious rulers
Vigilance: constant alertness against dictators
Isolationism: setting oneself apart from others
Repealed: canceled
Infestation: a huge amount of harmful elements
Stock market: the buying and selling of shares of businesses as investment or profit

World War I haunted Americans long after the final shot was fired and the armistice was signed in 1918. Government policies were introduced in the 1920s to avoid another world war like The Great War of Europe.

President Woodrow Wilson attempted to prevent future war by forming the League of Nations, which *ostensibly* would resolve all conflicts peacefully. However, Congress considered the League of Nations too restrictive and chose not to join. The Kellogg-Briand Pact (1928), a treaty denouncing war, was signed by 62 major nations, including the United States. The League of Nations and the Kellogg-Briand Pact shared a common goal—to prevent a second world war. The objective was *noble*, but it discounted human nature. History has always reflected the evil attempts of *despots* to rule over masses of people. Alexander the Great, Atilla the Hun, Napoleon, Santa Anna, Hitler, Stalin and Hussein are prime examples. The price of freedom is *vigilance* against, and opposition to, dictators.

To avoid involvement in another world war, Congress adopted a policy of *isolationism*, which was designed to allow the American economy to operate without reliance on foreign markets. Additionally, Congress passed the Fordney-McCumber Tariff (1922) and the Smoot-Hawley Tariff (1930) which placed huge taxes on imported goods.

Isolationism also became a policy for immigration. Republicans feared supporters of Russia's 1917 Bolshevik Revolution would come to America and corrupt the U.S. government, while Democrats and labor unions feared the competition of immigrant entrepreneurs and workers. The Emergency Quota Act (1921) and the National Origins Act (1924) temporarily placed strict limits on immigration.

The years after World War I brought many changes to American culture. Public drunkenness was commonplace and crime ran rampant in the cities. Many concerned wives and mothers joined church groups to stop the negative effects of alcohol on husbands, sons, homes and businesses. The 1920s are often called the Prohibition Era. *Prohibition*, a ban on alcoholic beverages passed in 1919, was supported by Protestant ministers like former baseball pitcher Billy Sunday and temperance organizations like the Women's Christian Temperance Union.

Chicago gangster Al Capone controlled illegal, "bootleg" liquor sales and drug-running through organized gambling, racketeering and even murder. Public saloons were replaced by illegal, liquor-dispensing private clubs called *speakeasies*. Enforcing prohibition became difficult as Congress yielded to pressure from lobbyists representing the liquor industry. In 1933, national prohibition was **repealed**.

As liquor became a major American industry, opposition to it inspired women to become involved in politics. Passage of the 19th Amendment in 1920 finally gave women the right to vote and to participate in the election process. Women could not only vote, but they could also be elected to public office as mayors, representatives and judges. That changed politics as Americans achieved the highest living standards on earth during the period known as the Roaring Twenties. One reason for this prosperity was the relative lack of government intrusion into the economy. Private enterprise was a catalyst of the 1920s industrial explosion. Daring entrepreneurs in quest of profit developed new products and technology that propelled America to the forefront of industrial leadership. Electric motors replaced steam as an energy source for factories. Moving assembly lines and other technological advances led to efficient manufacturing in which great quantities of products were sold at low prices. Americans' wages could buy large quantities of products at reasonable prices.

A dominant industrial figure of the 1920s was Henry Ford. Mr. Ford wanted to provide efficient automobiles at reasonable prices. He introduced the concept of assembly line production that consisted of interchangeability of parts, a moving assembly line and a division of labor. Ford's innovative assembly procedure enabled him to mass produce the Model T. Instead of building a few cars and selling each for a large profit, Ford built hundreds of cars and sold each for a small profit. Any time Ford saw an opportunity to increase efficiency, he made sure the procedure was implemented. Henry Ford's motto was, "*Everything can always be done better than it is being done*." Mr. Ford built vehicles to meet the market demand. In the process, Ford Motor Company created thousands of jobs for Americans.

America became electrified during the 1920s. By the end of the decade, two-thirds of Americans enjoyed electricity in their homes. The electrification of America increased the demand for products like washing machines, vacuum cleaners, refrigerators and kitchen ranges. Like Ford Motor Company, appliance manufacturers produced items desired by housewives. In the process of providing practical household

Al Capone

Ford Assembly Plant

products, appliance manufacturers created hundreds of jobs and greatly reduced the work load of housewives.

The radio industry was also born during the 1920s. David Sarnoff, Commercial Manager of Radio Corporation of America (RCA), was the son of Jewish immigrants. Sarnoff believed radio could be used for entertainment by broadcasting sports and music. In 1922, a radio station aired a real estate firm's advertisement, and commercial radio was born. In 1922, only 33 radio stations existed. By 1923, 556 radio stations were broadcasting across the airwaves.

Another impact of industrialization was its effect on black families in the southern regions of America. Because of difficult relationships in the South and the boll weevil *infestation* that was destroying southern sharecroppers' cotton crops, blacks by the hundreds of thousands migrated to the North in the 1920s. During World War I, many black families moved to cities like New York and Chicago to work in war industries. The migration to

Detroit intensified after the war, as Henry Ford's auto factory became a popular destination.

Southern Negroes (the common term for African-Americans before 1960) were generally less educated and cultured than northern Negroes. When Southern migrants reached the North, they found themselves ridiculed by both blacks and whites. Large groups of Southern blacks settled in crowded city neighborhoods which implanted the seeds of loneliness, restlessness, fear, poverty and illiteracy.

However, the industrial North's economic opportunities outweighed the difficulties blacks faced in the South, and the migration continued. More than 750,000 blacks moved North during the 1920s, a number comparable to the great wave of Irish immigrants to America in the 1840s. The Great Depression of the late 1920s brought the black migration to a temporary halt. Employment opportunities dried up after the *stock market* crashed, forcing thousands of businesses to shut down.

Late in 1929, when the stock market began to falter, speculators rushed to sell their stocks and pay off their business loans. On October 24, 1929, a record 16,410,030 shares of stock were traded, and stock prices *plummeted*. Even non investors recognized the crisis, and rushed to banks to withdraw their savings. A banking crisis erupted as hundreds of banks closed their doors in *bankruptcy*.

To understand the four-year banking crisis that followed the 1929 stock market crash requires you to know how banks worked in America. U.S. banks operated on a *fractional reserve system*. When a customer deposited money in a bank, only a fraction of

Family on porch in the 1920s

VOCABULARY

Plummeted: fell dramatically
Bankrupt: legally out of money
Bank run: when people who have money in a bank fear that the bank will fail and they all withdraw their money at once—causing the bank to fail
Self-fulfilling prophecy: because of fear that a thing will happen, the event really does occur
Recession: withdrawal, temporary failure
Catastrophe: great and sudden disaster
Jumpstart: to help start then leave alone

that deposit went into the bank's reserves. The rest of the money was used to pay expenses or was lent out to other customers. Banks made money by charging interest on those loans. The amount of money in a bank's reserves never equaled the sum of the deposits made by customers. Banks routinely loaned more money than was actually available in the loan departments. However, if too many customers tried to withdraw their money at one time, a *bank run* occurred. The bank could only hope to meet a sudden demand for money by pressing other customers to repay their loans or by borrowing from other banks. An actual banking crisis occurred when many banks faced bank runs at the same time.

Great Depression Family

A banking crisis is a classic example of a *self-fulfilling prophecy*; the fear of bank failures actually caused banks to fail. First, depositors feared that the banks were going to fail; so depositors rushed to banks to withdraw personal savings; consequently, banks were unable to meet sudden client demand for currency; finally, the banks failed. Frightened bank customers demanded more money than was available, thus the American banking system collapsed.

The banking crisis affected everyone, regardless of their wealth or social status. Businesses needed bank loans to stay afloat, so when the banks failed, businesses failed also. When businesses failed, employees lost their jobs. When businesses failed to make profits, they paid fewer *taxes* (money collected to support the government). The "spin-off" effect of bank failures reached every aspect of U.S. culture in the 1930s.

Before 1913, banks had handled banking crises by collectively agreeing not to pay currency to depositors who wanted to make withdrawals, but to use bookkeeping entries instead. That method was effective, but clumsy.

Some financial experts believed that only the U.S. Government could prevent a nationwide failure of banks, thus the Federal Reserve System was established in 1913. It consisted of a central Federal Reserve Board in Washington, D.C., and 12 regional Federal Reserve Banks in various cities. If a crisis occurred, the regional banks would lend money to commercial banks, and the commercial banks would repay the loans after the crisis passed. The plan seemed infallible until October 24, 1929.

The stock market crash plunged the nation into a terrible *recession*, but bank failures actually caused the Great Depression. In 1930, bank runs occurred in the South and Midwest. On December 11, 1930, a commercial bank called the Bank of the United States failed. Although the Bank of the United States was a commercial bank, its name sounded like something of national significance. The failure of the Bank of the United States set off a panic. In the month of December alone, 352 banks failed. The failures continued through 1931, 1932, and early 1933.

Throughout the crisis, the Federal Reserve System was ineffective (at best). The Federal Board and the regional banks were involved in a power struggle to see who would get credit for making good decisions. Because commercial banks thought the Federal Reserve System was solving the crisis, local commercial banks did nothing to relieve the crisis.

The only way to end the crisis was to close banks. New York state closed her banks on March 4, 1933, the day of Franklin Roosevelt's inauguration as president. Thirty-seven other states quickly followed New York's example. On March 5, President Roosevelt, nicknamed "FDR" declared a national banking holiday. By March 13, the banks began to reopen. The closing of the banks in order to deal with the crisis was an admission that the Federal Reserve System had failed in its original purpose.

Today, the Federal Reserve System, usually called the "FED," is used mainly to regulate the amount of money in circulation. The head of the Federal Reserve Board holds extremely powerful economic authority. His job is a difficult balancing act. If he allows too much money in circulation, money will lose its value, and inflation will result. If he does not allow enough money in circulation, interest rates will rise, restricting ability to start businesses and make large purchases.

In response to the massive bank failures that produced the Great Depression, the Federal Deposit Insurance Corporation was established in 1934. The FDIC insured bank depositors' savings. Consumer confidence, not centralized decision making, was the key to preventing another *catastrophe*. Since 1934, bank runs have occurred on individual banks, but no runs have compared with the panic that led to the Great Depression.

In 1929, before the crisis, 25,000 commercial banks operated in the U.S. After the crisis, only 15,000 remained. As banks failed, Americans watched their savings disappear into thin air. Their jobs soon followed. By 1932, the unemployment rate was up to 25%. Former business owners sold apples and pencils on street corners. Some people lived in shelters after losing their homes. Soup and beans replaced meat and potatoes as the traditional meal.

The Great Depression shook Americans' respect for the free enterprise system that had made the nation great. President Franklin D. Roosevelt's federal government policies urged public reliance on Washington, D.C. to solve America's economic and social problems.

President Hoover had actually started the trend with farm subsidies, corporate welfare, higher taxes and government work projects, but he stopped short of providing direct aid to individuals and businesses. President Franklin Roosevelt's policies, collectively called the "New Deal," sent American's speeding toward personal dependency on government.

VOCABULARY

Utopia: the perfect place

Socialists: people who support government control of industry, education and private property

Destitute: terribly poor; without necessary means to live

Nazis: Germans who obeyed the commands of Hitler

Fascists: Italians who believed in harsh government control of citizens

Communists: military controllers of government, economics, religion, private property and education

The New Deal was inspired largely by British economist John Maynard Keynes, an advocate of government spending to *jumpstart* an economy, and socialist author Edward Bellamy, who had envisioned a *utopia* in which citizens depended on the government "from cradle to grave." The New Deal under President Roosevelt was modeled on existing, centralized governments in Britain, Germany and Sweden.

Though presented as temporary responses to a temporary crisis, many New Deal policies became permanent institutions. The Wagner Act of 1935 guaranteed recognition of labor unions, the beginning of the union age. The Social Security Act of 1935 created both social security and unemployment insurance (which hardly proved temporary). The Fair Labor Standards Act of 1938 created a national minimum wage. Every minimum wage increase since has been an extension of this policy.

The New Deal's basic approach to solving America's problems was to tax people who worked (employers and employees) to provide funds to employ idle men. The Civilian Conservation Corps (flood control, soil conservation, forestry), the Public Works Administration (construction of schools, highways, etc.) and the Tennessee Valley Authority (dam building) created government jobs for unemployed persons.

The New Deal did not end the Great Depression. The worst effect of the Great Depression was its impact on the American attitude toward government. *Socialists* were quick to blame business owners and bankers for the depression. Many unemployed people lost confidence in the free enterprise system and became more willing to accept government intrusion into their lives and the economy. Franklin Roosevelt won four landslide elections as he promised a car in every garage and work for every man. FDR's socialistic policies passed Congress, and the New Deal became the forerunner of the modern U.S. welfare system.

But not everyone went on welfare during the Great Depression. In New York, 23.9% of blacks and 9.2% of whites were receiving federal aid—both alarming numbers. But the numbers were only 1.2% for Chinese immigrants and a mere .1% for Japanese immigrants. Chicago, Los Angeles, Philadelphia and San Francisco were similar. Chinese and Japanese-Americans stayed off welfare because of close family unity and involvement in community-based organizations such as the Chinese Six Companies and the Japanese Kenjinkai. These volunteer organizations provided work for the unemployed and relief for the *destitute*. Asian-Americans valued family loyalty and community involvement and scorned welfare dependency. Thanks to these truly American qualities, welfare dependency remained minimal among Chinese-Americans and practically nonexistent among Japanese-Americans during the Depression.

Chinese working in field

The Depression was not confined just to America. Europe and Asia also experienced difficult economic times. Masses of people became discouraged, and dictators assumed control. Hitler in Germany, Mussolini in Italy and Soto in Japan began to expand their authority. In 1939, World War II erupted in Europe. War-torn European armies needed tanks, planes, ships and trucks to fight off *Nazi* Germany and *Fascist* Italy. Americans went to work building vehicles. The most terrible war in world history began, and with it came demand for American products and weapons. The massive effort to stop Hitler's Nazi forces brought an end to the worst economic crisis in American History. The Great Depression ended about the time World War II began.

In 1943, as a wartime policy, the federal government began withholding income taxes from workers' paychecks to help finance the war. After the war, however, this temporary policy remained in place and became permanent.

During FDR's presidency, government had intruded into many areas of American's lives, but the wave of government expansion crested with the 1946 Employment Act that made the U.S. government responsible for maintaining maximum employment. Voters rejected this Democrat sponsored government expansion bill in 1946 and elected a Republican Congress. The newly elected Congress stopped President Truman's efforts to continue Roosevelt's socialistic policies.

The Republicans, in turn, scored two points of their own: The Taft-Hartley Act, which passed over Truman's veto in 1947, ended *closed shop labor unions*—the union policy that required all new employees to become union members, and the 1949 Labor Act helped purge labor unions of *communists* and also monitored union tactics to prevent abuse of power.

In the early 1900s, Americans were becoming more mobile. The next lesson tells about the beginnings of industries that put America on wheels.

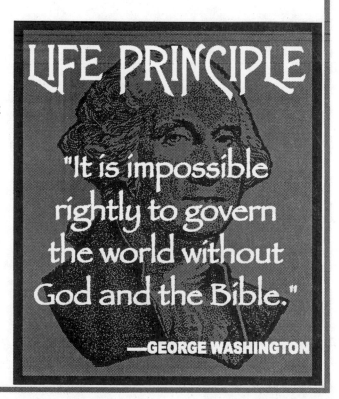

LIFE PRINCIPLE

"It is impossible rightly to govern the world without God and the Bible."

—GEORGE WASHINGTON

The Defending of America

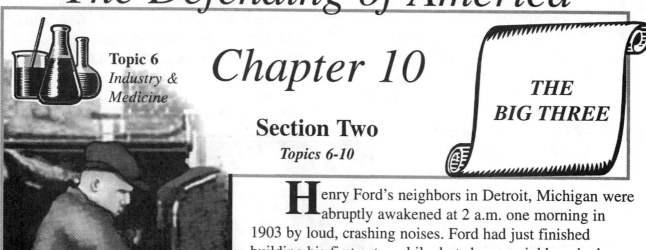

Topic 6
*Industry &
Medicine*

Chapter 10

Section Two

Topics 6-10

**THE
BIG THREE**

Henry Ford's neighbors in Detroit, Michigan were abruptly awakened at 2 a.m. one morning in 1903 by loud, crashing noises. Ford had just finished building his first automobile, but sleepy neighbors had not heard a celebration. Ford's "*quadri cycle*" would not fit through the doorway of the backyard shed where the car had been built. Ford simply tore down the wall to allow passage of his car. The quadri cycle was a forerunner of the sturdy little horseless carriage, popularly known as the "Tin Lizzie" or the Model T. Perhaps having to demolish the door frame and wall with an ax in order to free his creation inspired Ford's intense attention to detail in the decades that followed.

Henry Ford was an *eccentric* mechanic-turned-entrepreneur who put America on wheels. Ford's adaptation of mass assembly techniques to the manufacture of automobiles revolutionized the automobile industry and laid the foundation for "The Big Three" auto makers in 20th century America: Ford, General Motors and Chrysler. These auto makers dominated the U.S. automotive industry for more than four decades.

By 1925, Ford was turning out hundreds of Model T cars by using the moving assembly line that made him famous. The Model T was introduced in 1908, five years after formation of Ford Motor Company. The Model T was *reputed* to be so inexpensive that ordinary people could afford it, and so simple that inexperienced car owners could repair it with hand tools.

In 1908, the same year Ford launched his Model T, William C. Durant, another inventor, combined the Buick, Oldsmobile and Oakland companies to form General Motors. Durant later added Cadillac and Chevrolet, hoping to incorporate the best features of each. In 1909, William Durant offered to purchase Ford Motor Company for $8 million, but the deal fell through when Durant's financial backing collapsed.

VOCABULARY

Quadri cycle: having four wheels
Eccentric: different from the average; odd
Reputed: regarded or rumored as
Expertise: possessing the skill or knowledge of an expert
Inextricably: unable to be removed from
Enmeshed: to be caught in, tangled up in
Ball bearing: small steel balls that revolve freely in a track
Friction: intense heat caused by resistance to motion

Walter P. Chrysler founded the Chrysler Corporation in 1925. Captivated by automotive technology, Chrysler had dismantled and reconstructed a car before he ever learned to drive. Walter began training as a machinist's apprentice in the railroad industry at age 17. By the time he was 33, Walter Chrysler held an important superintendent's post for the Chicago Great Western Railway. Chrysler bought his first automobile in 1910. Two years later, his fascination with cars led to Walter Chrysler's initial job in the automotive industry. Later, as head of Chrysler Corporation, he was recognized as an inspired entrepreneur and one of America's automotive geniuses. Chrysler introduced four wheel drive Jeeps in WWII. The 1/4 ton vehicle revolutionized military tactics and introduced the world to recreational vehicles.

While establishing the company's reputation for engineering *expertise*, Chrysler bought Dodge Brothers, Inc. Dodge, which was known for rugged dependability, captured public attention by building the first car to drive into and out of the Grand Canyon.

In 1954, Englishman James Morris, wrote, *"The American civilization is **inextricably enmeshed** with the internal combustion engine. . . . It is an old joke that Americans are soon going to lose the use of their legs . . . but it is true that few Americans will walk anywhere if they can help it."* Morris' comments still hold true, but the relatively simple internal combustion engine of the mid fifties has evolved into a complex piece of machinery.

Computerization and power equipment assured high tech performance in late 20th century vehicles, including military machines and space age missiles. Seat belts and air bags, sleek styling, plush seating, push-button climate control and CD players are a few of the features that address automobile consumer demands. Minivans, pickups and four-wheelers, as well as sophisticated sport cars and convertibles, have joined the parade on America's highways. Henry Ford would scarcely recognize the descendants of his famed Tin Lizzie.

Henry Ford

General Motors, the number one auto maker in the world with sales of $158 billion in 1996, headed the Fortune 500 list of top corporations in America. The Ford Motor Company was number two on the list with sales of $147 billion. Chrysler Corporation, number nine on the Fortune 500, had sales of $51 billion. In 1998, Chrysler and Germany's Daimler Benz combined to create the Daimler Chrysler Corporation. It became the world's biggest industrial merger. Electric cars were introduced in California in 1998. Ford, Chrysler and General Motors each initiated programs to modify their vehicles for use by the physically disabled.

Strong international competition combined with competition among American manufacturers, stimulating research and development departments. Such competition lead to improved vehicle quality and lower prices. Fuel shortages, labor problems and environmental issues also made an impact on the Detroit-based auto industry, which by 2000 remained one of the most powerful economic and social forces in the world.

The secret to the growth of the vehicle industry rides on a hidden ball. The next vignette tells about the manufacturing development that led to major industrial advancement.

RIDING ON A BALL

The 1926 Indianapolis 500 mile auto race was won by Frank Lockhart who sped around the track at 95 miles per hour. Lockhart's #15 car, like all the cars in that famous race, depended upon *ball bearings* to keep mechanical parts functioning throughout the demanding competition. In 1926, auto racing was gaining popularity as a spectator sport. Industrial development had made great progress since Henry Ford assembled his

Ford Model T

Model T Ford. Engineers had improved the gasoline combustion motor, gear boxes and steering devices. New discoveries in the use of oil as lubricants, rubber for tires, sparks for ignition and foot brakes combined to enhance development of automobiles into high speed race cars. Development progressed in harmony with inventions and production of other related mechanical devices. One of the "break through" inventions was anti-*friction* bearings developed during the early 1920s.

Most spectators at races give no thought to the significance of ball bearings in race car engines, transmissions or steering

wheels. Race cars in the mid 1920s were manufactured from numerous parts that required metal to rub against metal. Friction was minimized through the use of oil and bearings. Ball bearings were enclosed in a metal cage (or retainer) that allowed the bearings to rotate along a metal track.

Manufacture of ball bearings for automobiles also led to other inventions in America. The simple ball bearing allowed industrial inventors to produce high speed motors and transmissions (gear boxes) for cars, trucks, ships, tractors and airplanes.

By 1930, one of every 4.9 Americans owned automobiles. Manufacture of automobiles encouraged development of related industries. Factories were established to produce heavy equipment for road building projects, clothing designs for travelers, gasoline refineries, petroleum products and trucks for long distance hauling.

In the next vignette, you will learn how big trucks were built to keep America supplied.

TRUCKING INTO THE FUTURE

When World War I began, the U.S. trucking industry was competing with well-established railroads for a share of the long distance freight market. During the war, the federal government depended heavily on trucks to haul supplies and equipment for military troops. Extensive military use and improved highways gave the trucking industry a major boost, swelling truck numbers to one million by the war's end in 1918.

By the mid 1960s, 75% of all goods transported in the United States were hauled at least part of the way by truck, and local freight was **monopolized** by the trucking industry. Railroads were unable to compete with the faster delivery and flexible routes that trucks made possible.

More than 8,000,000 people worked in the U.S. trucking industry by the 1980s, making it the nation's largest private industrial employer. More than 40 million trucks were registered in the 1980s. Two leaders in developing big rigs were C.L. Cummins and T.A. Peterman. Cummins founded Cummins Engine Company in 1919 and installed the first diesel engine in a truck in the early 1930s. Today, Cummins provides more motors to power heavy duty trucks than any other motor manufacturer.

While Cummins was developing diesel engines, other innovations in rig design were also under development. The popular semi-tractor trailers (also known as *semi*s or *18 wheelers)* were developed in the 1920s. Those big rigs (standards of the modern trucking industry) consisted of a tractor unit with ten wheels pulling a trailer with eight wheels.

In 1939, the year World War II broke out, T.A. Peterman, a logger and plywood

1940 18 wheeler truck

manufacturer from Tacoma, Washington established Peterbilt Motors Company. He intended to build logging trucks for his own use, but soon began considering other possibilities. While Henry Ford's assembly lines were turning out hundreds of carbon copy trucks a day, Peterbilt sent its engineers into the field to determine the needs of long-haul truckers. Based on those findings, Peterbilt developed rugged, high performance, low maintenance vehicles designed for long distance hauling.

Peterbilt became an industry leader and has maintained its reputation through high quality custom manufacturing of new models. Modern semi trucks are the result of engineering and technological advances which emphasize economy, efficiency, environmental impact, safety and driver comfort. Innovations included fiberglass bodies, sleeper cabs, air conditioning and 24-hour roadside assistance to *facilitate* vehicle service.

As in other industries, need inspired invention and modification of trucks and trailers. During the 1960s, Texas ranchers were shipping thousands of live cattle to California and Arizona markets then hauling empty livestock trailers back. Texas truckers were also hauling fruit and grain to California and returning with California produce. Several truckers collaborated to design a two-way trailer that would haul live cattle from Texas and fresh produce from California.

VOCABULARY

Monopolized: completely controlled
Facilitate: to make easy or easier
Containers: huge metal boxes loaded onto ships for transporting items across the ocean

E.B. Little and Fred Pierdolla of San Antonio, Texas contacted several different trailer manufacturers but were refused production because the special ordered two-way trailers required too much investment money and were heavier than regular trailers. In 1958, Hobbs trailers in Fort Worth, Texas agreed to manufacture the two-way trailers that Little and Pierdolla had designed. The two truckers purchased two cattle-produce trailers each and began to haul small, light calves to the west where the trailers were unloaded, steamed out and arranged to haul produce as a return load. This new design allowed Texas truckers to save money by transporting good pay loads in both directions. Soon, other companies took advantage of the newly designed two-way trailers.

Later, railroads and ocean liners adopted the piggy-back policy. Trailers and *containers* were loaded with cargo to haul on trains and ships to major cities and across the ocean. Railroads, container ships and trucking companies learned how to take advantage of opportunities to deliver products by land and sea. The trucking industry supports the American way of life by transporting everything from hair bows to hot dogs, mustard to motorcycles and jelly beans to jet skis.

Just as America's freight rides on wheels, progress in construction also depends on wheels as we will discover in the next vignette.

MOVING THE EARTH— AND BUILDING A DREAM

Caterpillars do an astonishing job of moving the earth. Not those fuzzy little creatures that munch their way through the garden, but huge, highly specialized earth movers that transfer gigantic loads of dirt and rocks from one spot to another. Before the end of the 19th century, Daniel Best and Benjamin Holt began experimenting with steam tractors for farming. The families of these two men united to pioneer track-type tractors and gasoline-powered tractor engines, and eventually formed Caterpillar, Incorporated in 1925.

Caterpillars' track-type tractors were in great demand for hauling equipment through muddy battlefields during World War I. During World War II, Caterpillar's tracked vehicles played an important role in designing military vehicles. America's expanding peacetime economy after WWII created the need for new products such as backhoes and other excavators, cranes, graders, bulldozers and power shovels. The company's equipment lists doubled between 1981 and the mid 1990s, with more than 300 products available toward the end of the 20th century.

According to company literature, *"Caterpillar makes the machines that allow the world's builders and planners to realize their dreams. . . . It's not only what we make*

1930 Track-type Caterpillar Tractor

that makes us proud—it's what we make
possible in every corner of the globe."
Caterpillar equipment, weighing as much as
50,000 pounds per unit, moves dirt at mine
sites and construction projects such as
airports, dams, roads, water systems and
sewer plants in nearly 200 countries around
the world. Headquartered in Peoria, Illinois,
Caterpillar, Inc. is a major U.S. exporter, with
1998 exports of more than $5.5 billion out of
sales totaling $16.52 billion. The seeds
Daniel Best and Benjamin Holt planted more
than one hundred years ago have blossomed
into the world's largest manufacturer of earth
moving equipment. Cooperative efforts of
their families established Caterpillar as a
Fortune 500 company that is well positioned
to bulldoze its way through the 21st century.

As the United States became more
mechanized and industrialized, new forms
of fuel were needed. The next vignette tells
where they were found.

LIFE PRINCIPLE

"LET YOUR
POLICY BE
QUALITY."

—H. JACKSON BROWN, JR.

The Defending of America

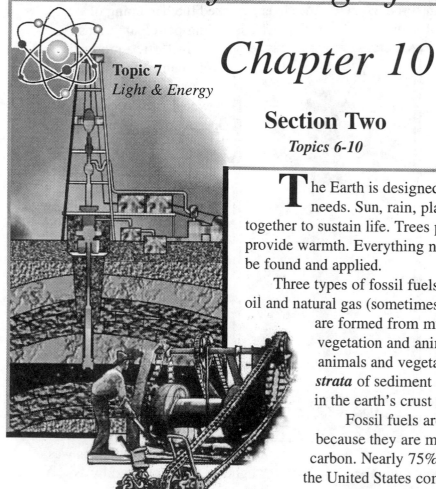

Topic 7
Light & Energy

Chapter 10

Section Two
Topics 6-10

FROM MARINE LIFE TO PINE KNOTS

The Earth is designed to provide for all human needs. Sun, rain, planting, harvest—all work together to sustain life. Trees provide shelter and fossil fuels provide warmth. Everything needed is right here. It just must be found and applied.

Three types of fossil fuels have been discovered: coal, oil and natural gas (sometimes called petroleum). Fossil fuels are formed from multiple layers of dead vegetation and animals. When the layers of dead animals and vegetation were covered under many *strata* of sediment and soil, pressure and heat deep in the earth's crust formed fossil fuels.

Fossil fuels are also called hydrocarbons because they are made primarily of hydrogen and carbon. Nearly 75% of all the energy produced in the United States comes from petroleum products. Oil and gas are vital for operating electric power plants, heating our homes and powering our vehicles. In a previous vignette, we examined how coal is mined and used; now, we will take a look at oil and natural gas.

Oil and coal are created by much the same process. However, oil is made from marine life that has been deposited, decayed and covered by layers of clay and *silt*. Through time and tremendous pressure, marine life is transformed into tiny oil droplets. These oil droplets collect in *impermeable* layers of rock to form oil pools, called petroleum or crude oil. Oil pools can be found in shale beneath silt or in off-shore areas of oceans indicating that the earth's surface may have been covered with water several thousand years ago.

Once a location which may contain oil is chosen, a large *oil derrick* is built. Original derricks were built of wood; contemporary derricks are made of steel and range from 80 to 200 feet tall. The derrick supports machinery and pipes for extracting oil from deep beneath the earth's surface.

VOCABULARY

Strata: several layers of dirt and rock
Silt: sand and salt deposits in water
Impermeable: unable to break through
Oil derrick: a tower over a well that supports machinery used to pull liquids from the well
Instinct: an inborn, natural tendency
Reservoir: underground area containing oil

Only about one in ten wells drilled produces oil or natural gas, thus production is a very expensive process. Offshore drilling rigs are even more expensive to construct. Crews on the offshore rigs live in small apartments constructed on rigs. Helicopters and boats bring supplies and occasionally take crews back to land.

Some drillers, called "wildcatters," sought oil as much by *instinct* as by science. Many of their wells were drilled where small amounts of oil had seeped to the ground's surface. The term wildcatters comes from the early 1920s when West Texas drilling crews encountered problems with wildcats. They would shoot the wildcats and hang their hides on the oil derricks.

The Middle East holds the greatest quantities of crude oil in the world, but large deposits are also found in the Soviet Union. America's richest oil supply is found in Prudhoe Bay, Alaska.

One American oil well that gained worldwide fame was drilled near Oil Creek, Pennsylvania, by Colonel Edwin L. Drake. The year was 1859, the *reservoir* was shallow (only 69.5 feet deep) the petroleum

Spindletop

was easy to *distill*. Colonel Drake's discovery marked the beginning of America's booming petroleum industry.

In 1901, a productive oil well, named Spindletop, was discovered in the western town of Beaumont, Texas. Derricks soon were placed so close together a man could step from one to another without stepping on the ground. Oil was quickly depleted from that field, but other areas of Texas were found to be rich in crude oil. Natural gas is formed where oil droplets receive especially strong heat and pressure, which converts the oil into a gas. Sometimes the gas reaches the surface of the earth and escapes into the air. More often, it is trapped by impermeable rock.

In the mid 1800s, natural gas was used for lighting. Once crude oil was discovered, the popularity of natural gas diminished because it was highly explosive and hard to transport safely. Uses were found for natural gas in making plastics, explosives, dishes and paints. Today, natural gas heats homes and fuels gas ranges and water heaters. Natural gas is also odorless and colorless. In 1937, tragedy struck the small oil town of New London, Texas. An undetected gas leak under the junior-senior section of the New London school caused an explosion. More than 300 teachers and students were killed; hundreds more were injured. The whole world shared the small town's grief. *Condolences* by the thousands were received, including those from American President and Mrs. Franklin Roosevelt and (ironically) Germany's

VOCABULARY

Distill: to boil, strain, remove impurities
Condolences: expressions of sympathy and grief
Odorous: smelly

Adolph Hitler. After this tragedy, natural gas companies added an *odorous* agent to the gas so leaks could be easily detected (a safety measure still used today).

With modern pipe systems, natural gas can safely be transported all over the country. However, care must be taken to ensure the safety of the pipeline. In early 1997, a pipeline near Fort Worth, Texas sprang a leak that was ignited when two teenagers started their truck. The resulting explosion and fire killed the two young men and destroyed property in the neighborhood.

As you have learned, Americans are an inventive group of people. With the availability of crude oil came the internal combustion engine. Gasoline, used to fuel this new engine, came from refining crude oil. The automobile and motorized vehicles for World War I brought demands for petroleum products that established the American petroleum industry.

As automobiles gained popularity, continued improvements increased their efficiency. More and more people owned cars, and gasoline to fuel them had to be readily available. Refineries produced gasoline for fueling stations which stored fuel in large holding tanks. Pumps delivered gasoline to each vehicle, and customers paid for fuel by the gallon.

Gasoline stations once performed only services like filling fuel tanks and making repairs. Along with pumps and repair facilities, today's gasoline stations may include gift shops, grocery stores and fast food restaurants which accepted credit cards.

High demand for fuel is depleting natural resources in some regions of

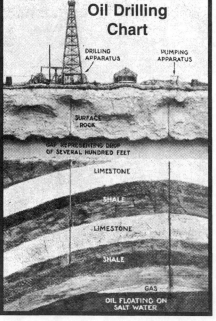

Oil Drilling Chart

DRILLING APPARATUS
PUMPING APPARATUS
SURFACE ROCK
GAS REPRESENTING DROP OF SEVERAL HUNDRED FEET
LIMESTONE
SHALE
LIMESTONE
SHALE
GAS
OIL FLOATING ON SALT WATER

America. While conserving available resources, Americans are seeking new energy sources. The rural Texas town of Jefferson exemplifies the American spirit of resourcefulness. In 1869, Jefferson's small gas company used coal in a process called *carbonization* (burning coal for energy) to produce gas for the city's gaslights. Then townspeople discovered *pine knots* (natural joints formed in the pine as the wood grows) could be carbonized to produce gas at less cost.

America is truly a land of opportunity—a place to try new ideas and make new discoveries. We can travel in the 21st century because of American ingenuity that provides energy sources for our country.

Just as advances were occurring in land transportation during the early 1900s, our next vignette will show how quickly air travel was developing.

Life Principle

"If your life is free of failures, you're not taking enough risks."

—H. Jackson Brown, Jr.

GREETING
THE VICTOR
OF THE
ATLANTIC

42

The Defending of America

Topic 8
Transportation

Chapter 10

LUCKY LINDY

Section Two
Topics 6-10

An old proverb claims, *"Luck occurs when preparation meets opportunity."* By this definition, Charles Lindbergh was a lucky man. Working hard while others slept, Lindbergh was the first man to fly solo across the Atlantic Ocean. Charles Lindbergh earned the nickname, "Lucky Lindy," on that trip in 1927.

Charles Lindbergh developed creative skills early in life. At nine years old, he devised a system of slides and pulleys to move ice blocks from the icehouse into the Lindbergh home. Later, Charles built a garden hut, raft, stilts and suspension bridge over a creek. Charles drove his mother's Model T Ford when he was only 11 and could repair it by the time he was 14.

World War I altered Lindbergh's educational plans. With many men fighting instead of producing food, teenagers were offered academic credit for growing crops. Charles farmed to earn his high school diploma. Teachers admired Charles' mechanical genius, but *deficient* English skills kept his grades so low he quit school.

Deciding to become a pilot, Lindbergh learned in only two months to fly and repair airplanes. He bought a cheap plane for *barnstorming* at rural fairs. The daring young pilot practiced wing-walking, parachuting, and selling airplane rides to earn money.

Lindbergh knew that he was different from other pilots. He did not smoke cigarettes. He drank neither alcohol nor coffee. While other pilots partied, Charles was busy disciplining himself. Each night, Charles Lindbergh graded himself against a list of 65 character traits. These outstanding qualities included honesty, alertness, precision, unselfishness and *tact*.

Eager to learn more about flying, Lindbergh joined the Army Flying Cadets. Eighty percent of the students in the cadet class failed, but the young Lindbergh graduated first in the class.

VOCABULARY

Deficient: lacking in skills necessary to function
Barnstorming: stunt flying; flying an airplane through a barn
Tact: skill and grace in dealing with others in order to maintain good relationships and to avoid causing offenses
Formidable: frightening and undefeatable
Treacherous: dangerous and life threatening

As a reserve military pilot, Lindbergh needed a job to earn money. At 24, he was hired to operate an air mail service between St. Louis and Chicago. The mail route provided valuable flying experience during Chicago's *formidable* winter weather. Airplane engines were unreliable in cold weather, and open cockpits were uncomfortable in freezing temperatures. Ice on a plane's wings made flying *treacherous* because the frozen water affected the lift from air flow over the wings.

While at an airfield on his mail route, Lindbergh saw a magazine article that changed his life. A Frenchman, realizing the potential benefits of air travel between continents, suggested a race, offering $25,000 to the first pilot who would fly solo across the Atlantic. No plane existed that could withstand such a long trip.

Inspired, Charles Lindbergh went to work designing a plane that could make a *transcontinental* flight. Charles knew he must overcome several obstacles blocking his path to success. Carrying sufficient fuel added extra weight to the plane. The extra weight of the fuel required a larger engine on the plane. As the gas tanks emptied, the plane needed to maintain its balance. The size of the wings had to be adjusted to accommodate the extra weight of additional fuel and a bigger engine. Charles took each of these items into consideration as he worked on designs for a plane.

Lindbergh could not afford to buy or build a plane capable of trans-Atlantic flight. No prominent airplane manufacturers would sell a plane to Lindbergh because the manufacturers had chosen their own experienced pilots to represent their companies in the race. Finally, a small manufacturer in California agreed to build a plane for Lindbergh. His plans helped engineers design a plane that cost less to build than his competitors' planes. Lindbergh persuaded businessmen in St. Louis, Missouri to pay for the plane, which he named the *Spirit of St. Louis*. The race was on!

One rival's plane disappeared over the Atlantic Ocean before Lindbergh's plane was built. Three competitors had accidents during their test flights. Two other plane crews were ready, but bad weather prevented their departure. Lindbergh's expertise in predicting weather during his mail route job gave him an edge. After hearing a positive radio announcement regarding the weather, Charles believed the clouds would clear. On faith, Charles Lindbergh headed for the airport at 3:00 a.m. in pouring rain. He fueled up the plane, checked the wheels and wings, then rolled down the runway.

The heavy load of gasoline and rain-soaked fabric of the wings slowed Lindbergh's takeoff. Despite the mile-long runway being almost too short, Charles was airborne by 8:00 a.m. on May 20, 1927. In the 23 hours before his departure, the exhausted pilot had not slept. Although the constant

Charles Lindbergh

demands of navigation kept him awake, Lindbergh became drowsy and drifted off the course. Estimating his direction and location by the stars, Lindbergh corrected his position and reached the Irish shoreline only 3 miles off course. Seeing the plane, people radioed the news to Paris. At night, 33 hours after his takeoff, Charles Lindbergh landed in Paris. Thousands of people greeted the courageous 25-year-old pilot. Lindbergh won not only the prize, but also the affection of the world.

Lindbergh's aviation triumph meant financial security. After his return to America, he collected $5,000,000 in *endorsements* from manufacturers. Charles accepted offers to endorse airplane products, but rejected ads for cigarettes and items he considered harmful or immoral.

Suddenly Lindbergh was a wealthy man, but he chose not to retire. Instead, he planned international travel routes. Charles also advised Henry Ford in manufacturing airplanes. After teaching U.S. Army pilots safety and fuel conservation, Lindbergh was promoted to Brigadier General in the Army Reserve. A man of many talents, Lindbergh even helped design an artificial heart pump. The lad who dropped out of school with deficient English skills continued to learn and eventually wrote six books.

VOCABULARY

Transcontinental: across the ocean between continents
Endorsements: financial support
Daydreaming: pleasant, dreamy series of thoughts
Inattention: refusal to pay attention
Anticipate: outsmart and act ahead of a person or situation
Vulnerable: unprotected from danger or harm

America was blessed when Lindbergh proved trans-Atlantic flight was more than just a dream. Air travel around the world became possible because of a determined and skilled young man, Charles Lindbergh.

Not everyone who attempted to fly across the ocean was as successful as Lindbergh. In the next vignette, you will learn what happened to a woman pilot who disappeared in the Pacific Ocean.

THE WOMAN WHO VANISHED

Radio audiences listened attentively as Amelia Earhart Putnam reported her progress on an attempted solo flight around the world. Near the end of her scheduled flight Amelia radioed a request for guidance to a refueling station in the Pacific Ocean. That transmission was the last the world heard of Earhart. Because she had not taken time to equip the plane with a trailing antenna, her radio could not receive an answer from ships that had been tracking her progress. She disappeared somewhere in the Pacific Ocean.

Amelia was born in Kansas in 1897 and grew up a tomboy. When most girls wore long dresses, she wore bloomers. Dresses were not practical for the sports and activities she liked. Amelia's father taught her to shoot, fish and play baseball. Her mother allowed little Amelia to collect worms, butterflies and frogs. Grandparents encouraged her to read books. With family support, Amelia performed above average both in the classroom and in sports.

At age 23, Amelia's first plane ride convinced her to become a pilot. She was a good student, but **daydreaming** and **inattention** to details threatened disaster. Amelia left on one trip without fueling the airplane. She often confused procedures on different airplane models. Friends grew concerned when she blamed faulty equipment for minor accidents. She constantly lived on the edge of disaster and adventure.

One day Amelia accepted a daring challenge from a publisher named George Putnam who invited Amelia to cross the Atlantic Ocean by air. Putnam wanted to sell the story of the first woman's flight across the Atlantic. Two other pilots consented to accept Miss Earhart as a passenger. They would not let her fly, however, because she lacked experience with multi engine planes. Upon arrival in England, Amelia was given more recognition than the pilot and navigator simply because she was a woman.

With newfound fame came money from lectures and books. Amelia shared her money with family members, a habit she continued as long as she lived. Putnam's excellent publicity made Miss Earhart's book earnings soar. When Putnam and Earhart married, she continued to use the name people recognized—Earhart.

Amelia became offended when newspaper articles hinted that she was not a good pilot. Deciding to prove her expertise by flying solo across the Atlantic, Amelia Earhart took off on May 20, 1932, exactly five years after Lindbergh's historic flight.

Four hours into the trip, a broken altimeter and gas leak made the lady pilot uneasy. Struggling to rise above a storm, her plane went into a spin when slushy ice covered the wings. Amelia brought the plane under control just above the waves.

Reaching the Irish coast, Amelia did not take time to hunt for an airport. She feared fumes from leaking gas would be ignited by engine heat, so she landed safely in the nearest cow pasture.

Amelia earned new honors for solo transcontinental flights, but she wanted to complete a daring trip over the Pacific Ocean. She planned a trip from Hawaii to California. Because strong West to East winds prevented Amelia from making the flight from California to Hawaii, her plane was shipped to Hawaii, and Amelia flew it back to California. Once again, Amelia Earhart was honored.

Desiring adventure and even more fame, Amelia decided to become the first woman to fly around the world. To raise funds for the trip, Amelia agreed to test flight instruments invented by aviation corporations. Amelia invited a navigator and radioman along on the flight to assist with the tests. Help with those duties freed Amelia to devote full attention to the plane's demands.

Amelia's first attempt to fly around the world failed when she damaged the plane on takeoff during the second leg of her trip. The radioman who accompanied her on the first attempt was not available for Amelia's second try. Amelia was impatient to complete her flight around the world and never took the time to complete training on use of new radio and direction locator equipment.

Amelia Earhart

Amelia and a new navigator, Frederick Noonan, left Miami on June 2, 1937 without the recommended radio equipment or an experienced radioman. They were greeted by enthusiastic crowds when they landed in South America, Africa, India, and New Guinea, where Amelia was to receive a new trailing antenna for her radio; however, she grew impatient while waiting for the antenna to arrive, and she departed without it.

The large expanse of Pacific Ocean from New Guinea to the United States required refueling at a tiny island. A ship waited nearby to broadcast radio messages to help Amelia and her navigator find the island. On schedule, the ship crew heard Amelia's radio messages, but she could not hear signals from the ship. Amelia had failed to include the code for transmitting signals to identify her location. Amelia became lost and was unable to receive signals regarding her location from the ship or airport. Amelia Earhart was never heard from again. Neither she, her navigator, nor the plane wreckage were ever found. Amelia just seemed to vanish; her husband assumed that she had been "lost at sea."

Failing to take radio training and to pack necessary radio equipment was a fatal mistake. Amelia Earhart's impatience and inattention to details probably cost her life. But, Americans looked past Earhart's failures and recognized her successes. She is honored as an American hero.

An interesting footnote to this story comes from San Antonio, Texas. In 1997, a woman named Linda Finch attempted to complete the same course around the world that Amelia Earhart had planned but never completed. Linda followed the same flight plan and flew in the same kind of airplane as Amelia Earhart. Linda Finch was successful in her attempt because of careful planning.

In the next vignette, you will learn how a combination of ships and planes improved America's military proficiency in the Pacific Ocean.

AN ADMIRABLE DECISION

Strong leaders must make decisions and take responsibility for their actions. When Raymond Spruance trained at West Point, he learned to examine facts and make decisions. Raymond's attention to details and ability to assume responsibility helped the United States win World War II.

Japan, while at war with the United States, had taken control of many Pacific islands. If Japan could gain control of the whole Pacific Ocean, Japanese planes could strike any American city on the West Coast.

Military airplanes could not carry enough fuel to fight in the Pacific and return to Hawaii. Military leaders and innovative ship builders developed *aircraft carriers* (floating airfields and repair hangers). An aircraft carrier was a large ship with a long runway on the top deck.

Aircraft carrier

Steam powered catapults on one end of the ship launched airplanes. Arresting cables on the other end of the carrier helped catch and stop incoming craft so they would not fall off the edge of the ship. Large elevators moved airplanes between the deck runway and lower storage areas.

Linda Finch

47

Even though aircraft technology had enabled U.S. military forces to equip ships with guns, exposure to enemy aircraft and ships was still a serious issue. Bad weather sometimes grounded aircraft carrier planes, and a surprise enemy attack could catch American airplanes in the lower storage areas. The lives of the crew and the fate of the ship depended on the ability of the commander to *anticipate* enemy capabilities. Scout planes were usually sent out to locate enemy ships.

Admiral Raymond Spruance was commander of the carrier, *U.S.S. Enterprise* on June 4, 1942 when he learned that Japan planned to attack American-controlled Midway Island. The *Enterprise* was 300 miles from Midway and *vulnerable* to Japanese attack. U.S. scout airplanes left the *Enterprise* to locate the Japanese navy. The *U.S.S. Enterprise* planes were successful in locating and attacking Japanese ships. The Battle of Midway was one of the most dramatic encounters of World War II.

Fierce battles were fought there on June 4th, and ended after dark. American pilots indicated that Japanese carriers had been damaged, but no precise reports were available. Admiral Spruance had two options. He could take the damaged *Enterprise* to the combat area that night and be ready on June 5th to continue fighting, or he could remain

300 miles away to make critical repairs, then send scout planes at daybreak to gather accurate information.

Admiral Spruance made a decision to repair his ship. The Admiral was unaware of the total impact of his decision. If Admiral Spruance had approached the battle scene during the night of June 4th he would have been attacked by Japanese battleships sent out specifically to destroy the *Enterprise*. The repaired *Enterprise* engaged enemy forces on June 5th and played a major role in a United States victory over Japanese naval ships and planes.

Military documents record that U.S. forces destroyed four Japanese aircraft carriers that day—the entire convoy of Japan's aircraft carriers. *U.S.S. Enterprise* planes were credited with sinking two of Japan's aircraft carriers and assisting in the destruction of a third one. The elimination of all Japanese aircraft carriers was considered a turning point in World War II. Japan lost 17 ships, 275 planes and 4800 men. The U.S. lost two ships and 300 men at Midway.

The critical decision made by Admiral Raymond Spruance kept his crew safe and his ship from being destroyed. The *U.S.S. Enterprise's* pilots fought in nearly every battle in the Pacific Ocean, and the ship became the symbol of victory for the United States.

The next lesson shows you what a spinning top and a battleship have in common, and how one invention leads to another.

Deck of *Enterprise* ready to launch planes at Midway

Life Principle

"Keep away from people who try to belittle your ambitions. Small people always do that, but the really great make you feel that you, too, can become great."

\- Mark Twain

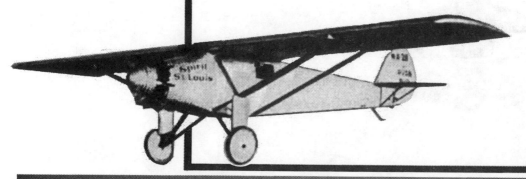

Gyroscope

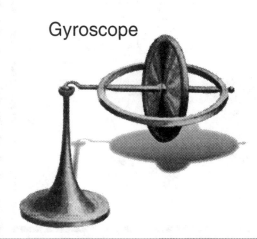

The Defending of America

Topic 9
*Discoveries &
Explorations*

Chapter 10

A PROMISE IN A STORM

Section Two
Topics 6-10

In the early 1900s, Elmer Sperry was busy in Cleveland, Ohio inventing things like electrical machines for digging coal and storage batteries for powering electrical cars. Once when Sperry was a passenger on a ship crossing the Atlantic during a storm, he was thrown violently on the deck as the ship tossed about in the waves. Scrambling to his feet, Elmer Sperry made himself a promise. He would discover a way to stop such upsetting motions of ships at sea. Sperry's two young sons shared his desire to understand the mystery of motion.

Back home in Cleveland, Elmer and his boys spent time sitting on the floor studying the motion of a spinning top. The threesome watched the top fall over when the spinning motion stopped. *"Why did this happen?"* they wondered. Turning a bicycle upside down, Sperry set the wheel spinning for the boys to watch. Elmer taught his sons how to feel the power needed to make the wheel change directions. As the boys grew older, they wanted to work in their father's laboratory finding answers to the mysteries of motion. They questioned why a spinning top always stayed level, and why a spinning object always stayed in the direction it was pointed.

When Elmer was ready to develop his idea for keeping a ship steady in rough water, the Sperry family moved to New York to be near the Brooklyn Naval Yard. Elmer's first project was to build a reliable ship compass. The compass normally used on huge warships could be pulled off its true direction by all the thick metal in the big guns and in the ship itself. Sperry found a way to use the **gyroscope** that the Frenchman Foucault had invented. The spinning part of the device gave Sperry the idea for making a **gyrocompass**. Once the gyrocompass was set in the right direction, it stayed on course and was not affected by the thick ship metal. Elmer Sperry's work was honored as the

VOCABULARY

Gyroscope: a rotating wheel that spins on an axis in all directions, helps ships maintain balance and direction
Gyrocompass: a compass driven by a gyroscope which bases its position of spinning on the rotation of the earth so that it is able to point true north
Stabilizer: an instrument that keeps ships steady and true to their course
Indebted: to owe someone for a favor they did you

20th century's greatest step forward in ocean navigation. Practically every vessel at sea today uses the gyrocompass to hold a steady direction.

Sperry and his sons studied a toy version of the gyroscope. They saw how the inner spinning part somehow held the outer metal frame in a level and steady position. Elmer explained how he would build a device to hold a ship steady by using the idea of a gyroscope. In 1913, Elmer Sperry installed his first *stabilizer* on the American destroyer, the *Worden*. Elmer worked hard to make many technical adjustments needed to steady the ship's particular roll. Sperry installed a total of 42 stabilizers on ships and submarines.

Elmer Sperry's son, Lawrence, worked hard on making the device light enough to work in airplanes. The French government offered a prize to the man who could stabilize an airplane. In 1914, Lawrence flew a stabilized plane to France and won the prize. Lawrence demonstrated the plane's stability by flying so low that the crowd on the field could see both his hands raised off the controls. The best evidence that the plane was stable came when his French mechanic stepped out onto the wing of the plane without causing it to tilt to one side. For the next nine years, Lawrence

Gyrocompass

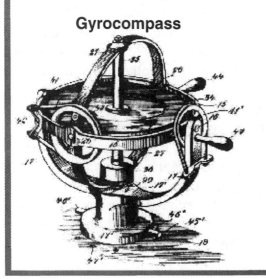

worked on making airplanes safer. Sadly, Lawrence Sperry died in 1923 when engine failure caused his plane to crash in the English Channel.

The Sperry family had always worked together; thus, after Lawrence died, his younger brother joined the family effort to make planes safer. The Sperry family worked together, and the Sperry Automatic Pilot System was made famous when a pilot named Wally Post flew solo around the world, navigating his plane with the Sperry Automatic Pilot.

America is *indebted* to two young boys and their devoted father who challenged them with a spinning top. Each of the Sperrys made great discoveries which improved instruments and made flying safer for pilots of passenger planes and explorers in remote regions.

AIRPLANES AND DOGSLEDS IN ANTARCTICA

Inventions like the gyrocompass, gasoline motor and battery powered radio gave Richard E. Byrd the technology and equipment he needed to explore the North Pole. Airplanes replaced the dogsleds of earlier explorations. The first successful flight over the North Pole was made by Rear Admiral Richard Byrd, accompanied by Floyd Bennett on May 9, 1926. The round trip of 1,440 miles took about 16 hours. Byrd then turned his attention to Antarctica, where he expected to make a successful flight over the South Pole.

As an American hero, Byrd received a huge amount of support for his 1928 *expedition*. His crew reached the Bay of

Whales in Antarctica with equipment that filled more than 12 supply buildings. Byrd organized the men to form tunnels through the snow. His men were able to move about as though they were in a city. They had electricity, telephones, and three radio towers to keep them in touch with the outside world. Byrd named the outpost "Little America."

Byrd was the first explorer to replace dogsleds with motor-powered machines. For his first trip, Byrd mounted a Ford engine and *chassis* on skis and tractor treads. This mechanical dog sled enabled Byrd to explore the ice-covered South Pole. Only penguins and a few birds lived along the outer rim of land. News of Byrd's findings was beamed by radio to Americans eager to learn about Byrd's discoveries.

The next year, Byrd flew over the South Pole. When blasts of air from the high frozen mountains kept the plane from rising, he ordered emergency supplies thrown overboard. Then, the plane scaled over lofty peaks higher than the Andes Mountains and soared out across the level space of the Pole. About that moment, Byrd later wrote: *"One gets there and that is all there is for the telling. It is the effort to get there that counts."*

Four years later in 1933, Byrd made another expedition with even more supplies and equipment. That time he had four planes, six motor vehicles and 153 dogs for doing trail work. Byrd successfully blended dog-power with technology. Not far from the first camp he built, Byrd set up "Little America II."

Byrd made sure that many scientific studies were carried out successfully. Planes flew over the region and discovered that Antarctica was one continent, not a series of islands. Its 500 million square miles made it larger than the U.S. and Mexico put together. Byrd's major scientific aim was to take readings of the winter climate. He wanted facts and figures about the icy air that pours off the two-mile high polar *plateau* and has a strong effect on the world's climate.

Byrd spent the winter alone in his small 9' x 13' cabin, which was dug into the ice 125 miles south of Little America II. One day he went outside to take a weather reading and a blast of wind slammed shut the trap door to the house, leaving

VOCABULARY

Expedition: a voyage or journey that requires courage and a lot of planning
Chassis: supporting frame of a vehicle
Plateau: a large, flat hill
Harmony: working together peacefully and productively

Byrd stranded outside in the sub-zero weather. Byrd struggled to survive until he finally pried the door open with a shovel found in the snow. Another day, Byrd lost his direction in a howling blizzard. He walked in larger and larger circles until he found the guide posts that marked a safe return. Before the end of seven months, he almost died of carbon monoxide poisoning coming from a leak in his oil stove. The near-death experience changed Byrd's life. He returned home, determined to spend the rest of his life helping people to face conflicts peacefully. In 1936, Richard Byrd spoke in 156 cities to more than 600,000 people. In 1939, Byrd wrote a book, *Alone*. In it, Byrd revealed detailed information about the experiences that changed his life.

President Franklin Roosevelt also decided in 1939 that another expedition should go to Antarctica. Byrd, who was then an Admiral, was selected to organize the trip. The purpose of Byrd's third Antarctica expedition was to establish a permanent base. He claimed the land between longitude 80 W and 150 W for the United States. New tools and new methods made that polar expedition less risky than previous endeavors. Vitamins prevented diseases. Planes dropped food and supplies and lifted out any men who became ill. By 1941, however, World War II demanded America's attention and the men assigned to the Antarctica base returned home.

The following excerpt is from Byrd's book, *Alone:"Real peace comes from struggle that involves such things as effort, discipline, enthusiasm. The **harmony** of a man's life-course is expressed by happiness; this is the prime desire of mankind, I believe. When a man achieves a fair measure of harmony within himself and his family circle, he achieves peace; and a nation made up of such individuals and groups is a happy nation."*

People who could not participate in adventurous expeditions liked to read about them. In the next vignette, you will learn what else Americans were reading in the 1920s and 1930s.

Life Principle

"Man's mind once stretched by a new idea, never regains its original dimension."

-Oliver Wendell Holmes

54

The Defending of America

Topic 10
Education, Music & Literature

Chapter 10

Section Two
Topics 6-10

GATSBY, GHOSTWRITERS, AND PILOTS WITH PENS

After World War I, America roared into the 1920s with newspaper headlines focused on gangsters, flappers, and bootleggers. The Roaring Twenties brought dramatic changes to American lifestyles. F. Scott Fitzgerald wrote about the glittering society life of that time. After his boyhood days near Chicago's elaborate homes, Fitzgerald dreamed of a fancy lifestyle. While he was a student at Princeton University, magazines published his stories about wealthy people having fun to excess. Fitzgerald had clearly researched his subject—he partied so much himself he could not write a successful book. Many of Fitzgerald's admirers believed he could become a great writer if he learned to discipline his talents correctly. The young writer left school after some major disappointments, closed himself up at home and wrote his first successful novel, *Tender is the Night*.

Success and status enabled Fitzgerald to storm high society in the lifestyle he craved. He and his beautiful young wife entered the fast lane, a glamorous couple who ***hobnobbed*** with famous people in the best nightclubs of New York, London, and Paris. During that time Fitzgerald wrote his most famous novel, *The Great Gatsby*. The book's characters chased wealth and high society so much they never found lasting love. Fitzgerald ended the story by letting the ***protagonist***, Gatsby, finally realize how his bad choices had destroyed real happiness. Fitzgerald's book revealed how Gatsby's lust for riches had pierced his soul with sorrows and disappointments.

During the Depression of the 1930s, Americans no longer enjoyed reading about rich, carefree people. Much like his protagonist, Gatsby, Fitzgerald himself paid a great price for his excesses. He lost not only his wealth, but also his wife, who entered a New Jersey mental hospital as an alcoholic. When

VOCABULARY

Hobnobbed: to associate with
Protagonist: main person in a story
Resurrect: bring back to life
Ghost writers: someone who writes books for someone else
Espionage: spying
Cliffhanger: a scene that entices the reader to keep reading
Tundra: the semi-frozen grass lands in arctic regions
Circumnavigate: to go around

Fitzgerald died in the 1940s, he was working on a novel about powerful men behind the motion picture industry titled *The Last Tycoon*. Published years later, the book shows how Fitzgerald tried to **resurrect** the talents he had ruined by following reckless habits. F. Scott Fitzgerald's brilliant earlier work from the 1920s earned him a lasting place in American literature.

During the early 1900s, young teenagers read thrilling adventure books written just for them. One man alone sold 200 million copies of such books from 1900 to the 1930s. Edward Stratemeyer's clever mind created ideas for 1,300 books in his popular series. However, his name never appeared as author of a single book. Stratemeyer set up a system that used **ghost writers** who agreed to write books, never using their real names.

Stratemeyer sent 3-page outlines to writers who wrote the stories and returned them to Stratemeyer within a month. He paid them $50 to $250 for each book. Before sending it to the publisher, he made sure the plot moved the characters smoothly from one book to the next. Stratemeyer's amazing genius flooded the market with heroes and heroines such as: the Hardy Boys, Nancy Drew, Dave Fearless, the Bobbsey Twins, the Rover Boys, Dave Dashaway, the Carewell Chums and Tom Swift. These clever and courageous characters solved mysteries and had grand adventures all over the

Zelda & Scott Fitzgerald

world. Their wholesome, exciting lives provided good role models for young people who wished they could grow up to be like their literary heroes.

Ghost writers for these books are still writing today. Ghostwriters for the *Hardy Boys Mysteries* series must follow a rule book sent to all modern-day writers. Crimes the characters solve must be realistic and dangerous, and can include everything from terrorist attacks to **espionage**. Each chapter ends with a **cliffhanger** to keep readers turning the pages. A cliffhanger is something like the following: *"An assassin's bullet penetrates the boat's fuel tank while Joe is at the helm."* As the chapter ends, the craft erupts into a ball of fire. Readers discover in the next chapter that Joe dove into the shark-infested Gulf of Mexico just seconds before the explosion.

Even in today's liberal times, writers of teenage adventure stories are expected to follow the morally sound traditions of earlier episodes. Dialogue must never use vulgar words, off-color double meanings, cursing, or taking God's name in vain. The character's romancing is limited to a very rare friendly hug or kiss.

And while young men were reading about the Hardy Boys, other brave young men and women in the 1920s were actually experiencing adventure in the skies. These adventurers later wrote beautiful and meaningful books. Early days of railroading did not spur exciting books, but this is not true of the first aviators. These daring pilots wrote about flying into the rising sun . . . feeling the wind in their faces . . . looking down on green fields and wandering rivers. With great beauty and color, they wrote about touching distant corners of the Earth.

After Charles Lindbergh made the first nonstop flight from New York to Paris, he wrote the book, *We*. He described feeling himself becoming linked to the plane. He believed both man and machine had won a victory. The name of Lindbergh's plane, *The Spirit of St. Louis*, became the title of his next book. It won the Pulitzer Prize in 1926.

On later expeditions, Lindbergh's wife, Anne Morrow Lindbergh, flew as his copilot and radio operator. Their flight in 1931 took them over the great frozen *tundra* of northern Canada and Alaska. Anne's beautifully written book, *North to the Orient*, describes how she and Charles

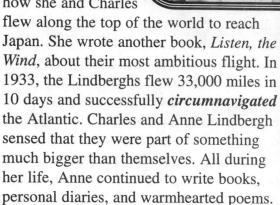

Anne Morrow Lindbergh

flew along the top of the world to reach Japan. She wrote another book, *Listen, the Wind*, about their most ambitious flight. In 1933, the Lindberghs flew 33,000 miles in 10 days and successfully *circumnavigated* the Atlantic. Charles and Anne Lindbergh sensed that they were part of something much bigger than themselves. All during her life, Anne continued to write books, personal diaries, and warmhearted poems.

These early pilots became some of America's greatest heroes. Amelia Earhart, the first woman to fly the Atlantic, wrote three books. *The Last Flight* was compiled and published by Amelia's husband after her mysterious disappearance in the air. The whole nation mourned her death.

Americans read these aviators' books as well as books by pilots from other countries. Like Charles Lindbergh, the Frenchman Antoine de Saint-Exupery began his career by flying the mail. He flew over the Sahara Desert and high across the Andes Mountains. His novel, *Night Flight*, became world famous, and his fable, *The Little Prince*, became a classic.

These aviator-authors saw how airplanes in the future would affect travel and relationships among nations. Near the close of his life, Charles Lindbergh made a speech in Minnesota, sharing some of what he learned from 50 years of watching airplanes change. Lindbergh said "nature should always be important to man." He believed that *"progress could only be measured by the quality of life; not human life alone, but all life."*

__During this time, a revolution was taking place in education. In the next vignette, we will see how the military influenced academics.__

How did Civil War uniforms revolutionize America's schools? The

STANDARDIZED TESTING—ONE SIZE DOES NOT FIT ALL

"revolution" started when many soldiers suddenly needed army uniforms at the same time. Prior to the Civil War, individuals had always made their own clothes or hired a tailor to make them fit properly. During the Civil War, recording body measurements of countless soldiers revealed a totally new concept—most bodies grew to be certain "standard" sizes. This collection of measurements was averaged into *standard* sizes and a chart was set up from these averages. For the first time, uniforms were cut to fit specific sizes. After the war, America's huge clothing industry sprang up from this simple discovery. People needed shoes, hats, shirts, and trousers that fit, and Americans began thinking of themselves as belonging to *sizes*.

Charts of body sizes inspired a new science called *psychology* to study ways of measuring a person's mind. Psychologists wanted to know if the mind could grow to a certain size like the body did. Many people made fun of the first mental tests of the early 1900s. When World War I began, the Army found an important use for these tests. Thousands of soldiers needed work assignments; the Army hoped the tests would help determine for which job each man was best suited. The Army conducted the most stunning single exercise in the history of testing: 13,000 testing centers gave the Stanford Achievement Test to 316,000 young men.

VOCABULARY

Standard: a basis for comparing certain required criteria
Core: most important, essential to learn
Subtle: sneaky, not easily detected or noticed
Consolidate: to add small parts to make one large amount

Soon after the war, psychologists made the Stanford Achievement Test available to schools. Schools tried to test and grade each child's abilities. Tests aimed to find abilities which seemed average for large numbers of students from certain age groups. Tests compared individual students to the average score. Schools began to base lessons and behavior guidelines on what most students, or the *norm,* did. The traditional concept of learning a specific *core* of values-based education was replaced by information which the "average" person should learn.

Inspired by the Army's mass testing, colleges began testing students before allowing them to enroll in classes. The College Entrance Exam Board was set up in 1924 and the first Scholastic Aptitude Test (SAT) was administered in 1926. By using such tests, colleges hoped to avoid wasting money when too many students

Classroom Testing

dropped out, and to avoid wasting talent by overlooking students with high abilities. By 1935, the tests used a new grading scale that no longer stopped at 100. The average was 500, with low scores dropping to 200 and high ones going to 800. A new design was set up so that machines graded the tests; students no longer had their work read by trained graders.

By the end of World War II, nationwide testing touched many aspects of American life. Government funds paid for thousands of veterans to enter college after the war. Before being accepted by colleges, the veterans were tested by the Educational Testing Service. That company also tested people wanting to enter programs offered by big businesses like Westinghouse and Pepsi-Cola.

Although mass testing offered some benefits, it came with *subtle* side effects. Americans grew comfortable with a system that measured and sized them up according to groups with minimum consideration of individuality and creativity. Perhaps no arena of American life demonstrated this side effect more dramatically than the public school system. The desperate need for educators to consider each student's individual abilities and talents was often sacrificed for the sake of group instruction. One room schools were replaced by large *consolidated* schools with classrooms for each age level.

This attempt at standardized learning offered administrative convenience for classifying and instructing students, but caused slower students to suffer defeat and humiliation while fast learners became bored. Creative writers, teachers, and editors who pursue ideas for improving education in America are often frustrated by the common policy of operating schools based on standardizing students to become average.

Fortunately, by 1998 alternative educational programs were widely available for students who were below average, average and above average. Alternative programs included private schools, home education, charter schools and vouchers. Some large school districts established magnet schools which offered specialized studies in career fields such as auto repair, cosmetology, media, computer technology and agriculture. Students in alternative programs currently have the option to learn from the Internet, computer CDs, audio cassettes, VCRs or printed materials available in graded classrooms or in individualized learning centers. By 2000, many educators were experimenting with individualize programs available in storefront schools, over wireless palm held computers and in industry site schools.

Just as Americans loved the written word, so were they intrigued with reproduced sounds and pictures. During this time period, many advances were made in the fields of communication, as you will see in the next vignette.

Life Principle

"Hold yourself responsible to a higher standard than anyone else expects of you. Never excuse yourself."

-Henry Ward Beecher

The Defending of America

Topic 11
Communication

Chapter 10

Section Three
Topics 11-15

CAN YOU HEAR WHAT I HEAR?

Only 125 years ago, Americans did not have telephones, radios, CDs, personal computers or the Internet—inventions we take for granted today. In the past, Americans communicated primarily by the spoken word or written language. Colonists visited with each other at church or town meetings. Settlers waited anxiously for the pony express rider to arrive with mail.

Today, Americans can communicate with each other by simply sending a "fax" or E-mail. Technological inventions and advances over the years have expanded methods of communication both to local and global levels. The following overview gives some examples of how technology has helped us "keep in touch" with each other and the world.

VOCABULARY

Sabotage: to destroy intentionally
Electromagnetic waves: waves generated by electrical charges
Profound: intense, deeply felt
Orbit: a circular path
Image dissector: a camera tube necessary for transmitting television pictures
Iconoscope: similar to the image dissector—a tube required for transmitting picture signals
Detrimental: a situation that is harmful
Coveting: wanting what someone else has due to being dissatisfied with ones' own possessions

The Telegraph:

Before telephones were invented, the telegraph was a major form of communication in America. Research that went into developing the telegraph laid the groundwork for the first telephone. In 1832, Samuel F.B. Morse became interested in telegraphy after hearing about experiments conducted in Europe. Using an electrical device similar to a doorbell, Morse designed a system of taps using dots and dashes combined with longer connections to represent the alphabet. That system became known as Morse Code.

Telegraphs made a dramatic impact on the communication world. For the first time, news could travel from one location to another almost instantly, affecting everything from family life to politics. By the Civil War years, America was so dependent on the telegraph that both Union and Confederate soldiers cut telegraph lines to *sabotage* military communications.

The Trans-Atlantic Cable:

In 1854, Cyrus Field attempted to lay an encased telegraphic cable from one side of the Atlantic Ocean to the other. The cable broke 360 miles offshore. Four years later, after three more attempts, the project was still not completed. Despite the complications preventing its success, Field was sure the system would work. He persisted, and in 1858 America and Europe were linked by underwater cable. Britain's Queen Victoria sent the first message to American President James Buchanan, but the cable broke again two weeks later. Finally, in 1866, Field was successful. Cyrus Field's determination paid off. At last, not even the ocean remained a communication barrier between countries.

The Telephone:

Americans seldom send a telegraph these days, but the telephone is probably the most widely used communication tool in the world. Most Americans are dependent on their phones; they would be lost without them.

The first telephones did not come in decorator colors and shapes. Nor did they have the many features of phones today. Each telephone on a system had to be connected to the next phone by wires. For 50 telephones, more than 1,000 wires could be necessary. Switchboards were the solution. The first switchboard was used by E.T. Holmes in 1877. He had a switchboard system connecting four banks and a factory. At night, the switchboard acted as a burglar alarm.

At first, telephones were used only for business and emergencies. Installation was expensive, and some geographic areas were impossible to reach with phone lines. Usually, a phone was located in the general store of rural communities.

Switchboard Operators

Today's mobile lifestyles create a market for highly sophisticated telephone technology. Cordless phones have independent handsets that can be used at a distance from the base unit. This means a person working in the front yard or relaxing by the pool can still receive important calls.

A major advancement in communication is the cellular phone. Geographic regions are divided into what are called "cells." As the caller travels from one cell to another, his call is instantly transferred to the next cell, enabling mobility with nationwide access.

American Telephone and Telegraph Bell Laboratories successfully developed the world's first digital optical processor in 1990. It allowed information to be processed by light rather than electricity. Optics can process at least a thousand times more information at once than electronics, efficiently handling the increasing demands for world-wide communication.

Radio Waves:

In 1895, an Italian physicist named Marconi discovered how to adapt sound waves for communication. When sounds are changed into *electromagnetic waves* and sent through air, they travel at the speed of light (about 186,000 miles per second). A receiver changes them back into the original sounds. At first, radio was used primarily for sending and receiving emergency messages, especially during World War I. The full potential of radio was later realized when the first successful station, KDKA in Pittsburgh, Pennsylvania, broadcasted the 1920 Presidential election results of Warren G. Harding's win over James Cox. Little more than a year later, more than 500 licensed stations existed in the U.S.

Radio flourished during the Great Depression when people found a diversion in radio entertainment. With sound effects only, creative producers communicated stories to listeners' imaginations. Listening audiences were entertained by comedy shows, dramas, music, mysteries, quiz shows, news, documentaries and children's shows. Many early television personalities launched their careers on radio programs.

Radio had a *profound* effect on Americans. Before, information could hardly be communicated to more than an arena full of people at one time. Now, the entire country could receive the same information instantly. Americans could listen to their radios and share these experiences as a nation. Gathered comfortably around their radios, families heard the latest Sherlock Holmes episode, Gene Autry songs, election returns or presidential speech. Radio brought American families together as they listened to dramatic presentations of "The Lone Ranger," "Johnny Dollar" and "The Shadow."

Satellite Communications:

Satellites are launched into space by rockets and placed into *orbit* around planet Earth. Satellites travel at a speed that enable Earth's gravitational pull to keep them at a constant location over the planet. Satellites pick up signals which are beamed into space by transmitting stations on Earth. Signals are then transmitted to receiving stations elsewhere on Earth—even on the other side

of the planet. Through satellites, radio and television waves are sent to any part of the world. Satellites produce better signals than ground systems. One satellite can cover only about a third of the earth's surface, but a network of several satellites enables instant global communication through radio, television and telephone communication systems.

English writer Arthur C. Clarke introduced the concept of satellites in 1945. On October 4, 1957, Soviet Russians launched the first satellite into space: *Sputnik I*. No one was on board *Sputnik I* because it was not known if humans could survive in space. November 3, 1957, Russian *Sputnik II* was launched. However, this time, a passenger was on board—a Russian dog named Laika who survived the trip, but had to be put to sleep shortly after her return. Laika proved a valuable point. Now, humans knew they too could survive in space. On January 31, 1958, America launched her first satellite— *Explorer I*—but no humans were on board.

The first man in space was an American named Alan B. Shepard. On May 5, 1961, Shepard was launched into space aboard the Mercury spacecraft, *Freedom 7*. Shepard's flight lasted only 15 minutes, but proved that humans could travel safely in space. The next step was to figure out how to perfect the technology to make space travel profitable and effective.

On February 20, 1962, millions of people watched in fascination as John Glenn was launched into space inside the Mercury *Friendship 7*. This time, America was successful. John Glenn was the first human to orbit the earth.

Men and women who dedicate their

lives to serve America are considered heroes and heroines. John Glenn was such a man. As a child and teen, Glenn had developed a strong determination to overcome tremendous obstacles. One year, Glenn survived a Scarlet Fever epidemic, but could not leave his house. Instead of being discouraged, he spent his time building and repairing model planes. His interest in model planes developed into a love for flying.

After three years of college, Glenn joined the Navy Aviation Cadet Program, and by 1944 had become a naval aviator and first lieutenant in the U.S. Marine Corps. John Glenn served his country during World War II and again in the Korean War, where he flew 90 combat missions. After the Korean War, Glenn became a test pilot and made several record-breaking flights.

In 1965, Glenn retired from the

John Glenn

Marines and started his own business. In 1980, he was elected as U.S. Senator from Ohio. In 1998, John Glenn, one of America's greatest heroes, was 72 years old. Glenn told his colleagues he was interested in flying in space again as a senior citizen. He decided to return to space in October of 1998. Glenn is proud of that honor—he took one more opportunity to serve his country. John Glenn's dedication and courage paved the way for others to go into space and to the moon.

In 1969, the whole world watched as

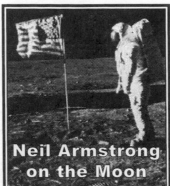

Neïl Armstrong on the Moon

Neil Armstrong placed man's first steps on the moon. The first television pictures from *Apollo 11* astronauts on the moon were seen live via satellites.

Movies & Movie Theaters:

Moving pictures were developed in 1889 and were in common use by World War I. The most popular movie themes were comedy and cowboy heroes. Movie theaters sprang up across America as families discovered the pleasures associated with "Saturday night at the movies." During the 1940s and 1950s movie theaters were favorite places for teenagers to date. Most of the movies were based on good prevailing over evil. Heroes were common and sex-explicit scenes were forbidden. Movie scripts were written to cause the audience to be attentive by following a plot rather than relying on action scenes enforced by technical effects. Actors and actresses such as John Wayne, Humphrey Bogart, James Stewart, Charleton Heston, Audrey Hepburn and Sophia Lauren popularized American movies.

Television (TV):

No single person invented television; many scientists helped develop the concept of television. In 1922, a 16-year-old American high school student named Philo T. Farnsworth developed the idea of an *image dissector*. Two years later in 1924, a Russian-American named Zworykin invented the *iconoscope*. In 1926, Scottish engineer John Baird built a television using ideas from Farnsworth and Zworykin.

While radio touched our ears and our imaginations, television commanded our entire attention—and left little to our imagination! World War II delayed development of TV for household use, but by

1948, television was on its way to being a household fixture. In the 1950s, a teenager riding a bicycle through his neighborhood could see television screens in nearly every house. Television created perhaps the greatest revolution ever known in the lifestyles of Americans. Some of the changes were positive, but others were extremely *detrimental*. Instead of living active lives, people watched an imitation of other peoples' lives on a screen. Many became confirmed *couch potatoes*, neglecting healthful exercise. Although families watched television together in the same room, communication skills suffered as people spent less time talking with each other. Young people grew up watching TV actors and actresses whose lives were inconsistent with reality, and program sponsors enticed viewers to buy products advertised on TV. Millions of Americans became materialistic, *coveting* the cars, clothes and homes of their television idols.

Advertisers found that television viewers were a great *captive audience*. Commercials persuaded people that life would be easier, more glamorous and fulfilling when certain products were purchased. A *phenomenal* rise in product sales expanded national businesses. Unfortunately, cigarette and beer commercials prompted countless people to start smoking tobacco or drinking alcoholic beverages. Glamorous actors and actresses were often portrayed lighting cigarettes or drinking liquor.

Television programs were expensive to produce, so network executives sold advertising time to businesses. TV marketing worked well because gullible viewers spent money on items advertisers enticed consumers to purchase. Advertisers targeted specific programs and baited buyers with a *plethora* of products.

During recent decades, cable and satellite television have become popular. Many households pay monthly fees to access a wide variety of programs brought into the home by wire or signal. Unfortunately, television offers violent and pornographic 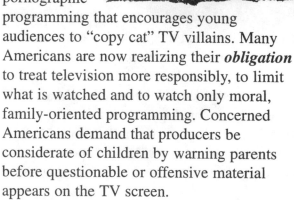 programming that encourages young audiences to "copy cat" TV villains. Many Americans are now realizing their *obligation* to treat television more responsibly, to limit what is watched and to watch only moral, family-oriented programming. Concerned Americans demand that producers be considerate of children by warning parents before questionable or offensive material appears on the TV screen.

Television has had many positive effects, too. Viewers are informed quickly about world wide current events. Thanks to television, viewers can share the joy of a rescued child, experience the capture of

---

VOCABULARY

Captive audience: an audience that is very interested or unable to avoid listening
Phenomenal: incredible, huge, beyond expectations
Plethora: a great amount, beyond imagination
Obligation: the state of being bound to a promise or duty
Modem: a device that converts data and prepares the data for transmission

terrorists, share in the relief when a murderer is brought to justice or prepare for bad weather. Volunteers can be rallied quickly to aid communities devastated by natural disasters. The whole world can share in triumphs of the Olympic games. Television has brought the entire world (both fantasy and reality) to most homes.

Cassette Tapes:

In 1898, the principle of magnetic recordings on wire or tape was developed. In 1963, a Dutch electronics firm introduced compact audio cassettes, using cellulose tape coated with iron oxide. Cassettes were available to the general public, purposely not patented so they would gain worldwide acceptance. Not only did the public accept them, everybody wanted to be able to play and listen to the tapes. Most homes, automobiles and offices have several compact audio cassette players.

VCRs:

In order to give videotapes both sound and picture, a more complex production system was developed. To produce sound, the tape has to move slowly. To produce pictures, the tape has to be scanned at high speeds. Tape moves slowly through the video playback machine, while internal heads scan the tape at great speeds, thus producing balanced sight and sound. This technology enables most American families to own at least one VCR unit on which to view videos of sports, musicals, documentaries or favorite movies.

CDs:

Compact disk technology revolutionized the recorded music industry. Developed in 1979, the compact disk is small, with a diameter of only 4.25 inches. Since CDs are played by laser light, wear-resistant disks last much longer than tape. Digitally recorded and encoded music has much better quality than old-fashioned phonographic recordings. Durable compact disks are used for studio recordings as well as programs for personal computers.

The Computer and the Internet:

People from different backgrounds and skills were responsible for inventing and developing computers and modern day

Babbage's Calculating Machine

Internet services. In 1822, Charles Babbage developed a mechanical calculating machine that operated on steam. In 1889, Herman Hollerith developed a computer that used paper *punch cards*. Punch cards were pieces of thick paper that told the computer what to do. Instead of using modern day disks, the first computers operated using paper punch cards. These cards stored programs and data that the computer needed to operate. Hollerith founded the *Tabulating Machine Company* in 1896. It later became *International Business Machines* (IBM) which manufactures computers.

Professor John V. Atanasoff and assistant Clifford Berry developed the first all-electronic computer in 1940. Their on/off switch system became the basis for all modern computers. By 1956 transistors were invented, allowing manufacture of small computers. In 1962, J.C.R. Licklider believed that a globally interconnected computer system could be devised, allowing anyone with a computer and a phone line to connect and access data and programs from any site. By 1963 all the components associated with modern computers had been developed: operating systems, memory, tape storage, disk storage, printers and stored programs.

What Mr. Licklider envisioned, Lawrence G. Roberts accomplished in 1967 through ARPANET which evolved into the World Wide Web (WWW or Internet). In 1972, Ray Tomlinson wrote the first electronic mail program messages over the ARPANET. Lawrence Roberts added the ability to read, file, forward, and respond to electronic mail (or E-mail) messages. Modern computers enable users to correspond with other computers using telephone lines and a *modem*. Today, the ability to access data, personal messages, and remote programs can all be done in most places with a local phone call. By 1998 voice activated computers allowed information not only to be at our fingertips, but on the tips of our tongues!

The value of communication in America cannot be measured by technological developments only. Computer-transmitted communication is valuable because it allows people to learn about each other: families sharing everyday joys and sorrows, and nations working together. Electric communication systems enable Americans instantly to see, hear and understand life-changing events around the world.

While Americans were improving the way they processed information, they were also changing the way they dressed and lived. The next vignette helps you look at a really new style.

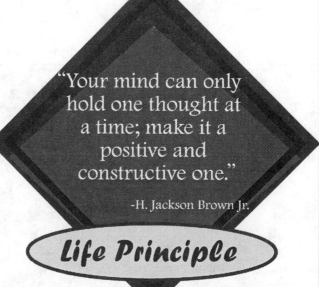

"Your mind can only hold one thought at a time; make it a positive and constructive one."

-H. Jackson Brown Jr.

Life Principle

Stage in the Radio City Music Hall

The Defending of America

Topic 12
*Art,
Architecture,
Fashions & Furniture*

Chapter 10

Section Three
Topics 11-15

THE NEWEST STYLE—ART DECO

VOCABULARY

Gothic Pinnacles: dark, high, pointing towers
Flying buttresses: arch supports of stone buildings
Opulence: great wealth
Chintz: shiny cotton cloth
Ousted: removed and replaced
Berets: woolen caps without visors
Synthetics: man-made products
Chinchilla: silver-grey fur of a small animal
Ibis plume: feather from an Ibis (a large wading bird)
Feather boa: scarf made of feathers

The 1920s-1930s were times of expansion of America's economy. Skyscrapers built in the late 1880s became great architectural symbols of U.S. wealth. Cities competed to build the tallest and most beautiful skyscrapers. In Chicago, Illinois, the Wrigley Building and the Chicago Tribune Tower won competitions for architectural beauty. Both buildings contained unique *Gothic pinnacles* and *flying buttresses*. The ultimate expression of an industrial design in architecture was the Empire State Building in New York City. It was completed in 1932 after two years of construction. The Empire State Building stands 120 stories above ground and remained the tallest building in the world for 39 years.

In addition to the Gothic designs built into tall structures, other buildings utilized designs of the Art Deco period; a period defined by lavish colors and extravagant materials. The American Radiator Building in New York featured black and gold colors throughout its design. Chrome, black glass, aluminum and the use of light and mirrors were abundant in other elaborate buildings. Art Deco design was especially popular in entertainment architecture. Both the cinemas and ballrooms built then were popular entertainment centers. Radio City Music Hall in New York City and Graumen's Chinese Theater in Los Angeles were known for their *opulence* in decoration: gilded ceilings, black glass, mirrors and polished metal inlays in walls and doors.

While skyscrapers were being constructed from 1924 to 1936, Frank Lloyd Wright created exceptional architectural work in houses and business buildings. He designed the Charles Ennis House in Los Angeles, California in 1924; the Arizona Biltmore Hotel in Phoenix, Arizona in 1927; and Fallingwater in Mill Run, Pennsylvania in 1936.

Fallingwater is considered Wright's masterpiece. The structure incorporated Wright's idea of a living place fused with nature. Resting across a small brook, called Bear Run,

Frank Lloyd Wright

Fallingwater seems to take roots from a ledge of rock. Several multilevel platforms of the house project out over a small waterfall. To Wright, the construction of Fallingwater echoed how a tree grows its own network of branches. In keeping with the Art Deco theme, Wright created an enameled steel chair with walnut arms for the house. He often produced furniture that complimented his buildings.

Art Deco style stressed machine-made furniture which was cylindrical, rectangular or cubical. Natural surfaces were replaced by smooth plastics, metal, artificial wood or stone surfaces.

Popular also during this time were designs by Elsie de Wolfe, who popularized the little known profession of interior decorating. She drew from 18th-century English styles, which popularized loose, floral-patterned *chintz* covers for upholstered chairs. Interiors were decorated with antiques, as well as white, beige or cream carpets, walls and upholstered chairs.

Accessories for men and women reflected the architectural and furniture designs of the Art Deco period. Clothes and upholstery were replaced with new items from man-made materials. Men's wristwatches *ousted* the pocket watch. For women, the major accessory was the *vanity box*: the first compact which held powder, powder puff and a mirror.

Both men and women wore *berets* for motoring. Decorative scarves or mufflers accented winter outfits. Artificial flowers, dangling earrings, lockets, necklaces and large pocketbooks were popular accessories in the 1920s.

New clothing fabrics included such *synthetics* as rayon, cellophane or combinations. Metal in fabric and *lamé* (a shiny, metallic fabric) was used for evening dresses and coats. Dresses were further decorated with detailed bead work.

The new culture in clothing, dominated by man-made materials, favored freedom for men and women. America's nine years before the stock market crash of 1929 marked the heyday of the shapeless, one-piece dress worn with silk stockings. The tubular effect of the dress was a change from the hourglass look of centuries past. The beginning of the women's suffrage movement further developed fashion freedom from bulky crinolines and restrictive corsets.

The waist belt of the simple dress slipped lower and lower until it reached the hips. A variation was the slanted or diagonal low waistline. Long tunic blouses enhanced the narrow, boxy line of women's clothing.

As a sign of the times, in January 1925, a fashionable lady named Miriam Ferguson became the first woman governor of Texas. For the inaugural ceremony, she wore a narrow hip-waist dress of black satin, her kimono sleeves trimmed with *chinchilla*. Wearing a wide-brimmed hat decorated with an *ibis plume*, Mrs. Ferguson completed the outfit with an ivory *feather boa* across her shoulders. Her inaugural ball gown was another boxlike style of orchid crepe embroidered with crystal beads and gold threads. The ankle length skirt was appliqued with seed pearls.

Mrs. Ferguson was not reelected in 1926, but was elected again in 1932. The depression of 1930 had a sobering effect on American fashions. Popularity of colorful, opulent dresses and extravagant accessories diminished. When Mrs. Ferguson took office again in 1932, her fashions reflected the times. Her inaugural ball gown was a black crepe dress with the waist at the normal level. Over her dress, Mrs. Ferguson wore a chiffon cape appliqued in velvet.

The Depression brought the clothes of wealthy and poor Americans closer together. Great design houses of Paris created fashions that were reasonably priced for nearly every woman. Textile manufacturers began using cheaper synthetic fabrics for clothing. Artificial silk stockings, made of nylon, were in abundance due to advances in production of synthetic materials.

No dominant trend appeared during the 1930s except for a nostalgic return to the tradition of more feminine clothing. Evening gowns were longer, tending to be backless like the new, backless bathing suits. Toward the close of the 1930s, women's styles changed. Skirts raised to knee length, and turbans or felt hats with tiny brims became popular. Women parted their hair in the middle and wore finger waves ending in a roll at the back of the head. Women experimented with clothing and accessories, wearing slacks, play suits, tennis dresses, bathing suits, ski costumes, low sandals, platform sandals and shirtwaist frocks. Late in the thirties, female factory workers wore zippered overalls, Levi's and dress pants.

For men, trousers were wide with one or two pleats at the waist and moderate to wide cuffs at the bottom of the pant leg. Cuffs on shirt sleeves were eliminated, along with vests for double-breasted suits. Men's suits were made from wool, cotton, or rayon. Eveningwear tuxedos were of midnight blue or maroon color rather than black. White dinner jackets and cummerbunds began to be popular.

Men's sportswear reflected more innovation. Pullover sweaters, cardigans, sports shirts in pastels, bright colors and even floral prints became popular. Shirts with straight cut hems were worn either tucked in or hung outside the trousers. For skiing, men wore the new, fashionable windbreaker jackets with gabardine trousers fastened at the ankle. Casual wear consisted of Levi denim pants and jackets that faded and shrank after washing.

America's 1920s and 1930s introduced the artistic ideals of Art Deco design and the practical ideas of the new machine age. Excesses of the Roaring Twenties were toned down by the Great Depression of the 1930s. Ready-made fabrics and synthetic materials gave different classes of people a wider variety of styles and opportunities to experiment.

What would the richest person in the world wear? Read the next vignette to find out how John D. Rockefeller earned his wealth—and what he did with it.

Life Principle

"The best building blocks in life are truth, honesty, integrity and moral principles."

—Ron Johnson

The Defending of America

Topic 13
Dominant Personalities & Events

Chapter 10

JOHN D. ROCKEFELLER

Section Three

Topics 11-15

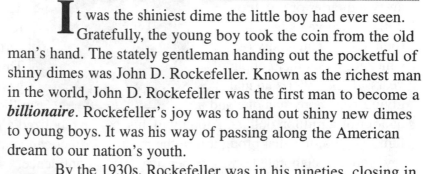

It was the shiniest dime the little boy had ever seen. Gratefully, the young boy took the coin from the old man's hand. The stately gentleman handing out the pocketful of shiny dimes was John D. Rockefeller. Known as the richest man in the world, John D. Rockefeller was the first man to become a *billionaire*. Rockefeller's joy was to hand out shiny new dimes to young boys. It was his way of passing along the American dream to our nation's youth.

By the 1930s, Rockefeller was in his nineties, closing in on his final days. Forty years had passed since he retired from the company he and a few partners had begun in the 1860s and built from the ground up. It was one of the largest and most successful companies in U.S. history. Nearing the end of his life, Rockefeller was still giving. For generations to come, he would exert a positive impact on *multitudes* through the philanthropic projects he funded.

By 2000, 60 years after the death of this charitable businessman, the foundations he began are annually investing millions of dollars in people around the globe. In 1997, his most prominent foundation, the Rockefeller Foundation, had a budget of $100 million.

Rockefeller knew the value and power of a dollar bill. Born poor, the son of a *peddler*, Rockefeller began working at age 16 and started his own business four years later. He believed that a good living could be made in the oil business, but only if this *fragmented*, young industry could be better organized. Rockefeller and a couple of partners did just that. They united small pieces of the oil producing business into one large entity: the Standard Oil Company. This resulted in lower prices and better service for consumers and personal wealth for Rockefeller. By the time he was 38 years old, Rockefeller and his company dominated the U.S. oil-producing industry.

VOCABULARY

Billionaire: one who owns one or more billion dollars
Multitudes: large crowds of people
Peddler: one who sells products house to house
Fragmented: in separate pieces
Flagrant: extravagant, bold, outrageous
Thrifty: economical management of resources
Staunch: uncompromising, standing firm in beliefs

Flagrant spending or being selfish was not Rockefeller's style. Even after attaining incredible wealth, he continued to live a *thrifty*, simple life. He and his wife raised their four children to be hard workers and to be generous. Rockefeller's *staunch* Baptist upbringing and Christian ethic influenced him to give away large sums of money. In his 48th year, he gave away a quarter of a million dollars; two years later he founded the University of Chicago; in another couple of years, Rockefeller's annual giving was more than one and a quarter of a million dollars. Along with his family, the things that brought him the most joy were *not* elaborate homes, expensive travel, or fancy automobiles, but church, golf and quiet motor drives through the countryside.

By the turn of the century, Rockefeller was donating so much money to charitable organizations he had to organize his giving through several foundations. Along with the already-mentioned Rockefeller Foundation, he founded the General Education Board, the Laura Spelman Rockefeller Memorial Foundation, and the Rockefeller Institute for Medical Research, which in 1954 became Rockefeller University in New York.

Rockefeller believed that money given away to help others was an investment in eternal rewards—an investment from which thieves could not steal and decay could not corrupt. Rockefeller's unselfish giving certainly accentuated the point. Throughout his life, Rockefeller gave away more than $530 million. Every one of those dollars symbolized a message of generosity to American youth in whom Rockefeller had confidence.

Other men also helped make America great, and four of them have been immortalized in a unique mountain sculpture known as Mount Rushmore.

John D. Rockefeller

VOCABULARY

Cascaded: flowed down dramatically or majestically
Precipitated: started an action
Showcase: an area in which something is shown off, displayed
Symbolism: an object or word that represents a deeper idea or belief
Lobbied: tried to persuade Congressmen to pass legislation in favor of the lobbyist's agenda
Estimate: a calculated opinion
Colossal: huge, magnificent

THE MOUNTAIN WITH FOUR FACES

An impressive crowd— thousands of interested citizens, dignitaries, photographers and reporters gathered at the base of the South Dakota moutains on July 4, 1930 to watch the once-in-a-lifetime event. Amidst the crowd stood President Herbert Hoover. The ceremony was unlike any other in history. A 72-foot American flag was draped dramatically across the mountainside. Suddenly the ropes were loosed, and the massive flag *cascaded* down revealing a 60-foot replica of George Washington's face carved out of solid rock on Mount Rushmore. Over the next nine years, the faces of three more American Presidents: Thomas Jefferson, Abraham Lincoln and Theodore Roosevelt, would be added to the mountain side.

That very moment, no one could have been prouder than Gutzon Borglum, the creator of Washington's likeness on that granite mountain. The idea that *precipitated* Borglum's moment of triumph began in 1923. A state historian suggested the possibility of a monument, a giant carving that would draw visitors to South Dakota from around the country.

Once Borglum was hired for the job, he scouted the South Dakota countryside for the perfect location. Where would he carve such a great tribute to some of America's finest heroes? Borglum chose the 5,725-foot Mount Rushmore for its broad wall of exposed granite facing southeast. It was the perfect *showcase*, lit by direct sunlight most of the day.

Mt. Rushmore Today

Then Borglum developed the subject matter for this one-of-a-kind project. Initially, he planned to include Washington, Jefferson and Lincoln as great leaders who brought America from colonial times into the 20th century. The decision to add Roosevelt came in the middle of the project.

"A monument's dimensions should be determined by the importance to civilization of the events commemorated," said Borglum. *"Let us place there, carved high, as close to heaven as we can, the words of our leaders, their faces, to show posterity what manner of men they were. Then breathe a prayer that these records will endure until the wind and the rain alone shall wear them away."*

The project was dedicated in 1927 by then President Calvin Coolidge, but it would be three years before the first face would be unveiled. America was suffering an economic depression; the challenge was raising funds. Fiercely believing in this monument's *symbolism* and the message it would give the American people, Borglum personally *lobbied* state officials, Congressmen, cabinet members, and Presidents to obtain finances. Finally, $836,000 of federal money was committed toward the $1,000,000 price tag.

Two things had to happen before Borglum and his crew could begin transforming Mount Rushmore into a monument. First, the work environment had to be prepared. A wooden staircase was constructed up the side of the mountain. Next came a workshop, dynamite storeroom and lunchroom on top. At the base of the mountain, other structures were built: a studio, a blacksmith's shop, bunkhouse, restaurant and custodian's house.

While the work site was under construction, Borglum was preparing models of each presidential figure. They were first sculpted in clay. Larger five-foot models were crafted out of plaster of Paris and wood shavings. The final figures stood five stories tall, about 12 times the size of Borglum's plaster models.

Each carving was completed in steps. First the heads were drawn and marked with one-inch squares in a process called *pointing*. At each "point" on the drawing, workers knew where to insert a drill and precisely how deep it should go. Into the holes went very specific amounts of dynamite which would blast away the appropriate amount of rock. This was very precise work. As Borglum told his crew, error was not an option.

Borglum's team spent six and one-half years of hard work to create Washington's likeness from the concept of the monument to its unveiling. After the first face in the rock surfaced, the faces of Jefferson in 1936, Lincoln in 1937, and Roosevelt in 1939 followed.

Remarkably, over the course of this dangerous project, no life was lost and only two accidents occurred. The years invested in building the monument were much longer than Borglum's original *estimate* of five years.

Today, Mount Rushmore stands as a symbol of men who helped shape America into the nation it is today: a proud, tall country with a *colossal* image. More than 2.5 million people from around the world visit the monument each year, attesting to the interest such an impressive undertaking generates. What began as Borglum's project now broadcasts a message of principles and moral leadership. A visit to Mount Rushmore is a history lesson and a form of recreation.

As America changed in the new century, so did forms of recreation. The next lesson is about athletic men and women whose faces were not carved in stone, but whose names are recorded in history.

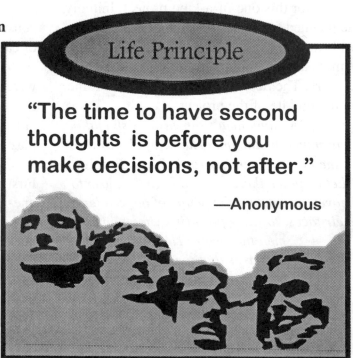

Life Principle

"The time to have second thoughts is before you make decisions, not after."

—Anonymous

The Defending of America

Topic 14
Sports & Recreation

Chapter 10

Section Three
Topics 11-15

GAMES
AND THEIR
CHAMPIONS

VOCABULARY

Perseverance: bravery and determination in overcoming obstacles
Endurance: the ability to continue in spite of pain and difficulties
Overwhelm: to crush, to overpower, to bury beneath
Unprecedented: having no equal; unheard of
Providential: planned by God
Benefactor: one who helps, usually through financial means
Benchmark: standard of quality
Commemorated: honored
Render: to cause to be

Glenn Cunningham was one of the few truly great athletes ever to compete. He is remembered not only as a record-setting runner, but for the determination and *perseverance* that marked his entire career.

Glenn was born in Kansas in 1909, the younger of two children. When Glenn was seven years old, his brother was killed and Glenn was badly injured while trying to light a wood stove to heat the local school. Glenn's legs caught fire in the accident and were badly scarred. The doctor told Glenn that he would never walk without crutches.

Glenn loved to run, so he refused to accept the doctor's report. Over the next several years, hope and perseverance sustained the young man. Glenn was determined to walk again. His mother spent long hours massaging Glenn's legs, and he worked hard doing exercises. By the time Glenn was ten, he was able to walk without crutches; his doctor said the recovery was a miracle.

Though trying to run was very painful at first, Glenn slowly built up *endurance*, disciplining himself to focus on the goal instead of his pain. Glenn was able to join his high school track team, and he did so well the University of Kansas awarded him an athletic scholarship. His sophomore year in college, Glenn set a new American record for running a mile in 4 minutes and 11.1 seconds. That incredible record made Glenn Cunningham famous across America, and for the first time, a lot of people became interested in track as a sport.

The high point of Glenn's career came in the summer of 1934. He and the other two top runners in the U.S. competed head-on in Princeton's Palmer Stadium. Cunningham ran the race of his life, beating out the next closest man by over 40 yards and setting a new world record for the mile—4 minutes,

6.7 seconds. His performance made people believe a man could run a 4 minute mile. It would be another 16 years before Roger Banister of England turned in a time of 3 minutes, 59.4 seconds.

Glenn Cunningham was not the one who set the 4 minute mile record, but he was the first man to cause other runners to dream about a 4 minute mile race. Glenn is remembered because he never gave up and because he never let the odds *overwhelm* him. He is one of the greatest track and field icons of all time because he persevered in spite of pain and great personal hardship.

One of Cunningham's contemporaries in track and field, Jesse Owens, is another man remembered for his defeat of impossible odds. Jesse Owens was the first black runner to make international headlines. During his sophomore year in college in 1935, Owens attended the Big Ten track championships where he had what is probably the greatest day any athlete has ever known.

A week before the meet, Jesse sprained his back wrestling with a friend. Owens was in such bad pain that he could not work out all week. He decided to compete anyway. When Jesse arrived at the competition, he had to be assisted out of the car. Owens could barely stand, much less run. Still, he never considered giving up. He determined to try; he entered six races and in the span of just 45 minutes, Jesse Owens set five world records and tied a sixth.

The next year (1936), Owens was part of the U.S.A. Olympic delegation to Berlin, where the Olympics were being hosted by white supremist Adolf Hitler.

Jesse Owens

Germany's Nazis sneered at America for allowing blacks to represent the U.S.A., but Jesse Owens made a political as well as an athletic statement in Hitler's own backyard. Owens won an *unprecedented* four gold medals in track and field and broke three Olympic records. Owens dominated the track competition and showed the world that blond Nazis were not the superior race. Perhaps it was *providential* that a black man would dominate the Olympic games right in the face of Hitler.

Back in his own country, despite his great track achievements, Owens was not able to turn his athletic abilities into financial advantages. In 1936, Jesse Owens, the greatest runner of all time, was employed as a playground janitor. Sixty years ago in America, four gold medals were of value to Jesse but did not generate financial support. Today, stars like Michael Jordan and Tiger Woods headline the news and earn millions in advertising. Jesse Owens was, however, honored by two United States Presidents. Jesse Owens was awarded the Presidential Medal of Freedom in 1976 by President Gerald Ford and the Living Legends Award in 1979 by President Jimmy Carter.

Another great athlete was Jackie Robinson, the first black professional baseball player. Robinson is credited with opening the door of opportunity for black athletes into all major professional sports.

In 1946, Jackie Robinson was signed to the Montreal Royals, a minor league farm team for the Brooklyn Dodgers. His *benefactor* was Branch Rickey, owner of the Dodgers and a visionary who believed that blacks could and should play major league ball. Branch Rickey, as much as Robinson, helped sports fans accept minority players.

Voted Rookie of the Year after a successful season with the Royals, Robinson moved up to the Dodgers. That move incited considerable controversy and hostility from other players. Opposing teams constantly yelled threats, shouted insults and attempted to hit Robinson with the ball. Even in those tough confrontations, Jackie Robinson remained a true gentleman. His positive, calm and collected attitude, along with his dynamic ability to play ball, earned him respect in the league. His first season, Robinson was named the National League's Rookie of the Year, and two years later he had his best year and was selected as the league's Most Valuable Player.

Over the ten years he played with the Dodgers, Jackie Robinson established a *benchmark* in professional sports. He inspired many young blacks to pick up the game of baseball. Robinson's positive attitude, wisdom and commitment to training earned him respect. He is *commemorated* in the Baseball Hall of Fame along with other "greats" of the era.

During the first half of the 20th century, many other names worth remembering overcame impossible odds and dazzled the world with athletic abilities. Pete Gray is remembered as an outfielder for the St. Louis Browns. He was not their top hitter or fielder, nor did he set any records, but he was the only one-armed man ever to play major league baseball.

Another man who made history was Ben Hogan, a golfer who dominated professional golf in the 1940s and 1950s.

Hogan was born in tiny Dublin, Texas. Tragically, when Ben was only age seven, his father died. At the height of Hogan's career, he was in a horrible automobile accident; the doctor pronounced Ben paralyzed from the waist down. Like Glenn Cunningham, Hogan was not a man to give up. With help and encouragement from his wife, Hogan devoted the next several years getting back into shape. To the amazement of the golfing world, Hogan later won the U.S. Open, the Masters, the P.G.A. and the British Open.

Babe Didrickson was another golfer who fought back against impossible odds and won. After a battle with cancer in the middle of her career, Didrickson claimed the Women's Open title in Miami. Babe was known not only as a golfer. She was named the greatest female athlete of the first half of the 20th century, and her accomplishments lived up to that reputation. At the 1932 Olympics, Babe set world records in several events. An expert at bowling, billiards and golf, she even beat most men at any sport she played. In her later years, Babe Didrickson established funds to promote women in sports and was instrumental in starting the careers of many young female athletes.

Babe Didrickson is another individual who overcame great obstacles to achieve her dreams. Perhaps in every sport, some athletes reached the top because of natural ability, but true role models are people who persevere over difficulties.

Some sports personalities became famous because their achievements propelled their sport into public limelight. Such is the case with prizefighting. During the early 1900s, boxing remained illegal in many parts of the United States. But in 1920, New York passed a law permitting prizefighting. Other states followed. Quickly gaining popularity as a spectator sport, boxing soon entered its golden age.

Joe Louis was a black man who became one of the most famous champion boxers. He held the heavyweight title from 1937 to 1949 when he retired as World Champion. His achievements in the boxing ring opened doors of opportunity for other black athletes. During World War II Louis joined the Army and conducted exhibition fights for U.S. troops.

Joe Louis

In the late 1930s, Henry Armstrong captured the welterweight, lightweight and featherweight titles—holding three world championships during his career. Henry Armstrong was ordained as a minister after he retired from professional boxing.

Lou Gehrig is another name remembered for more than his athletic career. This quiet, gentle baseball giant was somewhat overshadowed by his famous teammate, "Babe" Ruth. However, Gehrig's name lives on, inseparably linked to the rare and incurable nerve disease which forced him to retire—now known as *Lou Gehrig's disease.*

Sports and *recreation* are closely related. While organized sports came to the forefront during this period of American history, other forms of recreation thrived and advanced as well. Country fairs provided opportunities for people to join in festivities and contests. Fairs were not expensive, yet provided a variety of social events and recreation: dancing, tractor pulls, wrestling and mechanical rides.

Bicycling was also popular at the turn of the century. Early forms of the modern bicycle gear shift came into use after 1900. However, even with improvements in bicycle design, rapid development of the exciting automobile *rendered* bicycling less interesting. The growing automobile industry triggered growth in a related industry— tourism. Automobiles gave people a new way to go places, both for business and for fun.

Board games remained popular, and new ones were created. Monopoly was invented in the early 1930s by Charles Darrow, an out-of-work heating engineer from Philadelphia. In time, the game made Darrow a millionaire. In 1975, twice as much Monopoly money was printed in the United States as real money. Nearly 100 million Monopoly games were sold by 1985.

America is a place of enterprise, opportunity and achievements. She is a land where people with character, ideas, and dedication can become successful. The next topic puts into perspective the role of religion in America's history.

Life Principle

"In America anybody can become somebody."

~Jesse Owens

The Defending of America

Topic 15
Religion & Celebrations

Chapter 10

Section Three
Topics 11-15

RELIGION FOR A NEW CENTURY

VOCABULARY

Equate: to consider as equal to
Embedded: fixed firmly, stable
Debarked: stepped off a ship
Battalions: a large company of troops
Catapulted: thrown or launched into air
Fostering: helping to develop
Chaplain: a military preacher
Disillusioned: bitter, disappointed
Scores: a very large amount

*R*eligion? Who needs it?

Some Americans today would answer, *"No one."* For them, religious pursuit is a waste of time; they have other interests in life, like making money and watching the Sunday morning athletic game. They cannot bother themselves with thoughts of the national motto, *"In God We Trust."*

Compare this modern attitude with the mind set of our ancestors. For them, religion was life. They drew strength from deep spiritual wells as they bucked mysterious seas, fought impossible wars or plunged into hostile badlands. When the Founding Fathers laid the foundation on which to build America, they believed that Judeo-Christian values were essential for constructing a country that would remain strong and free.

The writers of our establishing documents showed wisdom when they adopted the First Amendment, which forbids the government to establish a national church. Yet our founding Fathers did not *equate* "free exercise" of religion with freedom *from* religion. George Washington, the Father of Our Country, commented, *"It is impossible to rightly govern the world without God and the Bible."* James Madison, author of the Bill of Rights and fourth President of the United States, wrote, *"We have staked the whole future of the American civilization, not upon the power of government, far from it. We have staked the future. . .upon the capacity of each and all of us to govern ourselves, to control ourselves, to sustain ourselves, according to the Ten Commandments of God."* Declaration of Independence author Thomas Jefferson firmly believed in a Supreme Being. He also asserted that our country needed the "glue" of religion to hold us together. During the War for Independence, Jefferson asked, *"Can the liberties of a nation be thought secure when we have removed their only firm basis, a conviction in the minds of the people that their liberties are a gift from God?"*

Religion continued to be a vital force in the 19th century. You have read about the Second Great Awakening, the city revivals of Finney and Moody, and the rise of religious aid organizations such as the Salvation Army and YMCA. Religion, though personal, was not private. Public figures generally did not suppress their religious convictions. Most U.S. Presidents in that century made direct references to God in their inaugural addresses. Rutherford B. Hayes, our 19th President, made a typical remark in his inaugural speech of March 5, 1877. Hayes acknowledged that he was *"looking for the guidance of that Divine Hand by which the destinies of nations and individuals are shaped."*

When America stepped over the threshold of the 20th century, religion was still *embedded* in her national consciousness. Churches dotted the countryside and towered on city corners. Many Americans spent all Sunday at church, attending worship and Sunday school and enjoying "dinner on the grounds" with neighbors. Principals, teachers and students prayed in public schools, and parents read the Bible to their children at home. Public figures spoke unashamedly about the value of religion and virtue. President Theodore Roosevelt said, *"A thorough knowledge of the Bible is worth more than a college education."* Yankee slugger "Babe" Ruth acknowledged that *"the appeal of God"* was a positive force in his life, giving him discipline and strength. Andrew Carnegie, the great steel entrepreneur, said that *"the man who dies rich dies disgraced,"* and so he donated over 7,000 pipe organs to churches across the nation.

As the 20th century opened, so did the floodgates of immigration, which swelled the ranks of the Roman Catholic Church in our nation. In 1890, American Catholics numbered 10.6 million. This number skyrocketed to over 12 million by 1906. The immigrants hailed from Europe where the Catholic church was strong. Catholic organizations helped many immigrants at Ellis Island. Greta Wagner was a German woman who *debarked* in New York in 1923. She was scared and single, without anyone to sponsor her. Immigration officials almost sent Wagner back to Germany until a Catholic charity agreed to provide free room and board until Greta could find work. Many religious aid societies came to the rescue of thousands of foreigners who probably would not otherwise have become American citizens.

In 1917, America marched into a world war. While soldiers, called "dough boys," fought in European trenches, American churches became their own *battalions* of action. Women huddled in church parlors to pray and knit socks and sweaters for the fighting men. Laymen mobilized a flurry of campaigns, from selling Liberty bonds to holding Red Cross drives. Clergymen held special patriotic services and prayer meetings where American flags were dedicated.

The decade after World War I ushered in a time of decline in religious interests. It was the Age of Prosperity, when the nation's industrial output doubled and wages steadily climbed. For a time the nation turned its attention to entertainment and business, but when the Great Depression struck, people again turned to the only remaining stability in their lives—their faith in God. During the twenties, Christians built beautiful, cathedral-like Church buildings throughout the land. Many of them contained large auditoriums, gymnasiums and Gothic-like sanctuaries. More churches were built during the ten years after 1920 than at any time in American history.

A popular book at that time was Bruce Barton's *The Man Nobody Knows*, published in 1925. The son of a preacher, Barton was an advertising executive who wanted to make Christ known among American businessmen. Using everyday language, Barton described Jesus as a fit, sun-tanned tradesman who *"led the most successful life on this planet."* Barton dubbed the moral tales that Jesus told as *"the most powerful advertisements of all time."* Because of its breezy, winsome style, *The Man Nobody Knows* became a best seller and **catapulted** its author into national prominence.

In His Steps by Charles M. Sheldon took America by storm in 1896. Millions of copies were sold in America, and the book was translated into 25 foreign languages and made into a movie. Second only to the Bible in popularity, *In His Steps* remained the American best seller for two decades. The story was about a small town preacher and his church members who revolutionized their town and surrounding communities by following the example of Jesus Christ. Each church member in the story responded to social situations and family events by asking, *"What Would Jesus Do?"* The modern slogan, "WWJD" derived from Sheldon's book and was made popular through *Paul Harvey News and Comments* in the spring of 1998.

During the Great Depression, several religious denominations flourished even as the economy fell. The Southern Baptist Church added nearly 1½ million members between 1929-1941. Pentecostal churches also enjoyed substantial gains. The foremost Pentecostal body, the Assemblies of God, expanded its membership from almost 48,000 in 1926 to over 148,000 in 1936.

President Franklin D. Roosevelt introduced his New Deal programs with inspiring speeches. In his first inaugural address he said, *"The only thing we have to fear is fear itself. . . .We face arduous days that lie before us in the warm courage of national unity; with the clear consciousness of seeking old and precious moral values."* Roosevelt then exclaimed, *"May God protect each and every one of us! May He guide me in the days to come!"*

In 1942, America was at war again. Churches and synagogues rose to the occasion, lending support to the war effort. The United States government took an active role in **fostering** spiritual well-being among U.S. soldiers. In the fall of 1940, one **chaplain** was required for every 1,200 servicemen. In the spring of 1941, Congress appropriated almost $13 million for building 604 Army post chapels throughout the world. The average chapel seated about 400 people and housed services for Protestants, Catholics and Jews. Numerous religious bodies, including the YMCA, Salvation Army, Jewish Welfare Board and National Catholic Community Service, sponsored the United Service Organization (USO) which provided outposts of entertainment and fellowship for war-weary soldiers. An association of military chaplains issued a book of prayers and hymns to "G.I.s," while the American Bible Society and Gideons provided free copies of the Scriptures for every U.S. serviceman. President Franklin D. Roosevelt cheered the soldiers with his remarks in a pocket Bible published by The Gideons:

"As Commander-in-chief, I take pleasure in commending the reading of the Bible to all who serve in the armed forces of the United States. Throughout the centuries men of many faiths and diverse origins have found in the Sacred Book words of wisdom, counsel and inspiration. It is a fountain of strength and now, as always, an aid in attaining the highest aspirations of the human soul."

On December 7, 1941, the U.S. cruiser *New Orleans* came under Japanese attack at Pearl Harbor, Hawaii. While sailors kept up a steady anti-aircraft barrage against Japanese planes, Navy Chaplain Howell M. Forgy repeated the phrase, *"Praise the Lord and pass the ammunition,"* which became one of the songs to come out of the war. A condensed portion reads:

> *Praise the Lord, and*
> > *Pass the ammunition,*
> *Praise the Lord, were on*
> > *A mighty mission,*
> *Praise the Lord, and*
> > *Pass the ammunition,*
> *And we'll all stay free!*

Another phrase that sparked a song was *"Comin' in on a wing and a prayer,"* referring to shot up planes. A condensed portion reads:

> *Comin' in on a wing and a prayer,*
> *Though there's one motor gone*
> > *We can still carry on . . . .*
> *While we sing as we limp*
> > *Through the air,*
> *Look below—there's a field over there!*

> *With our whole crew aboard*
> > *And our trust in the Lord,*
> *We're comin' in on a wing*
> > *And a prayer.*

During the most troubling days of World War II, Roosevelt met with British Prime Minister Winston Churchill in an Atlantic summit. Standing on the deck of an American warship, the President of the United States led a rousing chorus of the hymn, "Onward, Christian Soldiers."

The years immediately following the war brought a "baby boom" to America. In five short years, between 1948 and 1953, the national birth rate increased 50%. Young families flocked to churches during this time. Sunday school classes "packed out," increasing their attendance from 30 million in 1950 to almost 39 million in 1956. The *Sputnik* satellite was not the only thing blasting into space during the late 1950s; church membership soared as well. In 1956, sixty-two percent of all Americans claimed affiliation with a local church based on Judeo-Christian beliefs.

In the next chapter, we will see how religion fared in the turbulent '60s. Many of the Baby Boomers became *disillusioned* with American involvement in Vietnam. They rejected the traditional values of their parents and grandparents, including religion. But *scores* of them returned to church in the 1970s and 1980s.

Congratulations you have completed chapter 10. Now, request your quiz over this section.

LIFE PRINCIPLE

"THERE IS NEVER A RIGHT TIME TO DO THE WRONG THING."
—DR. BOB JONES

The Defending of America 1918-1996

The People, Places and Principles of America

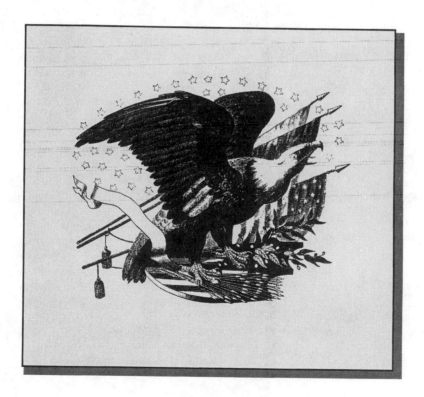

Chapter 11

TM

CHAPTER 11
TABLE OF CONTENTS

Chapter 11
Time Line 1918-1996

Use this time line for referencing important dates throughout the chapter.

1918 *World War I Ended*

1930-39 *The Great Depression*

1937 *1st Full Length Animated Feature Movie*

1941 *Japanese Bombed Pearl Harbor*

1945 *Atomic Bombs on Hiroshima and Nagasaki*

1945 *Ebony Magazine Began*

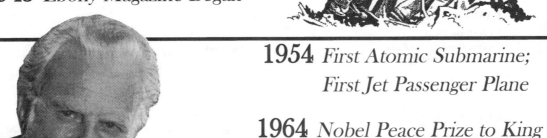

1954 *First Atomic Submarine; First Jet Passenger Plane*

1964 *Nobel Peace Prize to King*

1969 *First Man on the Moon (Neil Armstrong)*

1970 *Environmental Concerns*

1977 *Personal Computer (PC) Introduced*

1996 *Congressional Gold Medal Given to Graham*

The Defending of America

Topic 1
Industry & Medicine

Chapter 11

CRASH OF 1929 AND THE GREAT DEPRESSION

Section One
Topics 1-5

VOCABULARY

Luxury: a commodity which makes life more comfortable
Investor: one who places money in a company, property, or stocks for the intent of gaining profit
Substantial: big, plentiful
Abruptly: suddenly, without warning
Frenzied: frustrated, panicky, rushed, hurried
Expedite: to speed up, to perform without delay
Encroach: to intrude, trespass
Resilience: ability to adjust, change and recover in difficult situations
Alleviate: to soften, soothe; to make lighter or easier

Careless living became a way of life in the early 1920s. America's traditional social values took a back seat as young girls called *flappers* twirled their beads and danced the *Charleston* in bars and taverns. Caution was thrown to the wind in the business world, too. Buying on credit was introduced, enticing Americans to go into debt to purchase *luxury* items. Henry Ford and other auto manufacturers put wheels under a large segment of the population for the first time, allowing families to explore America from "sea to shining sea" on newly constructed highways and bridges. Gasoline stations and motels popped up across the country to serve the traveling public. Directly or indirectly, the automotive industry employed 3,700,000 people by 1929. America was enjoying financial prosperity while experiencing social carelessness.

Americans were optimistic, believing that prosperity would last forever. The financial structure of the United States seemed secure as banks accumulated a large share of the nation's income. Banks invested money in insurance, stocks and bonds. Corporations expanded, often too rapidly, using borrowed money. Companies anticipated they would grow over the long term, allowing *investors* to participate in the company's future profits. Rapidly advancing stock market profits encouraged people to borrow money from brokers for investing in the stock market. Investors hoped to sell quickly at a *substantial* profit, rather than holding their stock for future growth.

Feverish buying and selling on the stock market and other signs of inflation worried thoughtful investors. President Calvin Coolidge tried to calm public fears in March 1928, when he declared the country had never been more prosperous. Less than one year later, the stock market and banking industry spun out of control. Stock prices rose to sixteen times their value, far in excess of reasonable growth. Greed overcame reason. A market correction was inevitable, but speculators still hoped to ride the market to the crest of the profit wave and sell just before the market value of stock crashed.

On October 29, 1929, the price of stocks plunged *abruptly*. Panicky investors tried to sell their holdings as quickly as possible, but the crash caught people by surprise. The stock market had its worst day in history. During the rest of the year, prices continued to stagger downward with a $40 billion decline in stock values. Some discouraged business men who had poured their life earnings into the inflated stock market became so depressed that they jumped out of high rise building windows. Investors and their families suffered tragically. It was a difficult time for the new president, Herbert Hoover.

The Great Depression, began early in 1930, following the stock market crash. Many historians believe the depression resulted primarily from the massive over-extension of credit that financed the *frenzied* buying and selling in the stock market. After the crash, consumer buying power was no longer sufficient to keep industrial production and employment at high levels. People began to lose their jobs.

President Herbert Hoover believed the business community and the people could resolve the country's economic crisis if people were left to their own devices. In Hoover's annual address to Congress in 1930, he stated, *"Recovery can be expedited . . . by cooperative action. That cooperation requires that every individual should sustain faith and courage; that each should maintain his self reliance. . . . "*

Manufacturers and other employers, with no source of operating capital and a disappearing market for their products or services, were forced to lay off their employees and close their doors. Capable workers, many unemployed for the first time, were stunned by *encroaching* poverty and the loss of their homes. Schools closed because communities could no longer pay their teachers.

The construction industry virtually shut down and railroads went bankrupt. Even in the face of this great trauma, many Americans exhibited amazing strength and *resilience*. Those with spiritual resources learned from bad experiences and found strength to endure in times of hardship. Churches and private charities like the Salvation Army, which formerly had *alleviated* financial and social distress, set up *soup lines* and attempted to meet other overwhelming social needs. Americans pulled together to recover from the depressed economy.

Industry combined with federal legislation to stimulate economic improvements. The *advent* of World War II accelerated recovery as American businesses provided war materials. Industrial

VOCABULARY

Soup line: free distribution of soup to keep the poor from starving
Advent: the beginning or coming of an event
Stringent: harsh, severe, rigorous
Ventures: businesses established with borrowed capital (money)
Red tape: excessive government restrictions and regulations on free enterprise

production boomed in 1939 as the U.S responded to Allied wartime needs. The Federal government became heavily involved in American industry by contracting to build airplanes, trucks and cannons for the war. Additionally, federal legislation enacted during Franklin Roosevelt's first and second terms collected millions of dollars in taxes from businesses, and led to *stringent* government regulation and control over free enterprise. Government creates no money, except through taxes on businesses which make profits. Business profits have been taxed heavily since 1939 to provide revenue for government projects and programs.

The next lesson explains how the free enterprise system survived to allow entrepreneurs to build successful businesses that created thousands of jobs for Americans after World War II.

S mall businesses are traditionally seen as the backbone of American economics. There was a time when all that was needed to be successful in a small business was a good idea, a little capital and plenty of time to grow. Today, private *ventures* are born into an unrelenting environment of stiff competition, advancing technology, costly advertising and government *red tape*. While hard work and determination may still be the principle ingredients of success, the requirements of the current marketplace demand much more of the entrepreneur.

Purchasing an established business can be a shortcut to ownership of a small business. Another possible route is franchising, which has become a major

FRANCHISES

player in our country's expanding economy. A franchise is a privilege, right or license granted a person or group to sell or distribute a specific company's goods or services in a certain area. New franchise operations often achieve instant success with the aid of established public awareness, product recognition, training and advertising assistance. Some popular franchises are Wendy's, ACE Hardware, McDonald's and KFC.

Americans enjoy eating. Perhaps that is why some of the most successful franchises sell food. In 1926, Tennessee promoter Thomas Brimer, and his two brothers, purchased patent rights to a popular Cleveland ice cream business and started the Good Humor Corporation which became one of America's first franchise operations. McDonalds, which started as a hamburger stand in Pasadena, California in 1940, is the world's best known franchise.

A major non-food franchise pioneer opened in 1955. Kansas City accountants, Henry and Richard Block, developed a practice specializing in preparation of low-cost, mass-produced income tax returns. The brothers opened franchise offices in every major U.S. city. H&R Block became the country's largest tax preparation firm. It all started with an idea to help tax payers fill out federal and state tax forms quickly and inexpensively. In 1998, H&R Block's 8,300 offices in the United States prepared almost 15 million IRS tax returns. Block franchises operate 1,400 additional offices in 18 countries and territories around the world.

Today's list of franchise opportunities is almost endless. Carpet cleaning, auto windshield repair, pet sitting and grooming, home and office cleaning, handyman repairs and home inspection services are just a few examples of privately-owned businesses. In this type of franchise, an individual can become his own boss and succeed in business for a reasonably small investment.

Enterprises as diverse as public utilities and baseball clubs are often franchised. Sears and Roebuck, National Car Rental, Quick Lube and hundreds of other major corporations also expand through franchising. While the initial investment is much higher in these programs, the profit potential is also higher, and many new jobs are created as a result.

Franchises in the United States accounted for over $800 billion in annual sales by 2000—about 40 percent of all retail sales annually. Franchising provides more than 8,000,000 jobs and offers a viable opportunity for thousands of individuals to participate in the American dream of being their own bosses.

Some businesses merge or join other businesses to capture a larger part of the consumer market. The next vignette introduces you to the conglomerate—a large holding company that serves as a sort of umbrella for other smaller companies.

VOCABULARY

Subsidiary: a smaller company related to and controlled by a larger company
Vision: the ability to plan for the future regardless of present circumstances
Diversification: the combining of diverse (various) unrelated industries
Revenues: money earned
Mortgage: borrowing money against the value of owned property
Integrity: strong character
Modular: regular, standard, average

THE GE CONGLOMERATE

Thomas Edison would be amazed to see the gigantic conglomerate his invention of the light bulb helped spawn in the 20th century. A *conglomerate* is a company that consists of a number of *subsidiary* companies or divisions that operate in a variety of unrelated industries. The key to a conglomerate is its combination of "unrelated" industries, such as food and clothing, insurance and newspapers, leather goods and electronic equipment. These unusual combinations distinguish a conglomerate from other large corporations, like Ford and General Motors, that primarily engage in the single business or industry of manufacturing vehicles.

General Electric (GE) was initially formed by combining Edison General Electric Company and Thomson-Houston Company. By the late 1920s, GE was beginning to expand its production facilities and related industries. *Vision*, hard work and *diversification* combined to make GE the largest conglomerate in the United States with *revenues* in excess of $79 billion by 1996.

The typical American probably knows that GE makes dishwashers, lighting fixtures and refrigerators. But few realize it also owns companies which manufacture specialized medical equipment such as Magnetic Resonance Imaging (MRI) and X-ray machines, commercial and military aircraft engines, high-performance plastics, silicones and chemicals. GE also owns companies that market information, industrial power and transportation systems. GE Power Systems designs and manufactures world class steam and gas turbine generators and compressors. Several financial companies, including *mortgage* financing and specialty insurance, also come under GE's umbrella. GE acquired the National Broadcasting Network (NBC) in 1986. Since then, NBC expanded its broadcast market into a high-tech media powerhouse that stretched around the globe.

On any given day, a family in America may take dinner from the refrigerator or freezer and pop it into the 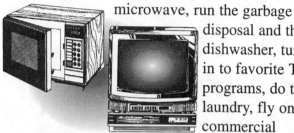 microwave, run the garbage disposal and the dishwasher, tune in to favorite TV programs, do the laundry, fly on a commercial jetliner or ride a train. If a family member needs medical attention, the doctor may order an X-ray or MRI. General Electric is so large and diversified that a product made by a GE company, or a service offered by a GE subsidiary, could be involved in every one of these activities.

The way a corporation runs its business and the ideals behind the scenes determines whether the industry is average or outstanding. According to GE literature, corporate leaders demonstrate *integrity* and a passion for excellence. They are open to ideas from anywhere and everyone. They see change as opportunity, not threat. When top level performance is expected, employees are encouraged to give their best. Consumers benefit because they receive high quality products, but the benefits do not end there.

GE businesses and volunteers take pride in helping others *"find a brighter future. . .and making the world around them a better place every day."* During 1996, employees from a wide variety of GE companies extended a helping hand to clean up debris and make repairs after a hurricane devastated Wilmington, North Carolina. GE also donated *modular* buildings to several churches that were destroyed by arson and refurbished a developmental center for children with multiple disabilities. During 1996, community service contributions from GE employees and a special company fund totaled $50 million.

Hundreds of Americans own stock in General Electric, but do not work for the conglomerate. Individuals may, however, own a private business franchise that sells or services GE products.

You have already learned how the Great Depression affected the country in various ways; next you will learn how it affected food.

"To be upset over what you don't have is to waste what you do have."

-Anonymous

Life Principle

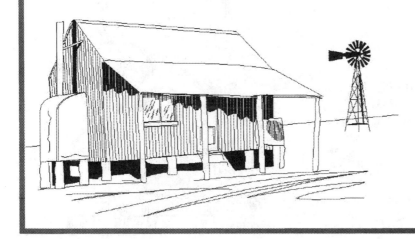

The Defending of America

Topic 2
Food

Chapter 11

Section One
Topics 1-5

CHICKEN FEET AND CARDBOARD SHACKS

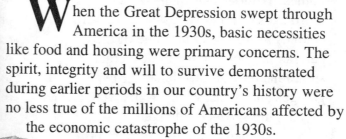

When the Great Depression swept through America in the 1930s, basic necessities like food and housing were primary concerns. The spirit, integrity and will to survive demonstrated during earlier periods in our country's history were no less true of the millions of Americans affected by the economic catastrophe of the 1930s.

Sad stories and heart-wrenching pictures emerged from the Depression years. For millions of Americans, life became one giant ten year struggle. Many families lost homes, businesses and jobs. With up to one quarter of the American population unemployed, people who had jobs and food were thankful. Hundreds of thousands lived in shanty towns dotted with cardboard boxes which served as homes. For families who were already poor, situations usually became critical. The middle class, which had enjoyed a steady growth of financial security during the prosperous 1920s, experienced emotional trauma and physical hunger.

Despite difficult economic conditions, the American family unit was strong. Mothers, fathers and children generally stayed together with home being the center of the struggle for survival. It was, in fact, a happy time for many families that learned to survive together. Some even recalled it as one of the most important times of their lives because they learned that personal relationships were more important than material possessions.

During the Depression, *frugality* and *resourcefulness* were practiced in all areas of life. Clothes and linens were recycled. A mother would often rip one of her threadbare dresses apart and then cut out pieces to make a smaller dress for one of

VOCABULARY

Frugality: wise use of money
Resourcefulness: creative use of resources (possessions, supplies)
Mesmerize: to hold the attention of, to cause the audience to listen intently
Sensation: excitement, interest

her daughters. Flour and feed sacks made of cotton cloth were regularly transformed into aprons, curtains, dresses, skirts, pillow covers, dish towels and even underwear. Shoes were precious items. Since everything had to last a long time, worn soles were commonly patched with cardboard. Many school age children simply went barefoot— and loved to feel dust between their toes!

Thousands of people lost their homes. Without jobs men could not pay for mortgages or rent. Thousands of married couples moved back into one of their parents' homes. Others in desperate situations moved into shacks or even garages and barns, where walls were created by hanging sheets or blankets.

Kitchens were much more primitive than today in terms of appliances, utilities and conveniences. Electricity was still fairly new; gas, kerosene and wood cookstoves were often used for heating and cooking.

Food was an important area of concern. The 7¢ for a loaf of bread or 49¢ for a pound of butter became harder and harder to obtain. Charities and churches did the best they could to help needy families. Bread and soup lines prevented people from starving. In 1933, several dozen breadlines were operated by charities in New York City. Poor families survived on a quart of soup and a loaf of bread each day. And people stretched what they did have to accommodate other people who were less fortunate. If someone visited at dinnertime, a little extra water made the soup go further.

Nothing went to waste in the kitchen. Every available part of a food source was consumed or used in some way. Even the feet of slaughtered chickens would be peeled, boiled with salt and pepper and eaten. The morning's leftover oatmeal became oatmeal soup at lunch. A common stomach-filler was homemade bread smeared with lard. Many people tilled gardens with new vigor, canning vegetables during the summer to provide food through the long winter months. Ground peach and apple peelings were turned into fruit butters and jams.

Toys and items of amusement for children during the Depression were simple. Children rarely played with store-bought toys; most were homemade from left-over products. Families became creative and resourceful in keeping children occupied with items such as scrap wood carved into toy boats and dollhouse furniture crafted out of food boxes. Catalogs provided hours of fun for young girls who would cut out pictures of furniture and people, using vivid imaginations to play games. Board games were popular, especially a new one called Monopoly. The radio was a great source of entertainment. Families would huddle around radios listening to tales of *Fibber McGee and Molly*, *The Lone Ranger*, *The Shadow* and others. Families with an extra ten cents could enjoy the picture show, *mesmerized* by such features as *Gone With the Wind* and *The Wizard of Oz*.

Children who grew up during the Depression learned important lessons about life. As one woman put it, *"Living through such a challenging time made me realize that possessions are not the source of happiness, but the peace which comes from inside."*

Typical of the folks who lived during that time in history was a 94-year-old great-grandmother who raised two boys during the Depression. In conversations about why she saved certain items, such as pieces of used aluminum foil or cotton string, the elderly lady sternly and stiffly proclaimed with a sense of pride, *"I lived during the Depression!"*

Amazingly, crime was much lower during the Great Depression with its poverty than during the 1980s and 1990s with prosperity. People lived under a moral code of ethics and respected private property. Rather than resorting to theft, people applied ingenuity and hard work to overcome poverty. Three men, Alderton, Thomas and Kloster illustrate how hard work helped Dr Pepper survive the Great Depression and become a major soft drink supplier.

In 1885, a young pharmacist named Charles C. Alderton devised a formula in Waco, Texas for a carbonated beverage that became one of America's most popular soft drinks. Carbonated soda drinks were fairly new to drug store fountains. The most popular drink was sarsaparilla. Charles experimented with various fruit juice formulas and finally settled on a combination that quickly became popular. It was named, "Dr Pepper."

Plant in Dublin, Texas

Demand was so high that the little corner drug store in Waco, Texas could not accommodate its customers.

Alderton and store owner Wade Morrison began to mix the formula in the store's back room for sale at other druggists' fountains. Customer demand grew and syrup production had to be moved to another location.

Wade Morrison formed a partnership with entrepreneur Robert Lazenly to produce and market Dr Pepper syrup. Lazenly retained bottling rights while Morrison retained rights to distribute the syrup for soda fountains.

Over a period of years the once-small company developed into a national *sensation*. By 1998, Dr Pepper was part of an economic giant that included Seven-up. In 1995, Cadbury Beverages purchased the Dr Pepper/Seven-up Companies for $1.7 billion. It ranked third in the soft drink industry, behind Coke and Pepsi.

The oldest franchise Dr Pepper bottling company is in Dublin, Texas. Until 1999 it was owned and managed by Bill Kloster who started working at the plant in 1933 when he was 14 years old. Bill's father had died, so Bill supported himself by working at the Dr Pepper plant. His hard work and careful attention to instructions earned him a series of promotions. After the owner died, Bill inherited the Dublin bottling plant.

Dr Pepper Soda Fountain

When Kloster began working for Dr Pepper, America was in the grip of the Great Depression. Sugar was scarce and times were hard. Then World War II broke out and the U.S. Government rationed sugar, glass and almost every ingredient used in soft drinks. Coke, Pepsi, and Dr Pepper felt the crunch of rationing. But like all other industries affected by the War, the soft drink industry rearranged management, cut production costs and altered marketing techniques in order to survive.

They did survive both the Depression and War and remain viable players in America's free enterprise system.

In 1969, Wendy's owner, Dave Thomas, put Dr Pepper drinks in all Wendy's Restaurants. Dave Thomas was adopted when he was six weeks old and his adoptive mother died when Dave was five years old. Dave Thomas was on his own since age 15. He was employed at restaurants, working 12 hours a day to sustain himself and to learn all the techniques of fast-food restaurants. He remarked years later, *"I would work until 8 in the morning, go home, fall into bed and sleep until about 3 in the afternoon. This work style set a standard for me. I became used to putting out a lot of volume when I was very young. I just thought that was the way you were supposed to do it. If somebody pays you, it was up to you to perform."*

During the Great Depression, people kept in touch through print media. The next lesson is about some magazines which were started during the 1930s.

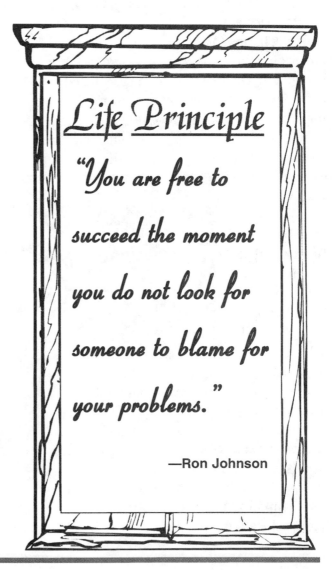

Life Principle

"You are free to succeed the moment you do not look for someone to blame for your problems."

—Ron Johnson

The Defending of America

Topic 3
Communication

Chapter 11

Section One
Topics 1-5

HAVE YOU READ THE NEWS?

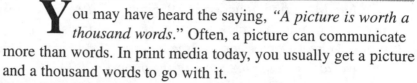

Y ou may have heard the saying, *"A picture is worth a thousand words."* Often, a picture can communicate more than words. In print media today, you usually get a picture and a thousand words to go with it.

Americans want to know everything. They want to know who, what, when, where, why and how—to see the news, experience it, understand it. The rise of literacy and prosperity in the later 19th century increased demand for printed materials. Prior to 1900, popular publications included scientific journals, gossip papers, newspapers and literary journals.

A great benefit to magazines and newspapers came in the 20th century with the development of advertising. Publishers learned that affordable publications could be supported by advertisers who wanted to market products or services.

Today, newspapers and magazines serve three purposes—reporting news, expressing opinions and advertising products. Historically, newspapers expressed news, but not political opinion. Before the 1776 War for Independence, publishers were *reluctant* to debate political issues in newspapers. In the United States, freedom of the press was guaranteed in 1791 with passage of the first article of the Bill of Rights.

American newspapers became more political in nature during the presidency of Andrew Jackson who understood the power of the press. At one time, President Jackson had 60 full-time journalists on the White House payroll. Various branches of our government learned to hold press conferences in which policies or official positions on issues were announced to the public. That policy continues today.

Within the pages of daily newspapers, readers find local, national and international news. Readers learn about births and deaths, winners of the World Series, Little League play-offs and

VOCABULARY

Reluctant: hesitant, not wanting to participate
Tidbits: small amount
Poignant: strongly moving to the emotions
Conservative: one who wishes to conserve (preserve, keep, save) the values and morals of America's heritage—the beliefs, standards and principles of our forefathers
Contemporary: modern day
Unscrupulous: dishonest and deceitful

movies. Other points of interest to the readers are new recipes for favorite desserts, stock reports, comic strips and hundreds of other *tidbits*.

While newspapers supply a broader range of news for general readership, magazines tend to specialize in news for specific audiences. No matter what your interest or hobby, you can probably find a magazine on the subject.

Life Magazine, founded in 1936 by Henry Luce, wanted people caught in the grip of the Great Depression to *"see life; to see the world; to watch the faces of the poor and the gestures of the proud; to see strange things."* Although *Life* used few words, its brilliant photography told the story to the reader. Vivid pictures depicted pain, pleasure, persecution and determination. *Poignant* moments of real life were captured forever on film and published to confirm or change the public's viewpoints. Since its beginning, *Life* Magazine has attempted to depict American life as viewed through the publisher's camera.

The *Saturday Evening Post* was a family magazine which became well-known for the artwork of Norman Rockwell. Each cover boasted a new color illustration depicting some aspect of American daily life. Readers identified with the people in Rockwell's art. Individually and in collections, his pictures still command admiration. With its *conservative*, well-

written articles, the magazine enjoyed a large readership.

The *Reader's Digest* was started in 1922 by DeWitt Wallace. The *Reader's Digest* presented shortened versions of books and articles to give the reader a general overview of American politics, economics, religion, disasters, families and humor. It printed real life stories of everyday people performing heroism and courage. *Reader's Digest* was so popular that it was translated into 17 different languages and had a circulation of more than 28 million in 2000.

Family Circle was originally published for Piggly Wiggly supermarkets in 1932. *Woman's Day* was begun by the A&P grocery chain in 1937. These magazines were initially handed out free at checkout counters. They featured articles of interest to homemakers, as well as product advertisements. These magazines are still available for a reasonable cost at grocery stores. Both still appeal to women's interests.

Contemporary newspapers and magazines hire reporters and columnists to write articles and features stories. Some reporters are *unscrupulous* or biased, seeking only to sell sensational stories, many of which bear little resemblance to truth. Respected journalists, however, care about truth. Print media usually reflects the politics or values of the publishers. Some are conservative. Some are liberal.

Do you use an Apple (Macintosh) or IBM computer? The tools of reporting have come a long way from early days when reporters telegraphed news to their editors and punched out articles on mechanical typewriters. Personal computers have streamlined communication, not only for America's print media, but for individuals and businesses as well.

Early computers were massive machines. American engineer Howard Aiken first designed and developed the IBM *Mark I* between the years of 1939 and 1944. Aiken's computer stood eight feet high and 55 feet long. Britain developed the first truly electronic computer in 1941, called *Colossus I*—a decoding machine used by the Allied Powers to break German codes in World War II. Few businesses owned computers, which were still too large to be practical.

55 Feet

Length of *Mark 1* Computer

The personal computer was introduced in 1977. The Apple II was the first marketed personal computer, made by Steve Jobs and Steve Wozniak in California. Competing for Apple's business, IBM Corporation introduced a personal computer in August of 1981.

More versatile than a typewriter, computers can create, edit, save and print documents. A few keyboard strokes can generate multiple copies. Constant competition among Apple, IBM and other computer companies to improve their products led to compactness, giving America and the world computers small enough to fit on a desktop or in a briefcase. By computer, businessmen can make phone calls, send faxes and connect locations all around the world by modem. By 1997, customers could buy computers that could fit in businessmen's pockets.

In recent years, Internet access has increased the capabilities of personal computing dramatically. A computer modem connected by telephone lines to various companies can coordinate access to a gold mine of information—everything from the stock market to libraries and encyclopedias to weather reports. Many major colleges and universities have databases—that contain libraries of historical, technical, medical and other information—available to anyone on the Internet. An individual sitting at a desk can link up with an entire universe of knowledge. Reporters and writers utilize research files from all over the world to gather data for their articles.

A very practical aspect of the Internet is electronic mail, affectionately called E-mail. Subscribers to Internet providers are given a *mailbox* and an *address* so their computers can send and receive mail. There is no additional charge beyond monthly service costs. Saving both time and money, electronic mail can send messages to anyone with an E-mail address.

E-mail is used by businesses and family members. Most magazines and newspapers can be accessed through the Internet, and readers can now E-mail letters to the editor or send entire manuscripts to publishers.

In addition to increasing the ability to communicate, technology enables Americans to disperse information that can make lasting differences in how people live world wide. One of the new frontiers for E-mail is education. Distant learning capabilities are challenging the conventional classroom—style of learning. Some students earn course credit without attending classrooms; all the lessons and assignments are transferred via E-mail.

Unfortunately, the American public cannot believe everything in print. A wise reader will search out the facts, intelligently discerning what is true and discarding propaganda and sensationalism.

Every U.S. citizen enjoys the freedom to think independently and to speak opinions. While some people abuse that freedom, freedom of speech is one of the cornerstones of America—a gift truly worth protecting.

You have already learned that America's industry provided military materials needed to win World War II. The next vignette answers the question: How could the whole world go to war?

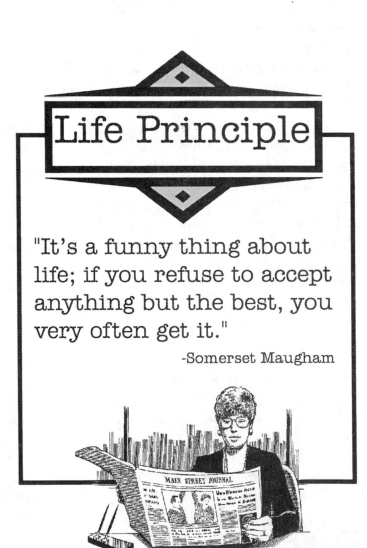

Life Principle

"It's a funny thing about life; if you refuse to accept anything but the best, you very often get it."

-Somerset Maugham

The Defending of America

Topic 4
Military

Chapter 11

Section One
Topics 1-5

WHAT PRICE FREEDOM?

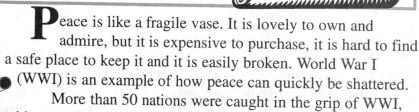

Peace is like a fragile vase. It is lovely to own and admire, but it is expensive to purchase, it is hard to find a safe place to keep it and it is easily broken. World War I (WWI) is an example of how peace can quickly be shattered.

More than 50 nations were caught in the grip of WWI, with scarcely a corner of the globe left unaffected. More than 16 million servicemen, from all nations on both sides, died in the conflict, and the number of civilians killed could not be *calculated*.

At the end of WWI, the Treaty of Versailles enacted harsh punishment on Germany for *escalating* the war. Germany was devastated by WWI and post-war conditions. She lost much of her territory, her army, navy, national pride and huge sums of money. The German people paid a high price for following leaders who attempted to rule Europe. Jobs in Germany were scarce, so were foods and products. Prices rose faster than paychecks could be earned. Inflation was so high that, literally, wheelbarrows full of money were required to pay for daily rations of milk and bread. Life was hard. The Germans blamed their hardships on the Treaty of Versailles and western foreigners who controlled the German economy.

Into this dismal scene marched Adolf Hitler, leader of the National Socialist Party, or Nazis. He promised to unite all German-speaking Europeans and restore Germany to its former glory. He taught that Germans were better than other people and therefore ought to rule the world. At the same time, Communism was building its power in Russia and flexing its military muscles toward Germany and the Baltic Region. The down-hearted German people gave up the liberties of a republic form of government in exchange for a restricted life under a dictator because of the promises Hitler offered. Hitler gained control of Germany in 1933 by one vote. And he ruled with an iron fist.

VOCABULARY

Calculated: counted, estimated
Escalating: increasing, intensifying
Integral: necessary
Devastating: horribly and overwhelmingly tragic
Hamper: to cause problems, to slow down progress
Paratroopers: soldiers who parachute out of planes into enemy territory
Precarious: unstable, insecure, likely to fail
Capitulate: to give in, give up, surrender

Meanwhile, in Italy, a dictator named Benito Mussolini came to power leading the Fascist Party in 1922. The Nazis in Germany and the Fascists in Italy represented a form of government called Fascism. Under Fascism, industry was privately owned but under strict government control. In fact, most aspects of life were rigidly controlled by the Fascists governments which granted few personal freedoms. Although intense patriotism was *integral* to the success of both Fascism and Nazism, these philosophies misdirected patriotism into warlike policies and persecution of minorities—especially Negroes, Christians and Jews. Conservative Germans and Italians who disagreed with Hitler and Mussolini were often murdered, imprisoned or exiled.

Benito Mussolini

Barely twenty years after WWI (1914-1918), thought to be "the war to end all wars," the world was again on the brink of all-out conflict. This time, it would be the most *devastating* war the world had ever known. World War II (WWII) began because dictators Hitler of Germany and Mussolini of Italy wanted to rule Europe and Africa. They used military force to take control of industry and to enslave foreigners and citizens.

On the other side of the globe, the Japanese empire was continuing a violent expansion policy started in the late 1800s. You may recall that Japan had joined the Allies in WWI to gain German-controlled territory in China and the Pacific. In WWII, Japan aligned with Germany and Italy to gain Asian territory controlled by France and other Allies. Japan was controlled by military officers, who used Emperor Hirohito to push Japan into war against Great Britain, France, China, Holland and other Allied nations.

By 1937, Japan controlled parts of Asia and much of the Pacific. In 1938, Japan began war with China. Although the United States was not yet part of the war, a group of American volunteer flyers under the command of Claire Lee Chennault formed a unit called the Flying Tigers to assist China's Generalissimo Chiang Kai-Shek against Japan. The Tigers became famous for defending the Burma Road, which was the Chinese supply route from India. After the United States entered the war, the Flying Tigers merged with the American Air Force.

While Naziism was assaulting Europe in 1935, Italy seized Ethiopia, an African nation. In 1938, the Nazis gained control of Austria and united it with Germany. Spain, although not a participant in WWII, became a Fascist state in 1936.

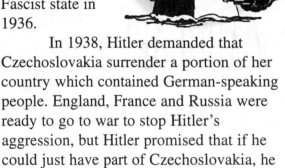

In 1938, Hitler demanded that Czechoslovakia surrender a portion of her country which contained German-speaking people. England, France and Russia were ready to go to war to stop Hitler's aggression, but Hitler promised that if he could just have part of Czechoslovakia, he would seek no new territory.

England and France appeased Hitler rather than oppose him. Hitler got his part of Czechoslovakia, but war was merely postponed. In less than a year, Hitler demanded that a portion of Poland be given to Germany. Europe learned not to make peace with a thug by giving him what he wanted. The Allied nations prepared to defend themselves against Hitler's open attempt to rule the world.

World War II officially began in Europe on September 1, 1939 when German troops invaded Poland. Britain and France realized they would not be safe if they allowed Hitler's aggression to continue, so they declared war on Germany. Italy honored its pact with Germany and declared war on Britain and France. Initially, the sides consisted of the Axis powers of Germany, Italy, and Japan against the Allies made up of Britain, France, a few smaller European nations, and members of the British Commonwealth such as Canada, India, Australia and New Zealand. Australian soldiers were some of the best fighters against Germany.

In the early days of the war, Nazi Germany and Communist Russia made a treaty not to fight each other, and to divide Poland between them, cruelly dominating the Polish people. (Hitler broke this agreement later in the war, and Russia joined the Allies.) Attacked by both Germany and Russia, the valiant Polish freedom fighters were crushed in just 26 days. Ruthless Communist and Nazi troops raped, plundered and devastated the Polish people. No sister, daughter, grandmother, mother or aunt was safe from abuse.

As in WWI, the United States tried to remain neutral. President Franklin Roosevelt wanted to provide some assistance for the Allies, but most Americans did not want to get pulled into another European war. The Neutrality Act of 1939 provided for European forces to purchase and transport American war materials. This worked in favor of Allied forces, whose naval blockades were set up to

German Nazi Soldiers

prevent Axis ships from *hampering* Allied trade with America.

German military leaders had devised a new type of warfare called the *blitzkrieg*, or lightning strike, which relied on rapid movements of air and land forces to conquer a country unprepared to defend itself. The blitzkrieg included the first use of *paratroopers*.

In April, 1940, Hitler turned north from Poland to conquer Denmark and Norway, then unleashed his terrible blitzkrieg

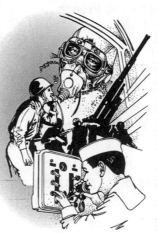

on western Europe. In May of that year, he conquered the Netherlands, Belgium and Luxembourg. In June, Germany and Italy attacked France. Although France had one of the largest armies in Europe, she fell in only 17 days. The German war machine appeared to be unstoppable. Its horrible military power terrorized Europe.

Wherever the Nazi's went, they carried with them their policy of terrible violence against Jews, Poles, Christians, Gypsies and minority ethnic people. Persecuted people were stripped of their property, placed in concentration camps, used for slave labor and randomly executed. Christians who were discovered protecting Jews received the same cruel treatment. Widespread destruction of Jews was called the *Holocaust*. An estimated six million Jews were viciously raped, tortured and murdered by Germans during the Holocaust. Meanwhile, Communist leader Joseph Stalin butchered over 18 million of his own people to secure Communism in Russia.

While war raged on the European continent, a battle was also raging in the North Atlantic. The Allies' blockade kept most German surface ships in port or close to Germany, but German submarines, called U-boats, attacked shipping convoys carrying supplies from Canada and the United States to Britain and other Allies.

In the bleakest moments of war were incidents of heroism. Between May 26 and June 4, 1940, the French seaport town of Dunkirk near the Belgium border was the scene of many heroic acts. Thousands of Allied troops had retreated to Dunkirk, France where they were trapped by advancing German troops. Forty miles across the rough waters of the English Channel were the white cliffs of Dover, England and safety—but no boats were available in France to transport the stranded troops.

The British navy sent every available ship to rescue the trapped soldiers. British civilians were so touched by the Allied troops plight that they joined in the rescue effort. Towns sent ferries, wealthy people came with their yachts, fishermen and youths joined the rescue with their small fishing boats and canoes, ordinary people appeared in row boats—anything that would stay afloat joined the effort to cross the channel and bring back Allied soldiers.

All the while, German fighter planes and bombers attacked the boats. About 338,226 Allied troops were rescued. The evacuation was called the *Miracle of Dunkirk*. A famous movie, *Mrs. Minerva*, was made to depict the heroic action of the British civilian rescue of troops.

Another event that shaped the war happened in 1940: Britain elected Sir Winston Churchill as Prime Minister. Promising the British people *"nothing . . . but blood, toil, tears and sweat,"* Churchill's

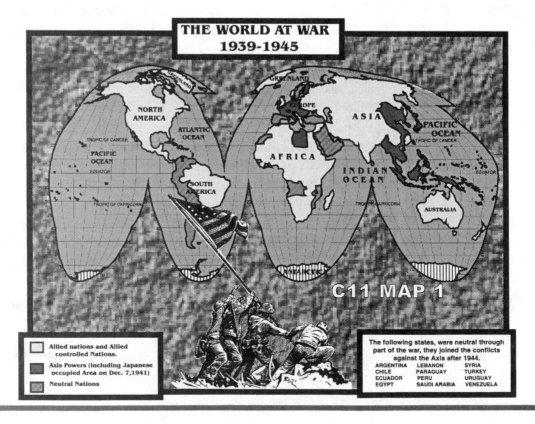

THE WORLD AT WAR
1939-1945

NORTH AMERICA

ATLANTIC OCEAN

PACIFIC OCEAN

SOUTH AMERICA

GREENLAND

EUROPE

ASIA

PACIFIC OCEAN

AFRICA

INDIAN OCEAN

AUSTRALIA

C11 MAP 1

Allied nations and Allied controlled Nations.

Axis Powers (including Japanese occupied Area on Dec. 7,1941)

Neutral Nations

The following states, were neutral through part of the war, they joined the conflicts against the Axis after 1944.

ARGENTINA	LEBANON	SYRIA
CHILE	PARAGUAY	TURKEY
ECUADOR	PERU	URUGUAY
EGYPT	SAUDI ARABIA	VENEZUELA

dogged determination and speeches inspired the British and Americans to continue fighting. In one speech the Prime Minister said, *". . .You may come to the moment when you will have to fight with all odds against you and only a **precarious** chance of survival. There may even be a worse case. You may have to fight when there is no chance of victory, because it is better to perish than to live as slaves."* Churchill proved to be an extremely capable leader whom many believed was divinely appointed to lead England during war against Hitler.

Another interesting heroic incident occurred in the life of Eddie Rickenbacker during WWI and WWII. The incident involved both air and sea. Captain Rickenbacker was the American fighter pilot "Ace of Aces" during WWI. He was credited with twenty-six official victories against German aircraft during WWI and was awarded the Congressional Medal of Honor. After WWI Rickenbacker bought and managed the Indianapolis Motor Speedway and became president of Eastern Airlines. During WWII, Rickenbacker was aboard a B-17 bomber that crashed in the Pacific Ocean while on a secret U.S. military mission to New Guinea. Rickenbacker and his six companions survived twenty-four days afloat on life rafts. After he was rescued he remarked that he and his men survived by quoting Bible verses, praying and eating birds and fish. He recorded that *"sea gulls and fish mysteriously landed in the rafts, enabling the crew to avoid starvation."*

Having conquered most of western Europe between April and June of 1940, Hitler focused his evil hatred on destroying Britain. Using nightly air attacks, Hitler expected England to surrender in two months. In mid 1941, after nearly a full year of daily bombing raids, Britain still refused to **capitulate** to the dictator. Hitler believed he had sufficiently destroyed England's military resources, so he turned his attention to Eastern Europe, a mistake that ultimately cost him the war.

In late 1940, Germans and Italians marched across eastern Europe. Communist Russia, meanwhile, was advancing westward, still under the treaty with Germany and independently pursuing her own expansion. Communists ruthlessly captured Finland, Estonia, Latvia and Lithuania on the coast of the Baltic Sea. Hitler broke his treaty and invaded Russia on June 22, 1941. As a result, Communist Russia, under the control of the cruel dictator Joseph Stalin, joined Allied forces against Germany and the Axis powers.

Deciding to add Asia to her territory, Japan attacked French Indochina in Southeast Asia. Japan soon began conquest of other French, British and Dutch territories in the Southeast Asian region.

The Japanese also wanted the Philippine Islands, which were protected by the United States Naval fleet stationed in Hawaii. On Sunday morning, December 7, 1941, Japanese bombers and fighter planes launched a surprise attack that destroyed much of the U.S. Pacific naval fleet while it was anchored at Pearl Harbor near Honolulu, Hawaii. While the attack was in progress, Japanese diplomats were in Washington D.C. discussing peaceful trade agreements with U.S. officials. It was this vicious surprise act that brought the United States into the war against Japan and the other Axis powers.

Former President Teddy Roosevelt once made a statement that America *"should speak softly and carry a big stick."* Now it was time to "carry the big stick."

Once in the war, Americans focused all available resources toward defeating the cruel Axis powers. Thousands of men between the ages of 18 and 45 joined the military before being drafted. The automobile and machine tool industries began heavy production of essential war goods: airplanes, trucks, tanks, ships and guns.

To finance the war, Americans were called upon to buy "War Bonds." Individual taxes were increased. Food, gasoline and cars were rationed—specific quantities were allowed per household. The entire nation united to assure victory over evil and to maintain freedom.

Women joined the Women's Army Corps (WACS), the Women's Air Force Service Pilots (WASP), and the Navy's Women Accepted for Volunteer Emergency Service (WAVES). These women served in non-combat capacities, enabling men to assume responsibility for combat.

About a half million black men served in units in the Pacific Islands and Europe. The Tuskegee Airmen was a famous unit of black aviators who trained near Tuskegee Institute in Alabama. Aviators flew supplies to troops in Europe and the Pacific Islands. Dorie Miller was awarded the Navy Cross for heroism at Pearl Harbor—the highest honor awarded to a black serviceman in the war.

The Navajo Code Talkers were a specialized military group who developed a dictionary in which Navajo Indian terms were used to transmit U.S. military plans. The Navajo language was too complicated for Japanese intelligence forces to **decipher**.

Japan advanced across the Pacific ocean to capture Burma, The Philippine Islands, Malaysia, the large expanse of the Netherlands Indies (present day Indonesia), northern New Guinea and the Solomon Islands. Each country fell in quick succession in early 1942. Japanese forces destroyed Allied resistance forces and pinned down American troops in the Philippines.

WORLD WAR II EUROPEAN THEATER 1942-1945

Allied Nations and Allied controlled Nations

Axis Powers and Axis controlled Nations

Neutral Nations

ICELAND

NORWEGIAN SEA

NORWAY SWEDEN FINLAND

NORTH SEA

UNITED KINGDOM

IRELAND

DENMARK

ESTONIA LATVIA LITH.

UNION OF SOVIET SOCIALIST REPUBLICS

POLAND

ATLANTIC OCEAN

FRANCE

GERMANY

SLOVAKIA

AUSTRIA HUNGARY

RUMANIA

ITALY

YUGOSLAVIA

BULGARIA

SPAIN

PORTUGAL

MEDITERRANEAN SEA

TURKEY

C11 MAP 2

President Franklin Roosevelt ordered General Douglas MacArthur, the U.S. commander of Allied troops in the Pacific, to escape from the Philippines by submarine and to direct the American war effort in the Pacific from Australia. MacArthur left the islands as he was commanded, but promised, *"I shall return."*

James Doolittle

After MacArthur left the Philippines, about 60,000 American and Filipino soldiers were captured by Japanese troops and forced to march 70 miles under harsh conditions along the Bataan Peninsula in what became known as the *Bataan Death March.* Along the way, 10,000 U.S. and Filipino prisoners died from starvation, execution or mistreatment. A famous book, *Escape From Corregidor,* was written by Lieutenant Edgar Whitcomb who escaped the death march by swimming to Corregidor. You will read more about Lt. Whitcomb later.

Japanese government officials thought Japan was too far from U.S. forces to be attacked by air. In April 1942, sixteen B-25 bombers led by Lt. Col. James H. Doolittle took off from the carrier *U.S.S. Hornet* to attack Japan. The daring air raid surprised and terrified residents of Tokyo and other cities. The raid was designed to confuse Japanese military leaders and to be a morale booster to Americans. Lt. Col. Doolittle received the Congressional Medal of Honor for his *valor*. The Doolittle raid pumped new hope into Allied forces. The power to win began to shift to Allied forces.

The first major Allied victory in the Pacific was the Battle of the Coral Sea. It was fought May 4-8, 1942, north of Australia. In this clash between Japan and Allied forces, United States technology, courage and strategy conquered Japanese military strength. Japan's expansion to the South Pacific region was stopped, and Japanese officers were forced to change their war strategy.

The turning point in the war in the Pacific occurred June 4 and 5, 1942 at the Battle of Midway, a tiny island in the Pacific Ocean. By incredible diligence and ingenuity, American *cryptographers*, people who study secret codes to find out how to decipher them, managed to break the code in which Japan sent messages to its navy ships. Admiral Nimitz, commander of U.S. naval forces in the Pacific, learned of Japanese Admiral Yamamoto's plans to attack Midway Island. The large American naval force surprised the Japanese and met the attack of Midway Island with force that shocked the enemy.

Heavy losses inflicted on the Japanese fleet not only enabled the United States to win the Battle of Midway Island, but also kept the United States mainland and Hawaii safe from further Japanese attack. Although WWII continued for three more long years of gruesome fighting, just 6 months after the

VOCABULARY

Decipher: decode, figure out, translate
Valor: courage and bravery under pressure
Regime: a political force that controls others

attack on Pearl Harbor, the war in the Pacific had turned in favor of the Allies.

The years of 1941 and 1942 marked a turning point for the war in Europe as well. Britain held off Germany's air attacks, and Hitler's blitzkrieg toward Moscow froze in the harsh Russian winter. But the rest of the war was still not easy for the Allies. Three years of very heavy fighting on three fronts remained in Europe.

German troops advanced almost to Moscow before Russian soldiers and winter weather halted the Nazi invasion. In the spring of 1942, Communist troops began the counter offensive that slowly drove the Germans out of Russia. Another German invasion began in July 1943 and lasted two years before the Germans were forced back through Western Russia, the Ukraine and Eastern Europe. The angry Germans left a bloody trail of devastated homes, farms and villages.

To the south, Axis and Allied forces were equally matched in North Africa. The Axis were commanded by the brilliant German general, Erwin Rommel, called, *The Desert Fox*. The British were commanded by the capable General Montgomery. Opposing forces fought back and forth losing and re-gaining the same ground until a second Allied force commanded by American General Eisenhower made a surprise landing in Algeria and Morocco in November of 1942. By May, 1943, Axis troops had been driven out of North Africa. A major part of the credit for victory went to United States General Dwight Eisenhower for his brilliant and decisive combat strategies.

After victory in Africa, Eisenhower and the Allies drove north, invading Italy in late summer of 1943 and capturing Sicily.

Officially, Italy surrendered and joined the war on the side of the Allies in October, 1943, but German troops in Italy continued to fight against the Allies. The Allied advance up the Italian peninsula was costly and slow. Italians welcomed American soldiers with flowers, cheers, kisses and embraces. The U.S. Flag unfurled over villages previously marked by the German Swastika. The Stars and Stripes of America were gladly raised across Italy.

In the West, Britain remained unconquered. She became home base for Allied bombing raids against key Axis military and industrial targets in Germany and Western Europe. American planes bombed Germany and Nazi held territories by day, and British planes bombed by night. The Germans countered with two newly developed weapons—jet airplanes and bombs carried across the channel to England by missiles. But they came too late in the war to save Germany from defeat.

At 6:30 a.m. on June 6, 1944, known as *D-Day*, approximately 4,000,000 American, British and Canadian soldiers landed in Normandy on the north coast of France and effected the largest shore line assault in history. The Allied invasion was a unified assault to drive Hitler out of Western Europe. The Germans fiercely fought the invasion, but could not prevent the Allied forces under the command of U.S. General George Patton and Supreme Allied Commander, Dwight Eisenhower, from gaining a foothold in Western Europe. Patton's tanks and artillery

Erwin Rommel

spread across France and destroyed German strongholds in Western Europe.

The Allies began the hard drive east toward Berlin, liberating Nazi-controlled territory along the way, and stopping the horrors of the Nazi *regime.* The Germans made a massive and fierce counterattack called the *Battle of the Bulge* in late 1944, but their offensive was repelled by Allied troops in January 1945.

In early 1945, Allied armies were moving toward Berlin from all directions. On April 30 of that year, Hitler committed suicide. Berlin fell on May 2, and Germany surrendered on May 7. The war in Europe was over.

Battles in the Pacific focused mostly on Japanese efforts to destroy Allied bases in Australia, Hawaii and the Philippines. The few paragraphs that follow do not adequately convey the hardships of the Pacific. Each battle mentioned below involves tens of thousands of individual stories of heroism and sacrifice and not all the battles are mentioned. Time and space simply are not available in this course to convey the horrors, patriotism and heroism of WWII.

Americans at home learned the names of far away and unfamiliar places as brave U.S. servicemen fought their way across the Pacific to conquer the Japanese. The American strategy was to island-hop, capturing only key islands rather than every island the Japanese held. Guadalcanal, Guam, Iwo Jima and Okinawa were some of the many fierce and famous battlegrounds between 1942 and 1945. In June 1944, American forces began bombing Japan on a regular basis, but Japanese officials refused to surrender.

In October 1944, U.S. General MacArthur kept his promise to return to the Philippines. Upon landing, the general declared: "I have returned. By the grace of Almighty God, our forces stand on Philippine soil." Under the general, U.S. forces fought their way ashore, liberating the Filipino people from Japanese troops. Filipinos greeted the general and American troops with tears of joy, flag waving, dancing, parades and music. A year later, MacArthur reclaimed the entire Pacific region from the Japanese.

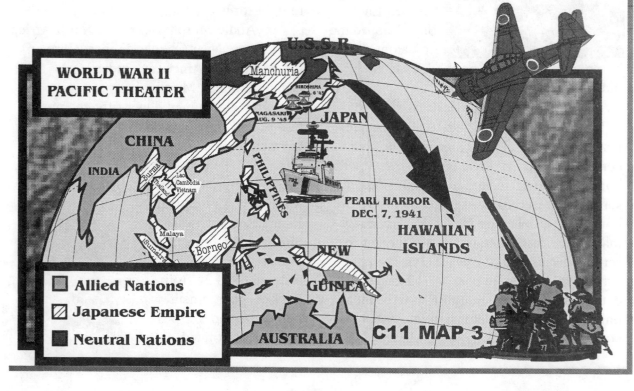

WORLD WAR II PACIFIC THEATER

C11 MAP 3

☐ Allied Nations
▨ Japanese Empire
■ Neutral Nations

On April 12, 1945, Franklin D. Roosevelt, President of the United States since the beginning of World War II, died, and vice-president Harry S. Truman became president. The new president faced a major challenge: how to end the war quickly. President Truman had the capability to make quick, monumental decisions based on wisdom and preservation of lives. The Allies had already won the war in Europe, and victory over Japan seemed likely. The only question was, how long would victory take, and how many brave soldiers and innocent civilians would sacrifice their lives because of Japan's greed? The planned U.S. invasion of Japan was still months away and the long and deadly conquest of Japan would be at a terrible loss of more U.S. soldiers.

The United States had developed a secret weapon called the atomic bomb. It was more destructive than any weapon developed in history. President Truman chose to use the bomb to bring a swift conclusion to the war.

B-29

On August 6, 1945, the United States B-29 bomber, Enola Gay, dropped the first atomic bomb used in warfare on the Japanese industrial city of Hiroshima.

That single bomb destroyed 4.7 square miles of the city and killed 100,000 people instantly. For weeks to come, people would continue to die from radiation released by the bomb. However, Japanese officials refused to surrender. Three days later, another atomic bomb was dropped on Nagasaki. Japan saw that further resistance was futile and began serious discussions for peace. Japan surrendered on September 10, 1945. To the date of this publication, those have been the only atomic bombs detonated in combat conditions.

The war was over. The world breathed a sigh of relief, combined with overwhelming grief. Generals and soldiers alike had fought bravely. Many heroic stories could be told. Men were called upon to put the war behind them and go home to their families for whose freedom they had fought. Eisenhower, Murphy and Whitcomb were such men.

American General Dwight Eisenhower was the Supreme Commander of all Allied Forces in Europe. His military assignments early in the war involved developing detailed plans for the defense of the Pacific and the invasion of Nazi-controlled Europe. His skill in developing and later carrying out these plans led to a rapid series of promotions over other generals to become the Supreme Allied Commander.

War required not only brilliant generals, but also combat soldiers. One such soldier was a 16-year-old Texas youth named Audie Murphy. His father had abandoned the family, and when Audie's mother died, Audie's two younger siblings were placed in the care of a relative. Young Murphy enlisted to fight for his country.

Audie Murphy served in North Africa and Europe. Near Colmar, France, German forces attacked American soldiers, who began to retreat. Murphy jumped on a burning tank, gunned down fifty enemy troops, and single-handedly held off a German force of six tanks and 250 men. For this action, he received the Congressional Medal of Honor. Over the course of the war, Murphy was promoted to Lieutenant and awarded three medals from France, one from Belgium, and 24 from the U.S. government, making Audie Murphy the most decorated

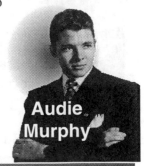
Audie Murphy

American soldier of World War II. His story, *To Hell and Back*, was made into a movie in which he portrayed himself.

Edgar Whitcomb grew up in a small Indiana town, and like a lot of young men in 1940, he volunteered for duty in the U.S. Army because he loved his country. Ed became navigator on a U.S. B-17 Flying Fortress bomber in the Philippine Islands. He refused to surrender when Bataan fell and made his way to the island of Corregidor.

Ed Whitcomb

When Japanese troops captured Corregidor, Whitcomb escaped back to the mainland by swimming for eight hours at night in shark-infested waters. He was later recaptured, tortured and shipped to China, where he was held in an internment camp for one year. He returned to the Philippine Islands to fly combat missions against the Japanese.

After the war, Ed wrote a powerful book, *Escape From Corregidor*. It helped elect Whitcomb as Indiana's Secretary of State and later as Governor (1970-74). Whitcomb's memories of war lingered. Many veterans of wars had to find ways to overcome the horrors and forget the tortures they underwent. Mr. Whitcomb believed his life had been spared by God for a reason. Governor Whitcomb found relief from torturous memories by studying the Bible to learn about two other famous prisoners—Jesus of Nazareth and Paul of Tarsus. Late in life, when Governor Whitcomb was 72 years old, he sailed around the world on a 30 foot boat. While sailing he wrote another book about WWII, *On Celestial Wings*, telling detailed accounts of heroes whose names have been forgotten, but whose actions helped preserve America's freedom.

Even though Ed Whitcomb grew up a poor farm boy and was tortured in a war, he decided to be thankful for his past and make his future successful. Ed Whitcomb was an American hero. He knew the cost of freedom is great, and that the value of freedom is matchless. Freedom was expensive for Ed Whitcomb and the men who fought with him. A recent war film, *Saving Private Ryan*, released in 1998, depicted the horrors and heroism many American heroes such as Eisenhower, MacArthur, Murphy and Whitcomb experienced in WWII. Director Spielberg effectively captured the essence of war against Germany—heroic American men and women fulfilling duty for a worthy and significant cause. They fought because they knew sacrifice, pain and even death are prices men and women pay to remain free.

The next vignette explains what was happening back home while American men were fighting the war in Europe.

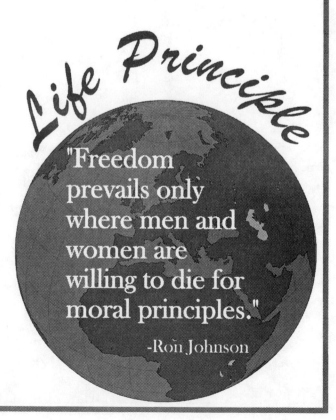

Life Principle

"Freedom prevails only where men and women are willing to die for moral principles."

-Ron Johnson

The Defending of America

Topic 5
Family & Home

Chapter 11

Section One
Topics 1-5

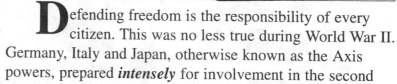

ON THE HOME FRONT

Defending freedom is the responsibility of every citizen. This was no less true during World War II. Germany, Italy and Japan, otherwise known as the Axis powers, prepared *intensely* for involvement in the second great world conflict. In 1940, while conflict was heating up in Europe and Asia, the United States was focusing on social and economic conditions. Thousands of families struggled to provide food, clothing and shelter. Throughout 1939 and 1940, American families were concerned not only about their "daily bread" but became alarmed over conditions in Germany and Italy. Japan's December 7th, 1941 attack on Pearl Harbor dramatically changed American families. Not only did the United States enter the war, it did so with astonishing efficiency. Within two years of the unexpected attack in Hawaii, America's war production equaled that of all three Axis countries combined, and exceeded that of the other Allied nations. By 1944, in an incredible display of free enterprise and capitalism, America's production output was double that of the socialist countries of Germany, Italy, Russia and Japan.

As U.S. soldiers and sailors headed into military service by the thousands, both industry and the United States government were left with a major problem—if the men were defending and protecting freedom, who would operate the factories and the shipyards? Young women were the logical choice, but would they leave children in care of aunts and grandmothers to work in factories that produce weapons of war?

America's plunge into World War II came on the heels of a decade of economic depression. Jobs had been scarce during that time, so a great effort had been made to encourage women to stay home in order that men could take the few jobs available. The role of women as ***homemakers*** was deeply ***ingrained*** in the American consciousness. A combination of economic needs

VOCABULARY

Intense: much energy, activity
Homemaker: a woman who stays home to take care of the needs of her family
Ingrained: deeply entrenched, a strong custom or practice
Icon: a symbol or image
Portray: to describe, to create an image
Render: to give or provide

Women Supporting the War

while husbands went to war, and a sense of patriotism to assist America's men at war encouraged women to leave their kitchens in exchange for factory jobs. Many women were already involved in war activity such as raising victory gardens and volunteering with the Red Cross, but available factory jobs became a new avenue for thousands of young women to express support of America in the war and to provide family income while husbands and fathers were away. Thousands of women traded cotton aprons for denim overalls.

One of the biggest factory needs was for riveters, a job vital in the production of tens of thousands of military aircraft. Usually working in pairs, one riveter operated a special gun to shoot small bolts (rivets) into metal, and another person flattened the rivets with a hammer. The need for so many riveters led to the *icon* "Rosie the Riveter." This promotion of women factory employees was popularized with a song and poster of a female riveter displaying strong muscles, a determined will, and a pretty face, next to the caption, "We Can Do It!"

As the war continued and production needs increased, women were the focus of targeted advertising. Radio and print advertisements appealed to the emotions of women to entice them to fill war jobs. Advertisers used catch phrases such as "Be the woman behind the man behind the gun," and "Victory is in your hands."

A popular women's magazine *portrayed* Hollywood fashion and beauty queens as female factory workers. The article explained how these production workers could go home at the end of a workday with dirty fingernails and smudged overalls, but transform themselves into glamorous ladies in the evening. This image was misleading because not only did these moms work in factories all day, but also had to maintain their homes and train their children each evening.

Housework in the 1940s took a great deal of time to complete daily chores compared to contemporary modern conveniences. In 1941, one-third of American kitchen stoves still used wood or coal—not electricity or gas. Many women still hauled water for the back-breaking work of dishwashing and laundry. According to estimates in the early 1940s, American women spent an average of 50 hours weekly on household chores. Along with raising children, employment outside the home became a major issue about which mothers had to choose.

Married women with children were emotionally pulled between raising their children or working in factories. The federal government made special efforts to convince women to put their families second to the war effort. Advertising messages connected war time needs to domestic abilities and the sacrifices made by families during the Depression years. One employment brochure compared operating a rivet gun or drill press to sewing. Women who made the sacrifice to become employees in the war effort were glorified in the media as home-front heroines.

Songs like "The Lady at Lockheed" and "We're the Janes Who Make the Planes" kept the war effort popular across the airwaves. In Seattle alone, one four-week radio campaign resulted in 2,200 women being employed at several defense production plants. Detroit auto factories which quickly converted to war production facilities recruited 142,000 women after employment registration forms were mailed to 500,000 households in a surrounding county.

Women made up half the workforce in the newest industry—aircraft manufacturing. Just prior to World War II, women made up only 25% of the industrial workforce in the United States. That number grew to 36% by 1944 as 5,000,000 women helped construct planes and other military equipment or worked in jobs which supported defense efforts.

The 15,000,000 American men who fought overseas, and the millions of women who manufactured planes, trucks and tanks were all crucial to the Allied victory in World War II. Women factory employees provided equipment and tools which husbands, fathers, sons and friends needed to fight in Europe, Africa and the Pacific islands.

While women were entering factories, support organizations were beginning to focus on building patriotism and character into boys and girls whose mothers and fathers were absent.

SCOUTING ORGANIZATIONS FOCUS ON CHARACTER BUILDING

America has always been a place where youth could pursue happiness and take advantage of opportunities to build character. Adult focus on developing morality and character in our nation's young people became a special objective in the early part of the 20th century. A strong belief in building positive values resulted in the founding of several youth organizations.

Boy Scouts of America, Girl Scouts of America, and Camp Fire (originally called Camp Fire Girls) all started between 1910 and 1920. These organizations focused on developing personal confidence through positive character. Using the great outdoors as the backdrop, groups focused on building leadership qualities and creating responsible citizens through service and education.

Both Boy Scouts and Girl Scouts have their roots in an English scouting movement launched in 1908. The program in England was so popular that it spread quickly to other nations such as the United States, Australia, Canada and South Africa. While Chicago publisher William D. Boyce was lost in a London fog, he reached his destination only with the welcome assistance of an English scout. Boyce's favorable experience with the English scouting program led the publisher to start Boy Scouts of America in 1910. By 1912, Boy Scouts were in every state.

That same year, Juliette Gordon Low and 18 young ladies started the first girl scouting program in Savannah, Georgia. Originally called Girl Guides, the name was eventually changed to Girl Scouts of America.

During WWII, Boy Scouts became more of a movement than simply an organization. The aim of Boy Scouts was to supplement character-building responsibilities with the home, church, and school by involving boys in healthy and creative activities—often outdoors. The Scout's motto was "Be Prepared." Through group comradeship and wholesome activities, the Girl Scout's program attempted to prepare and equip girls physically, mentally, spiritually, morally and socially to function as responsible adult women.

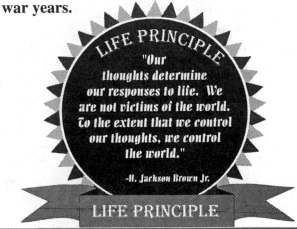

The Boy Scouts' attitude of service, which Mr. Boyce experienced firsthand in London, has been exhibited by American scouts over the years, from *rendering* nationwide assistance during the great influenza epidemic in 1918, collecting 2,000,000 items for destitute people during the Great Depression and collecting and recycling used rubber tires during World War II. The largest effort since World War II came in 1988 when more than 60,000,000 food items were collected by scouts and adult volunteers in a cross-country food drive for destitute and displaced families.

Camp Fire Girls was started in 1910 by a Maine medical doctor and his wife. Their goal: to teach young women responsibility and help them develop useful skills. In 1979, the name was changed to Camp Fire to allow for inclusion of boys. The name *Camp Fire* was selected carefully. *Camp* was used to represent beauty, health and happiness associated with the outdoors. The second word, *Fire*, refers to the fire in woodstoves in homes, symbolizing quality family time spent in nourishing healthy relationships among parents and children.

Male and female versions of various scouting programs are based on a merit system of earning awards—beads, patches and pins, depending on age-level. In more than 100 different potential career categories, the boys learn about, and earn awards for, achievement in sports, outdoor survival activities, science, history, citizenship, hobbies, occupations, medicine and safety. Each Scout learns to live by the twelve laws of scouting, including trustworthiness, loyalty, helpfulness, cleanliness, obedience, cheerfulness and kindness. Girl Scouts compete for their own awards in five category themes which include many of the same topics as the boys. Camp Fire also promotes a topic-based award program to earn beads and patches. In all three programs, the earned awards are displayed on military-like uniforms. During WWII, youths proudly wore their military-like scout uniforms as public displays of patriotism.

In 1938, the song "God Bless America" by the famous composer Irving Berlin became the official WWII patriotic song. It earned a fortune for Mr. Berlin, who donated all financial benefits to the Boy Scouts and Girl Scouts of America because scouts represented the basic values which made America a "God Blessed" nation.

All aspects of American life were affected by WWII—even agriculture. The next vignette tells how conservation that started early in the 20th century became even more important during and after the war years.

LIFE PRINCIPLE

"Our thoughts determine our responses to life. We are not victims of the world. To the extent that we control our thoughts, we control the world."

-H. Jackson Brown Jr.

LIFE PRINCIPLE

The Defending of America

Topic 6
Agriculture

Chapter 11

Section Two
Topics 6-10

A CENTURY OF CONSERVATION

Conservation has become an agricultural challenge for Americans in the 20th Century. Use of fertilizers and *pesticides* has spawned intense debate over conservation of manpower, resources, the environment and manufacturing costs. President Teddy Roosevelt's vision for conservation in the early 1900s ushered in a century of conservation awareness. Prior to Roosevelt's presidency, America's forests were damaged by careless mining, logging and farming. Dust storms stripped the soil from treeless land. Erosion began to eat away America's farmable land, demanding expensive fertilizers to *replenish* the soil. *Conservationists* became active to preserve the nation's forests and agriculture regions.

In the early 1900s, Congress, at the insistence of President Teddy Roosevelt, set aside 150 million acres of public land for National Forests. Public parks, presently managed by the National Parks Services, provided *erosion* control, wildlife refuges or game preserves and places of recreational enjoyment for the American people.

In 1908, President Roosevelt organized a Conference of Governors in Washington, D.C. They discussed ways to conserve and preserve our natural resources. Forty-one governors returned to their home states to set up conservation commissions.

The lessons in conservation were well timed. During World War I, Americans had to be resourceful, yet efficient, to meet the demands of war. While industries supplied the army with fuel and ammunition, farmers supplied the food. Both groups *extracted* resources from the land, yet attempted to preserve America's forests, ranges and rivers.

The Great Depression was a tragic irony for the farmer from 1929 until the beginning of WWII in 1941. He was able, thanks to advancements in technology, to produce *bumper crops*.

VOCABULARY

Pesticides: chemicals used to kill pests (insects, bugs)
Replenish: to restore, to make complete again
Erosion: the wearing away of soil
Extract: to take from
Irony: the opposite of what is expected comes true
Bumper crops: more produce than is needed
Scarcity: not enough, inadequate amount

But the excess of produce lowered prices, leaving the farmer with little spendable income. Congress provided assistance in the form of Agricultural Acts that paid farmers to store extra crops and to withhold extra farmland from production. Farm income increased, but so did federal taxes and regulations.

In the mid 1930s, President Franklin Delano Roosevelt (President Teddy Roosevelt's cousin) pushed government further into family and business involvement through creation of the Tennessee Valley Authority (TVA). The TVA was designed to conserve energy and provide affordable electricity through hydroelectric dams which helped restore the landscape of the Tennessee Valley. Soil erosion halted, the land surrounding the Tennessee River was reclaimed and the river no longer flowed uncontrollably. The poverty-stricken area was transformed into a fertile valley where agriculture flourished.

Then came World War II. The Japanese attack on Pearl Harbor instantly placed heavy demands on America's natural resources. America's efforts of conservation were tested to the limit. The voluntary rationing program of World War I was not sufficient to address the magnitude of WWII demands. When the war began, storage facilities had a two year supply of wheat, cotton and corn, and no shortage of food was foreseen. Yet, within six months of Pearl Harbor (Dec. 7, 1941), *scarcities* were very real.

In 1941, President Franklin Roosevelt established the Office of Price Administration and Civilian Supply (O.P.A.) to control inflation and to administer rationing programs. The federal government issued ration stamps that limited each family's quantities for *commodities* such as butter, gasoline, meat and sugar. Families learned how to conserve scarce items. Old toothpaste tubes were turned in for new ones. Ice cream came in only ten flavors. Everything had to be conserved and used wisely. America's armed forces needed supplies, and the folks at home had to do without some products so soldiers could have food and uniforms. A century earlier, the French dictator, Napoleon, had said that an army marches on its stomach. In order to keep the Allied forces marching, American farmers exceeded their production goals for 1942. Energetic farmers sweated their way into *prosperity*. All the wonderful new technology was put to use as farmers harvested bumper crops. Many farm mortgages were paid off during those war years.

Thousands of farm workers were *drafted* or *enlisted* in military service. The loss of farmers to the battlefield led to creative solutions to keep farms operating and to preserve farm investments. The New York state legislature permitted children over age 14 to accumulate a generous number of excused absences from school to help with spring planting and fall harvesting. A farm implement company trained women

TVA Hydroelectric Dam Diagram

Reservoir
Intake
Powerhouse
Generator
Penstock
Turbine
River
Long Distance Power Lines

Courtesy of TVA

VOCABULARY

Commodity: items people buy, goods
Prosperity: financially stable
Drafted: forced to serve in military units
Enlisted: volunteered for military duty

and girls to operate milking machines. Boy Scouts in Iowa were trained to do farm labor. City boys were trained for work by FFA (Future Farmers of America) groups. Farm neighbors worked together, pooling their labor and working longer hours.

Huge quantities of steel were needed for military equipment, thus, farm machinery clinics were conducted to keep existing machines working. In California, agricultural students used their welding classes to repair farm machinery. In Kansas, high school students repaired farm tools and taught at conservation clinics.

When WWII was over, farmers again faced the situation in which production was so efficient that staple products piled up in storage. National income had risen 50%, but the farmer's income had decreased by a third. The farmer was paying out more than he could earn. By 1956, one out of eleven farmers left their farms. Congress passed the

Soil Bank Bill, which paid farmers for taking twelve million acres of American farm land out of production. This legislation prevented the overproduction of staple crops and temporarily stabilized farm income, but made the American farmer dependent on the federal government for economic stability.

During the 20th century, agriculture became big business. Magazines such as *Farm Journal* kept farmers informed on everything from farm politics to fertilizers. Large agriculture operations took the place of small farms. One such example is the King Ranch in Kingsville, Texas. Founded in 1853 by a steamboat captain named Richard King,

the King Ranch became one of the largest working ranches in the world.

King's son-in-law, Robert Kleberg, and his sons expanded the ranch into a multi-faceted organization. They developed a new type of beef cattle by crossing Indian Brahmas with British Shorthorn cattle. The combination produced the hardy cattle called Santa Gertrudis. These cattle were red in color, tall, heavy and adaptable to the dry and hot Texas rangeland. In 1999 the King Ranch cultivated more than 60,000 acres in South Texas. The ranch grows a variety of agricultural products including citrus, grain and cotton. Because of its historical value, King Ranch also includes a museum and conducts tours. The ranch also has recreational sites, game preserves and hunting lodges. Although the King Ranch is an unusual example of big business in agriculture, it demonstrates the changes that American farming underwent during the 20th century as a result of technology and resourceful use of land.

Santa Gertrudis

Richard King

Modern technology has assisted American farmers in providing surplus commodities to meet foreign market demands for food and agricultural products. America exports more soybeans than any other nation in the world. Soybean meal is used as a meat substitute for people and feed for livestock. The oil is used in such products as salad dressing, soap, ice cream and explosives.

During World War II, American farmers produced large amounts of wheat and wheat products, not only for livestock and people at home, but also for Allied troops across the seas. America today remains the world's largest exporter of wheat. The Midwest states of Iowa, Nebraska, Illinois, Indiana, Wisconsin and Minnesota are considered to be the "bread basket" of America and the world. In the 1960s and 1970s, American scientists developed new wheat varieties with higher grain yields. Several poorer countries, such as Pakistan, India and Mexico, were able to use American technology to increase wheat production in areas with limited fertilizer and water.

America the beautiful is truly America the bountiful. Americans have learned to conserve and work hard to prosper as a nation. In any world crisis, Americans are always ready to send food, clothing and other necessities. The next vignette will introduce you to several important people during the middle 1900s.

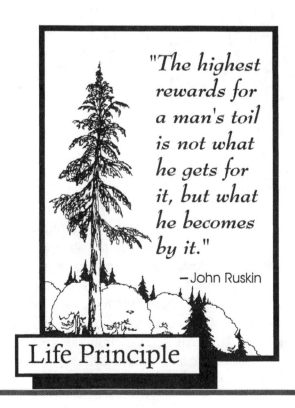

"The highest rewards for a man's toil is not what he gets for it, but what he becomes by it."

—John Ruskin

Life Principle

122

The Defending of America

Topic 7
*Dominant
Personalities &
Events*

Chapter 11

Section Two
Topics 6-10

FRANKLIN DELANO ROOSEVELT– (FDR) POLITICAL LEADER IN A WHEELCHAIR

By many standards, Franklin Delano Roosevelt (FDR) had a privileged childhood. Born January 30, 1882 to well-off parents, he spent his growing-up years on a large estate in beautiful Hyde Park, New York. Hundreds of acres of forests, fields and gardens served as his personal playground. Franklin was the only son of James Roosevelt and his second wife, Sara. Franklin received more than ample attention from a doting mother and a host of nurses, nannies and servants. The best private tutors were hired to teach young Franklin at home until he was fourteen. Then he enrolled at the prestigious Groton School in Salem, Massachusetts. His college career took him to Harvard in 1900, then on to Columbia University in New York City to study law. The man who would later become America's 32nd president grew up with the benefits of a thorough home education, prestigious colleges, financial security and social activities.

Influenced by distant cousin Theodore Roosevelt, who became president while Franklin was at Harvard University, FDR aimed for a career in politics. He met and fell in love with Eleanor Roosevelt, the favorite niece of cousin Theodore. FDR and Eleanor married in March 1905 in a *gala* wedding; President Teddy Roosevelt came from Washington to give the bride away.

Franklin had a steady early career—first as an attorney, then as New York state senator, assistant Secretary of the Navy, and vice presidential candidate on the Democratic ticket with presidential nominee James M. Cox. Even though the 1920 election was lost to Republican candidate Warren G. Harding, Roosevelt gained important national political experience and recognition. From there, Roosevelt became governor of New York and then U.S. president.

But Roosevelt suffered a great tragedy. In the summer of 1921 while vacationing at the family cottage at Campobello Island off Canada, Roosevelt became ill. At first FDR thought he had a simple cold, but later doctors announced a

VOCABULARY

Gala: festive, joyful, full of energy
Coincidentally: accidentally, but seemingly planned or arranged
Strenuously: forcefully, actively, vigorously
Mandate: an order from authorities
Enacted: established by law or with authority

devastating diagnosis—*polio*, an incurable disease which paralyzes and deforms muscles. The aspiring politician and father of six children was only 39 years old when he received the grim news that he would be confined to a wheelchair.

Many men would have crumbled emotionally at such a horrifying turn of events in their lives. But not Franklin Roosevelt. He had too much to accomplish to let polio defeat him. He was determined to continue his political career, and for 24 years he courageously endured great pain while living as a crippled man. After extensive rehabilitation, Roosevelt ran for governor of New York. Most of his campaigning was done from a wheelchair using a new media form—radio. FDR exhibited a fighting spirit which New Yorkers seemed to appreciate. He won the election and was sworn into office as governor on January 1, 1929, *coincidentally* in the same room where Teddy Roosevelt had assumed the same position 30 years earlier. During his two terms as governor, FDR became known for his progressive agriculture programs for farmers.

On October 24, 1929, just nine months into FDR's first term as governor, disaster struck America. The stock market crashed, plummeting the Unites States into economic depression. Times were desperate as many people—rich and poor—lost all their money, homes and businesses. The unemployment rate skyrocketed. Families struggled to feed and clothe themselves and keep a roof over their

Shack for family during Great Depression

heads. Roosevelt took immediate action to provide economic relief for the people of New York state. He believed the state government should create jobs. FDR introduced a government works program that put unemployed people to work in conservation and unemployment insurance jobs. Their tax-generated paychecks pumped money into local businesses, creating temporary cash flow in communities.

After two terms as governor, Roosevelt decided his tax and employment program could help the entire country, so he ran for president against Herbert Hoover who had been unjustly blamed for causing America's economic depression. Even though Roosevelt was the clear favorite, he campaigned *strenuously* across the country offering his "New Deal" of federal government involvement in agriculture, industry and education. He won by a large margin and became America's 32nd president in 1933. FDR accepted his election as a *mandate* to implement an aggressive socialistic program.

"The only thing we have to fear is fear itself," he told the American people. He sensed a feeling of desperation among Congressmen and quickly *enacted* tax-and-employ federal government programs to bring America out of the Great Depression. Banks were closed for four days until new legislation, called the Emergency Banking Act, could be pushed through Congress. Congress enacted government price controls on commodities and borrowed money to employ semi-skilled workers to build roads, reforest public land, improve national parks and build other public projects.

The Social Security system was instituted to provide retirement income for elderly people who could not perform hard labor for wages. FDR promised that Social Security would never exceed 3% of employees' paychecks. However, in 2000, Social Security taxes were 6.2% of paychecks. Roosevelt's policies established the Welfare system to bring economic relief to America, however, the cost was expensive for many employees whose paychecks were taxed to provide income for people who could not or would not work.

Roosevelt campaigned for reelection in 1936. Shadows of war in Europe and hope of economic relief through the New Deal put FDR back in the White House. He won the presidential election two more times (1940 and 1944), for an unprecedented *four terms* as president. In 1951 Constitutional Amendment XXII placed a two term limit on the office of United States President.

Even though the economy was experiencing recovery by the end of the 1930s, new troubles faced America. Conflict in Europe and Asia threatened to involve the United States in another large-scale war, something voters did not want. World War I and the effects of the economic depression were still all too fresh on most Americans' minds. Although becoming involved in another war was not what the American people desired, they agreed with Roosevelt who knew that the combined military power of Germany, Italy and Japan would threaten world trade and freedom. Roosevelt began preparing Americans for war by initiating a military draft and increasing production of military planes and ships.

The Japanese assault on Hawaii's Pearl Harbor on December 7, 1941 forced America into World War II. The United States declared war on Japan, and three days later, Germany and Italy declared war on the United States. Roosevelt had the tough job of leading not only his nation, but the entire Allied forces. America's free economic system, moral courage and work ethic positioned the United States as the World leader capable of effectively opposing Germany, Japan and Italy. And America raised up outstanding military men like Douglas MacArthur, George Patton, Dwight Eisenhower and Chester Nimitz. These brilliant military leaders combined their skills to lead allied forces against the Axis powers.

Chester Nimitz   Douglas MacArthur   Dwight Eisenhower

Any wartime president faces tough decisions. President Roosevelt complicated his role by relying on advice from Alger Hiss and Harry White, who were supporters of Communist Russia. Their influence on FDR directed United States strategy to help the Soviets gain control of Eastern Europe after WWII. Roosevelt's poor health left him vulnerable to Hiss and White whose advice often hampered U. S. strategy, but aided Communist Russia. At the critical time when Patton's tanks assaulted Germany, White and Hiss diverted fuel to Russian forces invading Germany from the east. Hiss and White were heavily involved in drafting the charter of the United Nations which gave special voting powers to Russia. Alger Hiss was eventually convicted as a Russian spy and sent to prison.

FDR never saw the end of WWII. He died of a stroke on April 12, 1945, just three months after being sworn in for his fourth term as president. One month later, Germany surrendered, and four months later, two atomic bombs were dropped on two Japanese cities. Japan's subsequent surrender ended WWII.

Roosevelt was a man of determination and persuasive leadership ability. He overcame physical difficulty with grace and courage. Although FDR skillfully led the United States to victory over Italy and Germany, unfortunately,

Albert Einstein

his administration edged America toward national policies directed from Washington D.C. His economic policies during the war established a pattern of government involvement in almost every aspect of American life.

The next vignette introduces one of the greatest minds in the 20th century—a man who did not do well in school, but was successful in life and whose brilliant scientific mind helped America win WWII.

VOCABULARY

Disheveled: in disarray, not neat
Physics: the study of proportions, matter and energy
Regimen: strict structure, routine
Stifle: to confine or control
Reputable: of good reputation
Inquisitive: curious and interested
Relativity: a scientific theory pertaining to motion, velocity and mass, and the relationship between matter, time and space
Physicist: one who studies the principles of physics
Collaborate: to work together

ALBERT EINSTEIN—A SCIENCE LEADER WITH A COMPASS

The elderly, *disheveled* man with age-whitened hair opened the small gift presented to him by a neighbor. The old gentleman was celebrating his 76th birthday. Inside the package was a small, mechanical toy. Despite the man's age, he laughed with the delight of a child. For this small toy, which operated under the basic law of gravity, was symbolic of the many great scientific discoveries made by brilliant Albert Einstein throughout his unusual and interesting life.

A life-long love of scientific study and exploration had begun seven decades earlier for the quiet, withdrawn Einstein. Albert was five years old when his father brought home a small, round object featuring a glass-covered needle. Young Einstein was absolutely fascinated by his father's compass and explanations of magnetism. Albert's growing fascination with the natural world around him, and his ability to master difficult mathematical concepts, set

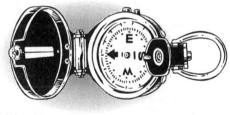

him apart from his peers.

Despite his advanced interest in *physics*, Einstein did not fare well in school. The disciplined *regimen* of the school in Munich, Germany *stifled* Albert. When his parents relocated to Italy for business reasons, Einstein halted his formal studies and spent a year enjoying the sights and smells of the Italian countryside. Because he was not in school during this time, he was free to daydream and process scientific thoughts.

After his year away from the academic world, Einstein finished secondary school and then entered the famous Polytechnic School in Zurich, Switzerland. He was dubbed a "difficult student" by the teachers of this highly *reputable* institution. Einstein wanted to think far beyond the boring scientific concepts taught at Zurich. His teachers mistakenly took his *inquisitive* nature as rebelliousness. Einstein often skipped science classes so he could study advanced physics. Using study notes supplied by a classmate, Einstein completed his course of study and graduated from the Zurich school in 1900.

Einstein accepted employment in the Swiss patent office. He did well at that job, but his greatest joy came in spare moments when he could scribble down notes about the things that were really important to him, like light and space and time—especially how they related to each other.

In 1905, at age 26, five years after graduation from college, Einstein received his doctorate degree from the University of Zurich and published five separate theories which forever changed man's view of the universe. Einstein's theories of *relativity* opened new avenues of thought regarding time, space, matter, energy and gravity. The fourth of these publications was Einstein's famous theory of relativity, which is summarized in the equation $E = MC^2$ (energy within an object equals its mass times the speed of light squared). This monumental scientific discovery later led to development of the atomic bomb. Einstein gained world wide recognition in the study of physics, and accepted several important teaching positions at universities in Europe, ending up in Germany. In 1921, Einstein earned the Nobel Prize for physics.

When Adolf Hitler came into power, the Jewish-born Einstein spoke out against Hitler's ideas of exalting one race of people

above other races. In 1933, Nazi's denounced Albert Einstein's views, seized his property and burned his books. That year, Dr. Einstein relocated to the United States, and in 1940, became a U.S. citizen. He joined the staff at the Institute for Advanced Study in Princeton, New Jersey.

In 1939, when WWII broke out, Einstein learned that two German chemists and an Italian *physicist* were close to discovering how to create an atomic bomb. Dr. Einstein and two other scientists *collaborated* on a letter to President Franklin Roosevelt warning him that this scientific knowledge could lead to Germany's development of an atomic bomb. Alarmed at the damage Hitler could do with such a powerful weapon, Einstein urged FDR to increase atomic research and to prepare America's own atomic bomb. Einstein sent two more letters to the president. The last letter prompted the president to initiate the Manhattan Project, which produced the atomic bombs in 1945 that brought Japan to the surrender table. Unfortunately, two Communist agents, Julius and Ethel Rosenberg, in the Roosevelt administration obtained atomic bomb secrets for the Soviet Union, enabling Russia to develop atomic bombs a few years after WWII. In 1953, the Rosenbergs were executed as Soviet spies.

On August 6, 1945, the United States dropped an atom bomb on Hiroshima, Japan. Another bomb was dropped two days later on Nagasaki: both cities were devastated. Japan promptly surrendered. Albert Einstein's alertness, patriotism and brilliance combined to enable American to defeat Japan. Einstein died April 18, 1955.

While war was raging, a crippling disease was causing great distress to parents. The next vignette tells how that disease was conquered.

JONAS SALK— THE DOCTOR WHO KILLED POLIO

I magine not being allowed to drink out of water fountains or play outside during the summer. That is exactly what many American's experienced before the 1950s. A deadly virus called *polio* was lurking in *temperate* geographic areas of the country. Thousands of parents were so scared that they sheltered their children from social contact during summer months. Polio often left its victims crippled and scarred for life. Some of those hardest hit became dependent on iron lung machines for survival. Most polio victims were children

Jonas Salk

between ages five and ten. Adults were hit too. In fact, one of the most famous adults to contract the disease was Franklin Delano Roosevelt, U.S. President from 1932—1945.

In 1952, polio reached epidemic proportions. By the next year, relief was on its way, thanks to the work of Dr. Jonas Salk. Already a leader in medical research, Dr. Salk previously helped create the vaccine that killed influenza in the mid 1940s. By the end of that decade, Dr. Salk turned his attention toward developing a polio vaccination.

Polio Shots

A *vaccine* is a liquid containing weakened or dead virus cells. It is injected into or swallowed by healthy people so their white blood cells will produce *antibodies*, natural substances that fight off the sick cells. People who have been vaccinated are usually protected because the resulting antibodies in the body neutralize the disease.

In 1952, Dr. Salk developed a vaccine from dead polio cells. After a successful trial test on monkeys, Salk was so convinced that the vaccine worked that he injected it into himself, his wife and children. He was right. With **March of Dimes** funding, Dr. Salk administered his polio vaccine to two million first, second and third graders. The vaccine made Dr. Salk a hero around the world.

But Dr. Salk had his critics. Some felt he was getting credit for developing a vaccine that was the culmination of several scientists' research, not just his own.

VOCABULARY

Temperate: mild, moderate climate, no extremes of hot or cold
March of Dimes: A health organization that fights against polio
Virologist: one who studies viruses and diseases caused by viruses
Jeopardy: danger
Enormous: huge, very large

Others criticized his testing of so many primary-grade children, calling it too risky. But the bottom-line result was that no longer did millions of people in this country suffer the damaging effects of the crippling disease. Interestingly, Dr. Salk did not patent the vaccine and so did not benefit financially from it.

The vaccine was given federal approval in 1955, and by 1961, the number of new polio cases had dropped *by 95 percent*! An American *virologist,* Albert Sabin, eventually developed another polio vaccine which in 1963 replaced Dr. Salk's vaccine in the U.S.

The Rotary Club International accepted the challenge to rid the world of polio and applied Dr. Sabin's vaccine to children throughout the world. Consequently, the disease called polio, which caused so much fear and heartache in the first half of this century, was almost non-existent by 1970.

Vaccine was dispersed at clinics. In the next vignette you will learn about a drug store owner who dispersed a new idea.

J ack Eckerd, who was born in 1913, loved to fly and was a barnstorming pilot in the days of open cockpits and cow pasture landings. When he heard about the bombing of Pearl Harbor on December 7, 1941, Eckerd's patriotism inspired him to sign up for military service.

Eckerd's life was in *jeopardy* many times as his plane transported bombs and gasoline in China during World War II. Eckerd came to realize the vital role of free enterprise (capitalism) to produce the weapons, uniforms, airplanes, gasoline and other items necessary for American troops to defeat the socialistic Fascists and Nazis.

JACK ECKERD—A BUSINESS LEADER WITH A DRUG STORE

Eckerd returned home to become a legend in the world of business. Starting with two drugstores in Jamestown, New York, Eckerd added three more stores in Florida. In time, his chain of drugstores grew to 1,700 locations across America.

Emulating his father's New York City discount drug methods, and importing new self-service concepts from California, Eckerd's chain of stores flourished. Under Eckerd's direction, neighborhood drugstores changed from small pharmacies offering limited products to a national chain that displayed a wide selection of items including candy, cards, hosiery and cosmetics. Business profits took an *enormous* jump when Eckerd added two-for-one photo processing (two rolls for the price of one).

Eckerd's concern for America's future led him to campaign for elective office three times. Although he lost each race, he became influential in the political arena and was appointed by President Gerald Ford to head the United States General Services Administration.

As founder and Chief Executive Officer (CEO) of Eckerd Drugs, he earned millions of dollars, and many of his loyal employees became independently wealthy as well. Eckerd sold his drugstore chain after 35 years as president; he could have retired to play tennis and sail his yacht. Instead, Eckerd turned his full attention to rehabilitating young people by exposing them to Biblical principles and values.

He and his wife, Ruth, began Eckerd Family Youth Alternatives (EFYA) in 1968, and by 1986, the Eckerds had helped redirect the lives of nearly 30,000 troubled boys and girls during that 18 year period. Year-long wilderness camps, designed to help young campers learn self respect, self discipline, teamwork and goal setting were the Eckerds' main point of focus.

EFYA helped 80% of the boys and girls who went through the program keep out of further serious trouble with Juvenile Court. Florida's Eckerd College and the arts community in Tampa Bay were other recipients of Eckerd's generosity.

At the age of 70, Eckerd became so concerned about the negative impact of pornography on youth that he requested all pornographic materials be removed from the Eckerd chain, then encouraged removal of pornography from more than 15,000 other retail stores. He also became a major force for prison reform in Florida. When Eckerd's autobiography was published in 1987, Warren E. Burger, retired Chief Justice of the U.S. Supreme Court, wrote *"this is the moving story by a man whose life and career exemplifies what an individual can do with the kind of freedom our system provides."*

The war years also brought great changes in fashions, furniture, and architecture as did the years immediately following the war. The next lesson reveals how Americans adjusted to war conditions.

LIFE PRINCIPLE

"Success is best measured by how far you've come with the talents you've been given."

-H. Jackson Brown Jr.

The Defending of America

Topic 8
*Art,
Architecture,
Fashions & Furniture*

Chapter 11

Section Two
Topics 6-10

THE WAR YEARS AND POST-WAR ERA OF THE 1940s AND 1950s

W ith the war years of the 1940s came rationing and a dire need to *economize*. Government war priorities on material goods imposed *constraints* on America's fashions. Women were encouraged to update or remake older clothing. Dressmakers advertised their ability to "make something new out of last season's wardrobe."

Even with creative economizing, some styles remained excessive. One fashion *indulgence* was the large padded square shoulders on dresses and coats which used extra material. In addition to the padded shoulders, dress waists were belted, and skirts extended just below the knee. Slacks were as popular as skirts for everyday wear, particularly among women factory workers.

Knitting was a popular pastime. Women knitted complete dresses, as well as "twin sets" of short-sleeved crew necked sweaters and matching long-sleeved *cardigans*.

Hairstyles for men were short, brushed flat on the head and held in place by hair gels or creams. Some men wore mustaches. Women kept their hair long or shoulder length, but up in net *snoods* during the day or while working. *Snoods* were hair nets which let the hair fall in a roll at the neck. In the evening, women brushed their hair up on top of their heads or swept it back into a roll, with another roll of hair on the forehead. African-American women wore their hair short or shoulder length and kept back in snoods. They often applied hair creams and gels.

Movies were popular during the war years, and film stars were idolized. War movies helped boost America's morale, and inspired new fads for fashion and hair. A famous movie star from the 40s was Veronica Lake. She popularized a hairstyle—

VOCABULARY

Economize: to use money and resources wisely
Constrain: restrict or confine
Indulgence: gratification, enjoyment
Cardigans: knitted sweaters or jackets
Trend: a short-lived fashion
Authentic: real
Novelty: new and different
Tie tack: an ornamental button that holds a tie in place
Cufflinks: ornamental buttons worn on shirt sleeve cuffs
French-cuff: a long cuff, turned back on itself and fastened with a cufflink

shoulder-length hair loosely parted on the left side, falling softly over the right eye. This quickly became the *trend* for most women, black and white, across the country. American women introduced the custom of shaving their legs and underarms to be fashionable. Swimsuit stars like Betty Grable and Esther Williams encouraged young women to display shapely legs and bare shoulders as fashionable.

Accessories for women included large pouch shoulder bags. Ladies carried vanity boxes and compacts with rouge, powder, eyebrow pencil and lipstick. Tinted fingernails, false eyelashes, and eye shadow complemented the woman's fully made up face. Gloves of suede, doeskin, calfskin or pigskin were worn for evening, sportswear or work. Costume jewelry replaced *authentic* gold, silver, diamonds, emeralds and other precious metals and stones. Matching sets of jewelry included earrings, hair clips, bracelets and necklaces. Animal pins, charm bracelets and hats with veils were popular. Sunglasses came in all shapes and sizes, along with *novelty* frames for regular eyewear.

Men's accessories included *tie tacks* and *cufflinks* for *French-cuffed* full dress shirts. Leather billfolds, wallets, key cases and walking canes were popular items for fashionable men. Innovations at the time of World War II were *transparent* plastic raincoats, rain hats and umbrellas, zippered fastenings for all manner of clothing and accessories, and rubberized, elastic swimsuits for men and women.

The Post War Era or the Cold War Era of the late 40s and 50s brought a *resurgence* of decoration and color to comfortable clothes. Several fashion designers came to the forefront with their new styles. In 1947, Christian Dior designed his *New Look in Paris*—a dress with a tight waist, no padding in the shoulders, a longer skirt, and a form-fitting bodice. Some fuller Dior skirts had several petticoats underneath. This look did not last, and other designers began to make names for themselves by creating *chemises* or sack dresses. At this time, high fashion designers allowed a few of their dresses for wealthier women to be used as inspiration for designers of more affordable clothing. European-designed fashions were welcomed by American women.

Coco Chanel was one of the designers who emerged from Dior's New Look. Chanel's designs tended to be more practical and comfortable for the modern, busy woman. In styles *reminiscent* of the 1930s boxy look, Chanel

VOCABULARY

Transparent: see-through
Resurgence: coming back to life or popularity
Chemise: a loose, shapeless dress that hangs straight down from the shoulders
Reminiscent: suggestive of pleasant, memorable experiences
Exert: to forcefully influence
Appliquéd: a handsewn design on another piece of fabric
Ensemble: a coordinated arrangement of color or sound
Synthetic: imitation materials
Contours: shapes, curves, angles
Utility: economic and simple
Exterior: outside shape and structure
Suburbs: areas where people live in communities outside large cities
Motoring: driving in motor powered vehicles

created business suits for the working woman in 1955. Double-breasted coats and pleated knee length skirts were some of the many Chanel fashions American women enjoyed.

In the 1950s, teenagers *exerted* a strong influence on fashion, especially sportswear or casual clothing. Bulky sweaters, striped or flowered blouses worn with sashes, knee-length capri pants or pirate jeans, and straight drain-pipe pants became popular. Brightly colored circular felt skirts made a splash on the American scene. These were known as *poodle skirts* because they were usually adorned with an *appliquéd* poodle.

Other trends or fads to strike during the 1950s included strapless tops with fitted waists, floor-length chiffon skirts over satin or taffeta, pedal-pushers or calf-length pants, bikinis, and halter top swimsuits. Women also wore a style that reappeared in the 1990s—*stirrup pants*, long pants with straps under the instep. Most hats had no brims and were based on the pillbox, dish, beret or bag shapes.

Ladies' shoes had pointed toes with high heels. Some shoes were sling backs, or backless. Nylon, which had been used in making military parachutes, proved popular for blouses, underwear and children's clothing. Nylon stockings were introduced at this time, and immediately became popular. Many women kept up with fashions as displayed by models in *Mademoiselle* or *Glamour* magazines.

In the 1950s, men's clothing focused on efficiency. Often made from gray flannel, suits became a two-piece single-breasted *ensemble* with narrow shoulders and lapels, and slim cuffless pants. Men wore knee-length Bermuda shorts, casual T-shirts and faded blue denim jeans and jackets. Leather flight jackets, army raincoats, fatigue jackets, and thigh-length car coats with hoods were popular fashions for men. Although hair for men remained short with minimal sideburns, some younger men sported a close-cropped crew cut similar to WWII pilots. A popular men's magazine was the *Gentlemen's Quarterly* (*G.Q.*).

Furniture was designed for practicality. Shapes were smooth and polished. Lines were geometric and tubular. Instead of leather, vinyl was used along with *synthetic* fabric upholstery. Solid colors were more popular than patterns or floral prints. Most households included plastic accessories and furniture, plain or geometric designed rugs and vinyl floor coverings.

A husband and wife team, Charles and Ray Eames, developed a plywood armchair that fit the *contours* of the human body. They made the chair in a simple form shaped over a cast-iron mold. A layer of foam rubber covered the form, with the upholstery fabric on top. By the late 40s, the couple made these same molded chairs out of glass-fiber-reinforced plastic. Inexpensive copies of these chairs were seen in almost every U.S. home and office by the mid 50s.

Utility furniture also made its way into American homes. This style included aluminum side chairs that could easily be stacked, metal tables and couches with foam-filled cushions.

The typical 1950s home had a front window, tiled bath, finished recreation room and an all-electric kitchen. *Exterior* designs were usually ranch-style, Cape Cod style, split-level or Colonial style.

Living in the *suburbs* of big cities was the trend. Men commuted to their jobs during the day. Most suburban homes took on a uniform look, commonly called *tract* living.

Some extraordinary structures were built at this time, including the famous Guggenheim Museum in New York City, the Marin County Civic Center in San Raphael, California and the Gammage Memorial Auditorium at Arizona State University in Tempe, Arizona, designed by architect Frank Lloyd Wright. Using his structural and spatial principles, Wright designed sky-lights and irregular geometric shapes that blended into the environment of the building site.

The family automobile was the chief mode of transportation, and hotels and inns became popular for travelers and vacationers. American hotel businesses boomed in the 50s and set the standard for international hotels. Prime locations for hotels were along coastlines and main highways.

Conrad Hilton, an American businessman, built an entire hotel empire that eventually stretched across the United States into Latin America, Europe and the Middle East. After his first hotel in Cisco, Texas became successful, Hilton began buying small hotels and inns that had been managed by families in various states. By choosing top managers and giving them complete independence to oversee his hotels, Hilton formed his successful hotel chain. The more famous Hilton hotels included the Waldorf-Astoria in New York City, the Palmer House built by Frank Lloyd Wright, the Conrad Hilton in Chicago and the Beverly Hilton in Beverly Hills, California.

With the increase of *motoring* came the rise of *motels*—a word formed by combining the words *motor* and *hotel*. Motels began as one-level lodging places where an overnight traveler could park his car just outside his room door. By 1952, Holiday Inns, Incorporated was founded as a motel chain. Holiday Inns soon became an incredible success, with motels in every state of the Union.

In the post war era, the nation focused on getting life back to normal. The idea of practicality carried over into fashion, furniture and architecture. The man in the grey flannel suit and the woman in the boxy jacket and skirt with her single strand of pearls; suburban tract living and cross-country motoring defined the era. The 1940s and 1950s reflected the true heart of American life: close families, private enterprise (men and women starting their own businesses), moral values and interest in a multitude of activities and events. In retrospect, the era has been labeled as the time of "Baseball, Apple pie and Chevrolet."

After WWII, America entered a time of prosperity. The next vignette shows the changes in government and economics during the 1950s and 1960s.

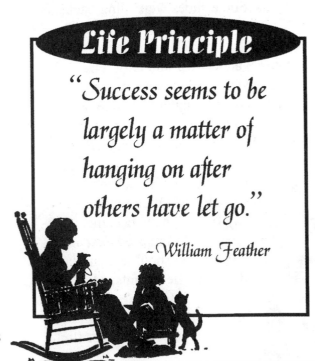

Life Principle

"Success seems to be largely a matter of hanging on after others have let go."

~William Feather

The Defending of America

Topic 9
Government &
Economics

Chapter 11

Section Two
Topics 6-10

SOCIAL AND ECONOMIC ISSUES

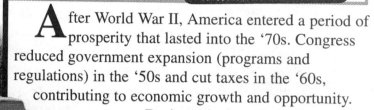

A fter World War II, America entered a period of prosperity that lasted into the '70s. Congress reduced government expansion (programs and regulations) in the '50s and cut taxes in the '60s, contributing to economic growth and opportunity.

During this time, suburban living became more popular. As young families moved to the suburbs, the national economy revolved around the family, and business owners marketed their products toward the mother and father with two or three children.

The free enterprise principle of *supply and demand* became evident in the construction business. Because residential tract houses were in *demand* (people demanded, or wanted them) by *consumers* (people who spend money), home construction boomed, especially among middle class families. And new houses needed electric refrigerators, window fans, washing machines and dishwashers. Manufacturers began to produce large *inventories* of household *appliances*.

Auto manufacturers began building station wagons to accommodate larger families. New cars even sported automatic transmissions, air conditioning and tubeless tires. Whereas during war years consumers spent money on necessities, during the post-war years consumers had extra money for conveniences such as TVs, electric skillets, washing machines and attic fans.

Immediately after WWII, radio king David Sarnoff began to promote the use of television in homes. By 1952, almost half of American families had television in their homes, and in the late '50s and '60s, color television sets were popular.

After WWII, many black Americans (at that time called Negroes) migrated from the South to the North. Between 1940 and 1970, 4,000,000 Negroes moved north where they obtained employment in factories. In the mid 1960s, income rose again among African-American families as more blacks attended

VOCABULARY

Supply and demand: products supplied by businesses to consumers to meet their demands
Inventory: products in storage, ready to be sold
Appliances: devices operated by electricity or gas
Blight: a negative aspect
Recession: a decline in economic status
Gold mine: a term referring to great potential and opportunity
Liberals: people who prefer that government agencies be empowered and funded to solve social problems
Integrate: to combine, to add together
Competency: ability to perform based on expectations

college and entered professions as teachers, lawyers, retail managers, pilots and doctors.

As blacks increased their economic status, they became involved in business enterprises. In 1945, *Ebony* magazine publisher, John Johnson, had trouble persuading white-owned businesses to advertise in *Ebony* magazine, designed specifically for black professionals employed in middle and upper class jobs. But by 1948, companies like Pepsi-Cola and Colgate were advertising in *Ebony*. The magazine became an unofficial standard for black fashion, social life and products.

A *blight* on African-American economic progress developed when government-imposed minimum wage increases forced many black teenagers out of jobs. Small businesses could not afford to hire teenagers who possessed little or no skills or experience, and pay the high wages established by government legislation. Unemployment among black teens was higher during the 1960s than during the *recession* year of 1949. Athletics however, provided some unexpected economic opportunities for young black men.

Until the 1940s, baseball and most other sports were segregated. In the 1940s, Brooklyn Dodgers team owner, Branch Rickey, noticed that the Negro League was an untapped *gold mine* of talent. Rickey decided to build a team of black superstars. The Dodgers' owner broke the color barrier in 1947 by hiring second baseman Jackie Robinson, the son of a sharecropper. Robinson was an outstanding player and a deeply religious man who did not smoke, drink or chase women.

During Robinson's first season, the Dodgers won the National League pennant, and Robinson was named Rookie of the Year. Before the season ended, Rickey hired 16 other Negro League players. Being the only team owner who would hire black players was good business for Rickey. While other teams divided the best white players among themselves, Rickey had the pick of the best black players. Consequently, more black sports fans attended Dodger games, setting attendance records for professional baseball and increasing the profits which benefitted both the owner and the players.

During the next ten years, the Dodgers won six National League pennants. Five Most Valuable Player awards and four Rookie of the Year awards went to black Brooklyn Dodgers. Other team owners had to start hiring black players or continue getting hammered by the Dodgers. Competition, with its supply and demand attribute, won over racism. Baseball fans of all colors soon enjoyed the talents of black players on all teams. Blacks and whites together enjoyed the games, laying aside and even forgiving past wrongs and misunderstandings. Even though economics opened new opportunities for black athletes, segregation did not die in other arenas. The Civil Rights Movement was a dominant force in the 1950s and '60s. Racial conflicts erupted over school attendance, employment and military service.

Jackie Robinson

The 1954 court case of Brown vs. The Board of Education of Topeka, Kansas struck down the "separate but equal" clause of the 1896 Plessy vs. Ferguson court decision. The court ruled that black students should not be bused across town to an all-black school when a white school was nearby if parents wished to send their children to the nearest school. Ironically, *liberals* later attempted to force desegregation by implementing busing—forcing black and white students to ride buses across town to *integrate* in schools, regardless of parental choice or *competency* of teachers and school administrators to educate.

The Civil Rights Movement accelerated on December 1, 1955 when an exhausted *seamstress*, Rosa Parks, refused to give up her seat to a white passenger on a Montgomery, Alabama city bus. Parks was arrested. Blacks *boycotted* Montgomery buses, preferring to walk or ride in carpools driven by sympathetic whites. A year after Parks' arrest, the Supreme Court declared Alabama's segregated seating law unconstitutional. That court decision opened other arenas of conflict, and through media coverage, national attention was focused on racial equality in sports, schools, entertainment and jobs. Black professional

singers like Nat King Cole, Louis Armstrong, Ella Fitzgerald and Marian Anderson raised public admiration for blacks. But generations of segregation in most communities was a difficult emotional barrier for both blacks and whites to overcome.

The National Association for the Advancement of Colored People (NAACP) helped usher in the Civil Rights Movement of the 1950s and 1960s. The NAACP was formed under the direction of a white man named Oswald G. Villard. He and several colleagues organized the NAACP in New York to promote economic and political opportunities for the welfare of black (colored) citizens. Villard was assisted by W.E.B. Dubois, a *mulatto* author and sociologist who published a political activist magazine, *The Crisis*. The Civil Rights movement encouraged the Civil Rights Act of 1964 which banned racial discrimination by employers and labor unions. This act proved difficult to enforce, and liberal legislators enacted *Affirmative Action* policies in an effort to establish economic

VOCABULARY

Seamstress: a woman who sews clothing
Boycott: an organized effort by a group of people to refrain from buying specific products
Mulatto: an individual of mixed Caucasian and Negro descent
Affirmative Action: the practice of hiring job applicants based on race
Preferential: giving privileges
Poll taxes: a tax required before a citizen could vote
Literacy tests: a reading test required to qualify a voter
Admission quotas: acceptance for college enrollment based on race
Liabilities: faults, problems
Entitlements: a right claimed by welfare recipients to receive government money based on gender, race or economic status

equity among ethnic groups. Under Affirmative Action, members of ethnic groups were given *preferential* treatment regarding employment or admission to college, regardless of skill, ability or qualifications.

The 24th Constitutional Amendment, passed in 1964, and the Voting Rights Act of 1965 struck down *poll taxes* and *literacy tests*, two longtime obstacles to black voters who wanted to use the legislative process to create employment opportunities.

In spite of the political expediency, the Civil Rights Movement proved ineffective at producing economic progress for minority groups. Government legislation alone could not raise economic opportunities for blacks, whites or any other ethnic group, because government cannot effectively create

products for consumers. Free enterprise proved to be the best avenue for raising the economic status of African-Americans. Private businessmen learned that segregation was not a smart business practice.

In the late 1960s, nonviolent civil rights speaker and leader, Martin Luther King, was ridiculed and shouted down by black militants such as Stokely Carmichael, Malcolm X, and the Black Panther party whose rhetoric closely resembled the hate speeches of the KKK. As race riots and *black power* tactics replaced nonviolent methods, legislators who supported the Civil Rights Movement became alienated, and the movement began to weaken. By the early 1970s, the Environmental Movement had replaced race issues as the newspaper headline of the day.

In the '70s, the Civil Rights Movement weakened into a debate over various social policies. Some of the debates were focused on

reverse discrimination—the name given to Affirmative Action by its opponents.

In 1974, Allan Bakke, a white man, claimed he had been denied admission to medical school because of his skin color. In 1978, the Supreme Court ruled in Bakke's favor. The decision stated that *admission quotas* were illegal, but that race was a legitimate consideration for admission boards—a vague decision that bewildered colleges. As late as 1996, Affirmative Action remained a heated issue on campaign trails. Prominent black leaders (called African-Americans by the 1970s) were divided over the alleged benefits or *liabilities* of Affirmative Action.

Conservative African-Americans such as Supreme Court Justice Clarence Thomas and economist Walter Williams did not agree with Affirmative Action, claiming that it undermined efforts to establish dignity and character in black Americans. Conservatives

Clarence Thomas

argued that giving blacks jobs based simply on race caused blacks to lose respect, be dependent on the government for success and not be self-reliant. By 1997, the U.S. Supreme Court ruled Affirmative Action unconstitutional. This decision motivated African-American leaders to refocus their efforts on education and employability.

The Civil Rights Movement changed Americans' view of rights. Originally, rights—such as those in the Bill of Rights— were viewed as granted by the Creator to protect private citizens from government abuses. In the 1960s, however, most media commentators and some politicians began to view minority rights as *entitlements* protected by government. Civil rights activists began to claim that all minorities were entitled to job and college acceptance regardless of education or employability. That policy further complicated efforts by responsible minority leaders to merge blacks and Hispanics into the free enterprise system.

Creative free enterprise consistently offered solutions to economic problems. In the late 1950s, an economically disadvantaged man started a business that eventually provided thousands of jobs for teenagers of all ethnic groups.

Harlan Sanders, who was six years old when his father died, learned to cook and care for the house while his mother worked. His religious mother taught Harlan to work and rely on self and God.

At age 66, Sanders had retired and was living on Social Security. The grey

Colonel Sanders

haired man decided to begin a new business.

He loaded his pickup truck with a pressure cooker and a 50 pound can of his own special blend of 11 herbs and spices and set out to persuade restaurant managers to use the special spices. During this time of traveling and marketing, Sanders began wearing a white suit, a black string tie and black shoes. He also carried a cane and grew a white moustache and goatee.

By 1963, more than 600 restaurants had adopted Sanders' method. The governor of Kentucky first called Sanders "the colonel," whose special chicken became known as Colonel Sanders' Kentucky Fried Chicken.

Using the money he earned selling his recipe, Colonel Sanders donated large sums of money to churches, hospitals, the Salvation Army and the Boy Scouts. In 1964, Colonel Sanders sold his Kentucky Fried Chicken company for $2,000,000, but stayed on as a symbol and a promoter.

Not everyone fared as well as Colonel Sanders, so the 1960s saw a second wave of government intrusion into private businesses. President Johnson's *Great Society* programs were promoted as social investments. Johnson believed an expansion of tax-supported government welfare programs would help poor people become employable and ultimately reduce their dependency on government money.

The Great Society expanded Social Security, unemployment insurance and ***direct aid***. It also created new welfare programs such as Medicare, Medicaid, food stamps and Aid to Families with Dependent Children (AFDC). The Economic Opportunity Act of 1964, much like New Deal works programs, attempted to end poverty and unemployment by putting citizens to work in government jobs supported by high taxes on employers and employees.

However, the Great Society did not reduce government dependency. Instead, the number of people receiving ***public assistance*** doubled between 1960 and 1977. By the '90s, Great Society hallmarks like Social Security and Medicare were on the verge of bankruptcy, and big government had failed to solve major social problems. Ultimately, the Great Society did not reduce the percentage of families dependent on welfare rather than on paychecks earned by working parents.

VOCABULARY

Direct aid: tax money given directly to persons for education or family assistance
Public assistance: financial or substance assistance to persons in poverty

Criminal *rehabilitation* became another topic of debate. A prevalent idea of criminal rights *advocacy* groups in the 1960s and 1970s was that violent criminals were not responsible for their crimes, but were victims of a corrupt society. Criminal rights activists focused on softer treatment of criminals rather than on quick and just punishment for crimes.

Supreme Court Chief Justice Earl Warren was a strong believer in the victim philosophy. He believed that therapy and education rather than punishment would reduce crime by *eliminating* "root causes." The climax of the criminal rights movement came when the Supreme Court banned *capital punishment* in 1972. Government advocacy groups provided free legal defense for violent criminals and enabled hardened criminals to live in prison with TVs, libraries, educational classes, carpet, health spas and other luxuries. Opponents of criminal rights pointed out that criminals were not victims, but had violated and abused others, and that shorter and softer prison sentences would not *deter* crime, but would rather increase it.

The emphasis on criminal rights failed to reduce crime. The murder rate, which had declined during the conservative

1950s, doubled from 1961 to 1974. By 1976, capital punishment was *reinstated*.

Many of the Warren Court criminal rights decisions were based on *judicial activism*, the process in which judges interpreted law based upon personal beliefs—in contradiction to enforcing law according to the constitutional principles of quick and just punishment.

In a *notorious* case of judicial activism in 1973, the Supreme Court ruled in Roe vs. Wade that individual states could not pass laws banning abortion. The decision split Americans into *pro-choice* advocates who believed abortion should be a legal choice, and *pro-life* advocates who believed abortion should be illegal because it was considered murder of innocent children. After Roe vs. Wade, over one million babies a year were aborted, often financed with federal tax money.

Pro-life advocates conducted a strong campaign to overturn the Roe vs. Wade decision. With support from President Carter,

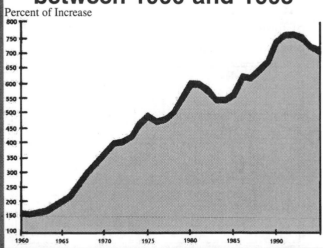

Violent crime rose 600% between 1960 and 1993

Percent of Increase

an amendment was passed which forbade the use of federal tax dollars to pay for abortions. Between 1973 and 2000, more than 38 million babies had been aborted in the United States—one third of those conceived. Less than one percent of abortions were based on rape. Most were the result of young women who did not want to assume responsibility for raising children.

By 1996, the Clinton administration and the National Organization of Women (NOW) *endorsed* the practice of *partial birth* abortions. This procedure was used between the 20th and 28th week of pregnancy (5–7 months). In partial birth abortions, the mother's cervix is dilated, the live infant is forcefully turned in the womb and brought out feet first—all but the head. The abortionist then forces surgical scissor points into the base of the baby's skull. The child's brain is then suctioned out, the head is collapsed, and the dead child is discarded. President Clinton vetoed a bill passed by Congress to forbid partial birth abortions. Many pro-choice advocates objected to the *deplorable* process. Conservative organizations such as Concerned Women for America (CWA), the Christian Coalition, Focus on The Family, Eagle Forum and the Family Research Council aggressively opposed the practice of partial birth abortion and President Clinton's veto.

Hispanics also affected social issues in the late '60s. During WWII, the gates of immigration reopened, allowing Mexicans to work in war industries. Mexican women introduced colorful clothing and Mexican food to American culture. Even though some Mexican immigrants were professional doctors, lawyers or architects, most Hispanic immigrants were skilled as farm workers, construction helpers and meat packers.

Many Hispanic immigrants settled in cities where they provided unskilled labor in factories. Cesar Chavez organized Mexican-American grape pickers and lettuce field workers into a union called the National Farm Workers Association.

During the 1960s and early '70s, Chavez led boycotts of farm products. He wanted to force farm owners to raise wages. The boycotts drew national attention but forced many farm owners to purchase machinery to replace field laborers.

Hispanics enjoyed the freedoms and opportunities America provided in the free enterprise system. Many Hispanics took advantage of the opportunities and started their own businesses. One such example was Romana Bañuelos, a 19-year-old divorced single mother of two sons, who immigrated from Mexico to Los Angeles to find work. By 1949, Romana had remarried and saved some money. With a small tortilla machine, a corn grinder, and a fan, she set up a tortilla factory in a small room. She and an aunt marketed the tortillas to Los Angeles restaurants. After five years of working 14 to 16 hour days, seven days a week, Ramona's Mexican Food Products—named for a California folk heroine—became a successful business. By the mid 60s, it was a booming business.

Bañuelos invested her profits in scholarships for Mexican-American college students. She also opened a bank that catered primarily to Mexican-Americans. In 1969, she was recognized as the Outstanding Business Woman of the Year. From 1971 to 1974, she was U.S. Treasurer—a position appointed by the president of the United States, and granted with the advice and consent of the Senate. Romana Bañuelos emerged from the depths of poverty by practicing her belief that people can achieve if they are *"willing to suffer and put up with inconveniences."*

Another woman, Mary Kay Ash, introduced women to successful business practices. Her efforts created thousands of jobs for women of all ethnic groups.

When Mary Kay was 28, her husband deserted Mary and the three children. Mary Kay supported her children by working in *direct sales*, selling books and cleaning products.

During her sales career, Mary Kay recommended challenging and creative ideas to her employers—ideas she believed would boost sales. By 1963, she had remarried and retired from full-time employment.

Retirement did not suit Mary Kay. She dreamed of working for a company that would incorporate her sales ideas, so she decided to start her own company. Mary Kay knew a woman whose father was a leather tanner. The man used a special formula to keep his hands moist. If the formula could keep a leather tanner's hands soft, Mary Kay knew it would be good for a woman's skin. Mary purchased the formula, and planned to start her own skin-care products company.

Mary Kay's second husband died just before the new company opened. Her children, however, encouraged their mother to pursue her dream. On September 13, 1963, Mary Kay Cosmetics opened in a rented storefront in Dallas, Texas with five products.

The company grew as women were hired to sell products. Mary Kay remembered her years as a young wife and single mother. She allowed her saleswomen flexible work schedules. She wanted women to work the hours that were best for them and their families. Nor did Mary Kay's saleswomen have fixed territories to serve. Mary did not want to force two-income families to choose between "his" job and "her" job.

In addition to high wages, Mary Kay offered rewards ranging from personal letters of appreciation to diamond rings to pink Cadillacs for her most diligent workers. Mary Kay constantly reminded employees that priorities should be *"God first, family second, career third."* In 1976, Mary Kay Cosmetics became the first company chaired by a woman to be listed on the New York Stock Exchange.

When people prosper, they usually have more time for recreation. The next vignette tells about recreational changes that swept America.

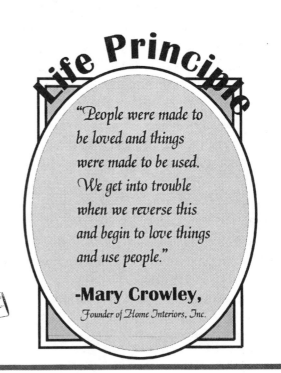

Life Principle

"People were made to be loved and things were made to be used. We get into trouble when we reverse this and begin to love things and use people."

-Mary Crowley,
Founder of Home Interiors, Inc.

The Defending of America

Topic 10
*Sports &
Recreation*

Chapter 11

Section Two
Topics 6-10

**RECREATION
ON THE
SCREEN
AND AT THE
ARENA**

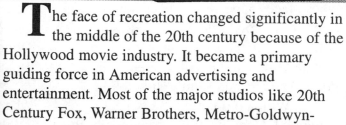

The face of recreation changed significantly in the middle of the 20th century because of the Hollywood movie industry. It became a primary guiding force in American advertising and entertainment. Most of the major studios like 20th Century Fox, Warner Brothers, Metro-Goldwyn-Mayer, Columbia and Paramount were founded in the 1920s and quickly became famous as they offered indoor recreation through high action movies.

Another dimension to film was added in 1937 when Disney Studios released *Snow White*, the first full-length *animated* feature movie. Since then, Disney proceeded to become the established standard for animation and children's entertainment, with landmark films such as *Bambi*, *Beauty and the Beast* and *101 Dalmations*. Millions of American children have been entertained by films in theaters and televisions in living rooms since the 1920s.

The rise of television during the late 1950s and early '60s changed Hollywood production themes and the American definition of entertainment. Hollywood spent more time creating *syndicated* daily shows than producing movies, and housewives accepted daily television episodes as a new way to spend free time. Television became the recreational activity of choice for children—and for adults who just wanted to sit back and not have to think after long days at work. Manufacturers learned to market products and services with catchy television advertisements. Viewers who sat down to enjoy movies became prime audiences for advertising commercials. Business and recreation found a common ground through television.

Television evolved into main areas for informing people of current issues, as well as providing *dynamic* action-packed sports coverage. By the 1980s, TV was characterized by

VOCABULARY

Animated: having motion or life
Syndicated: published through an agency or company
Dynamic: energetic, intense, and powerful
Glamorize: to make a lifestyle look appealing or exciting
Bronze: the third place metal rewarded at Olympic games
Boisterous: aggressive, spirited and energetic

situation comedy (sit-coms), talk show specials and soap operas that entertained audiences by *glamorizing* adultery, profanity and violence.

Television also created a new type of celebrity personality. Viewers often selected their role models from movie celebrities and athletes. Public idols included singers, musicians, actors, basketball players, football heroes, gymnasts and other stars whose faces appeared on television screens. Some were good role models and some were not, but media presented them to the world as entertainment. One of the stars who set a good example was Wilma Rudolph.

Wilma did not have a typical childhood. Complications from childbirth resulted in double pneumonia, scarlet fever and polio, which left both her legs deformed, causing her to wear metal braces. Other kids mocked Wilma, but she did not let cruel remarks destroy her determination. By age 11, Wilma had worked her way out of the braces and was walking alone. Over the next few years, with her older sister as a role model, Wilma became a basketball player and runner on the high school track team.

By age 14, Wilma had outdistanced every other female runner in her state. She was invited to compete in the 1956 Olympics. Wilma finished and earned a *bronze* medal, which fueled her determination to try even harder. Her goal was to become the greatest woman runner in the world. Over the next four years, Wilma practiced running numerous times each day. She was sure that no other runner would match her training and dedication, and that her hard work would pay off.

At the 1960 Olympics, Wilma astounded all who watched her perform. She became the first American woman to win three gold medals in one Olympics. Her

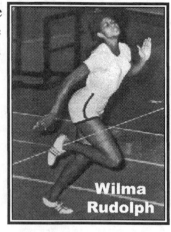

Wilma Rudolph

performances in the 100 meter dash, the 200 meter dash and the 400 meter relay were world record breakers. Her hard work had turned an unknown girl from Tennessee into the fastest woman in the world—and encouraged thousands of girls to dream of becoming track stars.

The popularity of television enabled the world to share in the excitement of Wilma Rudolph winning her gold medals and becoming an American heroine. Television is also responsible for the rise in popularity of many sports. Before television, people had to attend actual events in order to share in the excitement of their favorite teams and players. Television brought sports up close. Events which had previously captured the attention of relatively small audiences became popular world wide.

Boxing was a sport of increasing popularity on television. The relatively small audiences captured by 1930s and 1940s boxing champions Max Baer, James Braddock, Joe Louis and "Jersey" Joe Walcott widened profoundly with the introduction of television's coverage of Rocky Marciano who was the only undefeated heavyweight champion in boxing history. He began boxing in the Army in 1943, and later became a professional boxer. In 1951, Marciano wept after knocking out his boyhood hero, former world champion Joe Louis. In September 1952, in one of the most memorable matches in history, Marciano knocked out "Jersey" Joe Walcott and won the heavyweight championship. Rocky Marciano successfully defended his title six times in two years. He retired in April 1956 with a perfect record of 49–0, with 43 of those wins by knockout.

Twenty year old Olympic boxing champion Cassious Clay brought boxing to a new level of entertainment. His *boisterous* behavior and boxing precision captured audiences. After winning the heavyweight Olympic boxing title, he declared to be a black muslin and changed his name to Muhammad Ali. He became world champion in 1964. In 1968 he was barred from boxing for refusing to be drafted into the U.S. Army. After being suspended for five years Ali returned to boxing and regained his World Heavyweight Title in 1974. He lost and regained his world heavyweight champion title three times before retiring in 1979.

George Foreman was another young athlete whose boxing style and out-of-the-ring preaching entertained sports fans. As a child, George was constantly in trouble with the law and causing problems for his mother. He enrolled in the government funded Job Corps to try to get his act together. There, he met Doc Broadus who insisted that George compete in Golden Gloves boxing if he wanted to stay in the Job Corps. Boxing was a way for George to channel his anger and energy without getting into trouble.

In a few years, George, with barely any real fight experience, beat all his competitors to become the winner of the Heavyweight title in the 1968 Olympic games. After that, he turned professional and beat Joe Frazier, becoming the boxing heavyweight champion of the world.

During his 20s, when he was at the peak of his boxing career, George was not satisfied with his life. He had everything this world could offer, but he did not want any of it as much as he wanted emotional and spiritual peace—and peace was one thing he did not have.

In 1974, George Foreman lost the heavyweight title to Muhammad Ali in an eight round fight in Zaire, Africa. Foreman fought other boxers in an attempt to get another fight with Ali for the title. After one fight, Foreman was at the lowest point in his life. He was afraid and was sure he was dying. In desperation, the tough fighter knelt on his knees and asked God to take control of his life. He gave up boxing and devoted time to his children, but his marriage crashed, and again Foreman felt hopeless. He started attending a church and felt safe for the first time in his life. After a few years, he discovered he had a gift for preaching. He was ordained as a minister and began preaching to at-risk youth in schools and prisons.

In 1987, George Foreman began to work his way back as a professional boxer but this time his motive was different. Instead of seeking worldly fame, Foreman used his boxing career to tell people how God had changed his life. Fans were curious about the Preacher-boxer who was "too old to fight."

In November, 1994, George Foreman fought Michael Moorer for the heavyweight title. In the tenth round, Foreman won by a knockout. At age 45, Foreman became the oldest man to hold a world title. When he won, he went back to his corner, knelt down, and thanked God for giving him the strength to do what no one thought possible. Television audiences were both surprised and respectful. The 45-year-old preacher and boxer champion of the world had gained world-wide respect for his devotion to God. Foreman fought several contenders, including Evander Holyfield, another Christian boxer who beat Mike Tyson in 1997. Foreman finally lost his title in 1997, but in 1998, at age 50, George Foreman was still preaching and boxing—and enjoying life.

While changes were taking place in recreation, America was receiving an education in new forms of art and architecture.

The Defending of America

Topic 11
*Education,
Music &
Literature*

Chapter 11

**BUILDINGS
AND
MUSIC**

Section Three
Topics 11-15

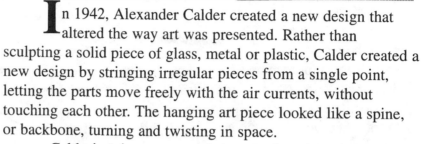

In 1942, Alexander Calder created a new design that altered the way art was presented. Rather than sculpting a solid piece of glass, metal or plastic, Calder created a new design by stringing irregular pieces from a single point, letting the parts move freely with the air currents, without touching each other. The hanging art piece looked like a spine, or backbone, turning and twisting in space.

Calder's spine art created an ever-changing design. As people looked at the floating pieces, new shapes constantly appeared. From this work came the idea for *mobiles*. People began hanging varieties of objects, and creating mobiles to decorate their homes and businesses. Colorful mobiles became popular art.

Buckminster Fuller was another creative artist. He brought a unique beauty to architecture. Until the 1940s, most of his ideas had been laughed at because they seemed wild and too futuristic. Fuller used a simple geometric shape, the triangle, to develop an entirely new concept in architectural design. Fuller placed many triangles together to form a *hemisphere* called a *geodesic dome*.

Fuller's dome was stronger and lighter and enclosed more space per unit of weight than any other architectural design. His domes could be put up quickly and easily. Traditional walls were not needed, and the geodesic domes supported themselves during construction. During the 1940s, new high-strength aluminum and steel became available for construction. Use of these new metallic materials made the dome of triangles appear as a silver bubble rising out of the ground.

During the 1950s, geodesic domes were built throughout the world. In 1958, a dome named Casa Mañana was built in Fort Worth, Texas. The new design created a theater-in-the-round with the stage placed at the center of the building. In 1982, Disney World in Florida chose the geodesic dome as the dramatic landmark for its Epcot Center. Silver-colored triangles

VOCABULARY

Mobile: (mō-bēel) a sculpture suspended in air whose parts are set in motion by air currents
Hemisphere: a half circle
Pall: a dark and dreary silence because of fear or uncertainty
Extras: non-actors (extra people) used in films
G.I. Bill: A bill that granted money to soldiers for educational studies
Gigantic: huge, massive, extremely large

147

with no other support were joined to make the gigantic ball-like building.

Just as changes occurred in art, changes also occurred in music, as you will learn in the next vignette.

ONCE IN A 100 YEARS

Music from the remarkable voice of Marian Anderson gave the world a special form of art. She first became famous during her concerts in major cities of Europe. Marian spent years of serious study to train her wonderful voice to reach the highest standards of vocal music. Audiences who heard Anderson sing were mesmerized by the rare quality of her voice. In 1938, the great classical conductor, Toscanini, attended Anderson's concert in Vienna, Austria. He said, *"A voice like hers happens only once in a hundred years."* His words of praise reached America even before Anderson returned to the United States.

The fame she enjoyed in Europe did not change her close feelings for family and friends. Anderson mastered many forms of music—from classical to soul. But her favorite songs were Gospel Spirituals she learned at church in Philadelphia. She used one of them for the title of her autobiography, *My Lord, What a Morning*. Love and support from church friends, combined with her mother's encouragement and Marian Anderson's own

Marian Anderson

hard work helped move her from poverty to a successful and dynamic career as a concert vocal soloist.

The highest honor paid to Anderson came when she was asked to sing with the Metropolitan Opera Company of New York City. She was the first black singer to perform there. The genius of her voice opened the way for other black singers to follow. Anderson never let prejudice change her positive attitude toward people. In 1939, she was not allowed to give a concert in Constitution Hall in Washington, D.C. simply because she was black. However, the president's wife, Mrs. Eleanor Roosevelt, helped schedule a concert for Marian to sing from the steps of the Lincoln Memorial. On Easter Sunday, over 75,000 people gathered on the steps and around radios to hear Anderson's voice. Years later, when she ended her career in 1965, Anderson had seen changes in race relations that undoubtedly accelerated because of her personal achievements and gracious attitude.

During the 1940s, Americans depended on their radios for special programs and music. News reports from World War II cast a **pall** over the nation. However, happy music brought cheer and hope. People everywhere thought about home and family when Bing Crosby sang "I'm Dreaming of a White Christmas." *White Christmas*, written by composer Irving Berlin, remained the number one best seller until the mid 1990s. Popular singers Gene Autry, Tony Bennett, Frank Sinatra and Doris Day sang about ranges and rural life as well as Chicago, New York, San Francisco

Bing Crosby

and other large American cities. Vocal songs were popular with soldiers away from home. During the 1940s, patriotic music helped the nation celebrate victories in the war. Composer Irving Berlin dominated the entertainment scene with his popular songs and musicals. His "God Bless America" sung by Kate Smith was America's most popular song during WWII and today stirs patriotism in the hearts of Americans. Duets, vocal ensembles and bands such as the Righteous Brothers, Glenn Miller, Platters, and Sons of the Pioneers brought hours of enjoyment to American families in the 1940s and 1950s.

In addition to radio, other media forms were expanding. Movie companies in Hollywood created action films that captivated audiences. Westerns starring John Wayne, Gary Cooper, Roy Rogers and Dale Evans, were extremely popular. Producers introduced new actors and technology to create audience interest. Producer D.W. Griffith often portrayed social issues in films. Producer Cecil B. DeMille used subjects from history like Cleopatra and Jesus. Producer Sam Zimbalist used thousands of **extras** to pack Roman streets with citizens for filming *Ben Hur*, an epic film starring Charlton Heston who portrayed the life of Judah Ben Hur, a follower of Jesus. *Ben Hur* received more academy awards than any other film until *Titanic* tied it in 1997 with eleven Oscars. Other popular films were the *Ten Commandments, El Cid, The King of Kings, The Greatest Story Ever Told, Antony and Cleopatra, African Queen* and *The Inn of the Sixth Happiness*.

In 1952, Americans flocked to stage musicals. Singing and dancing fit the mood of the country. *Little*

Abner and *Oklahoma* made happy times out of gold mining and frontier life. Famous Composers Rogers and Hammerstein wrote songs for *South Pacific* that told how Americans in the Navy learned a new way of life among the Pacific islands. *Showboat* was a satire on racial conflicts and advocated racial unity. Happy songs from *Camelot* made Americans believe their country measured up to the golden days of King Arthur's time. Two all time favorite musicals were *My Fair Lady* and *The Sound of Music*. Both remained popular as videos in the new millennium (2000).

During the time of the Great Depression and World War II, most people were not able to pursue higher education. The next vignette tells about a new focus of education after the war.

ADULT EDUCATION

American soldiers returning from World War II were offered a free education at public or private schools. The U.S. government established the *G.I. Bill*, which paid for adult education. Soldiers throughout the nation began to extend their education, equipping themselves for the hundreds of new career choices opened by war-related technology and creative entrepreneurs. By the 1950s, about half of America's adults were enrolled in some form of education. Many attended trade schools rather than large universities.

In 1946, R.G. LeTourneau started a trade school in Longview, Texas for war veterans. LeTourneau was a businessman whose company produced **gigantic** earth-moving machines. His own education had come from correspondence courses while he worked part-time in a garage in Stockton,

California. What LeTourneau learned from repairing tractors made him dream about building mechanized devices to bulldoze and scrape the earth. During the 1920s and 1930s, he moved from his first garage

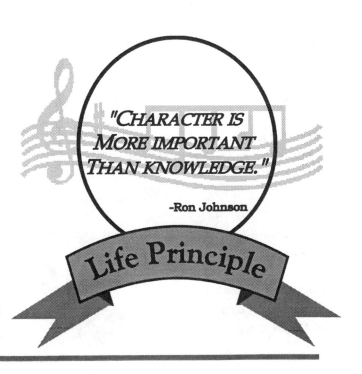

to operating a multimillion-dollar company. LeTourneau's company built more than 70% of the earth-moving machines used by America's armed forces during World War II. His equipment literally enabled U.S. troops to roll over enemy fortifications in Europe and the Pacific Islands.

He always gave credit for his spectacular rise in business to his "partnership with God." LeTourneau ran his factories with guidelines based on Christian principles and once said, *"God is chairman of my board of directors."* LeTourneau said that he liked to do two things: *"One is to design machines, turn on the power, and see them work. The other is to help turn on the power of the Gospel and see it work in people's lives."* In 1935, LeTourneau set up a foundation so he could give 90% of his personal income to finance missionary work abroad. He kept only 10% of his earnings.

When LeTourneau moved his company to Texas in 1946, he set up a mechanical training college associated with his company. Factory work was the lab part of school courses. The school grew and, in 1961, became a four-year college. The name changed to LeTourneau University in 1986. It has been rated in the top 10 most efficiently operated universities in America. Schools like LeTourneau University offer advantages for adults to gain employable skills to enhance opportunities for pay raises and job promotions.

While Americans were becoming better educated, they were also able to develop greater forms of transportation, as the next vignette shows.

"CHARACTER IS MORE IMPORTANT THAN KNOWLEDGE."

-Ron Johnson

Life Principle

The Defending of America

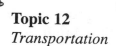

Topic 12
Transportation

Chapter 11

Section Three
Topics 11-15

UNDERWATER WONDER

Y ou do not have to invent, develop or manufacture a new product to gain fame. Admiral Hyman G. Rickover did not obtain a single patent, but he was credited with building America's first nuclear submarine, the *U.S.S. Nautilus*, between 1947 and 1954.

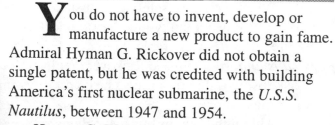

Hyman G. Rickover researched an idea for enabling the navy to operate submarines for sustained periods of time beneath the ocean surface. Diesel-powered submarines were able to remain under water for only three days at a time. Larger fuel tanks were heavy and caused the vessel to consume large quantities of fuel. Rickover wanted to reduce the space required for fuel and increase the range of submarines. He hoped that atomic energy (normally used for bombs) could be adapted to power submarines. The concept was brilliant but frightening.

Rickover faced obstacles to his plan. Defense officials did not want to invest money to develop atomic fuel or to redesign diesel-powered submarines. Atomic energy was compact, but dangerous to handle, and nuclear energy *emitted* radiation that required safety precautions that were untested in 1950.

Rickover convinced the Defense Department to finance the operation using the best scientists available. Admiral Rickover gave his time, energy and reputation to ensure success of the project.

Building a nuclear powered submarine was a major challenge. If not controlled, fuel combustion pressures could burst equipment. Materials had to be tested against salt water *corrosion* and water pressure damage. *Volatile* plastics and chemicals were prohibited inside the submarine, because toxic vapors could not be vented.

As a graduate of the naval academy, with a post-graduate degree in electrical engineering, Rickover studied every facet of the proposed nuclear submarine project. When the submarine

VOCABULARY

Emitted: let out, leaked
Corrosion: a chemical causing metal to deteriorate or be worn away
Volatile: highly explosive, dangerous
Malfunction: to cease to function properly, to quit working
Substandard: below standard, not the best quality
Fatigue: worn out
Fuselage: the main body of an airplane, excluding the wings and tail
Turbulent: rough, violent, unsafe
Longitudinal: north to south
Sheared: cut
Intact: safe and together, not broken or hurt
Free world: non-communistic countries

was completed, he knew how it worked and how to diagnose problems when it *malfunctioned*.

In the ocean depths, lives depended on the crew's ability to cope with emergencies. Admiral Rickover designed a special atomic-energy training program based on excellence, integrity, and the ability to use knowledge to provide working solutions during emergencies.

When money or safety was at stake, safety won. When a faulty pipe burst under pressure, all pipes were replaced to avoid any *substandard* pipelines. Rickover would not risk losing a ship or a life so he could save or make money.

Although Captain Eugene Wilkinson commanded the *Nautilus'* first voyage on January 17, 1955, Admiral Rickover was aboard. Careful testing of equipment did not prevent all problems. Oil and water leaks and small fires were minor irritations, but the nuclear fuel system performed as expected.

Three years later, the submarine slipped under the water at a Hawaiian harbor, traveled under the North Pole, and arrived in England. Rickover's sub surprised the entire world. Prior explorations under the polar ice cap had been impossible because diesel-powered submarines needed to surface every 72 hours for fuel.

Admiral Rickover guided America in producing its first nuclear reactors and submarines. More importantly, he taught men to work at peak performance level. Leaders in the navy noticed the *Rickover effect* in men who had worked under him. Even after Rickover retired, his men continued to demonstrate outstanding and excellent work.

Admiral Hyman Rickover

Rickover had a clear vision of his goal. Attention to details and willingness to accept responsibility helped him be successful.

While the Navy was developing highly sophisticated underwater travel, the Air Force was developing faster-than-sound aircraft. The next vignette tells about the jet plane chicken test.

CHICKEN TEST FOR A JET PLANE

Williiam (Bill) Boeing made a decision that could have cost his company millions of dollars and thousands of jobs. As you will learn in the next few minutes, he made an excellent decision that helped him and his country.

Bill Boeing produced his first aircraft in 1916. By the1960s, his plant was building the B-47 and B-52 military bombers used in Vietnam. During the 1950s, Boeing considered producing a jet passenger plane, but the U.S. Department of Defense did not need passenger jets, and commercial airlines saw no need for jet-powered aircraft.

A British commercial airline flew British-made passenger jets in 1952, but their planes failed when metal *fatigue* caused the *fuselage* skin to rip apart in flight. The public was skeptical of jet aircraft for passenger travel.

Boeing knew jet planes could be safe for passengers, but would travelers trust jet planes again and would commercial airlines buy his jets? He invested $16,000,000 to produce one jet passenger plane to prove his aviation theories. That was quite a decision.

The Boeing 707 was tested more than any other airplane had been tested. Boeing experimented with hundreds of body and wing shapes. Engineers designed and redesigned the plane fuselage and wings to reduce wind resistance. Wings were finally installed at a backward 35-degree angle. The *rudder*, an upright tail wing, also angled backward. Engines were suspended below the wings to avoid affecting air flow over the wings.

Freezing temperatures and low air pressure outside the plane at high altitudes posed special problems. Engineers tested the engines while spraying them with ice. The fuselage and doors were subjected to high air pressure on one side and low pressure on the other.

Boeing knew commercial airlines wanted their passengers to be comfortable. He installed ten tires and double-strength shock absorbers to cushion landings. Wings were built to flex in *turbulent* weather to provide a smoother flight. The fuselage was insulated to reduce noise.

The first test flight in Renton, Washington on July 15, 1954 thrilled the company. However, eight months later, no one had bought the new 707. Then, the government asked Boeing to redesign the 707 to carry fuel instead of passengers—to supply aircraft fuel to other planes in midair. Boeing built the KC-135 Jet air-refueling tanker which greatly increased the U.S. Air Force strike capability. It allowed fighter jets to extend air time over enemy targets without having to return to aircraft carriers or landing strips for fuel.

Boeing continued testing the 707 passenger model while engineers made improvements: cooler brakes, less vibration inside the cockpit and more stability in the air. As part of the testing, engineers built a machine to project chicken carcasses at 500 miles per hour toward the windshield to test its strength against flying birds.

The turning point for Boeing occurred when American Airlines purchased a large quantity of 707s. Publicity aided Boeing's sales when their test pilot broke a speed record from the West Coast to the East Coast with the 707. It crossed the country in less than four hours, causing airline companies to see the potential passenger market for rapid coast-to-coast travel. Flying Tigers, a freight airline, put the plane in the news again when their pilots made the first *longitudinal* flight around the world, flying over both poles.

Two accidents justified Boeing's extensive safety tests. A 707 engine exploded in midair and ripped 20 feet off one wing. The pilot, however, was trained for emergencies, and landed without a single injury to his passengers. Another 707 was hit in midair by another plane. An engine and 30 feet of a wing were *sheared* off. Again, the trained pilot landed the sturdy 707 with all passengers *intact*.

William Boeing's idea to build a safe plane was successful. Purchases of the 707 guaranteed financial security for his company and employees. In the next 10 years, Boeing produced nearly half the passenger planes in the *free world*.

Although Boeing has built newer models during the past 40 years, the Boeing 707 is still flown in many foreign countries; and the B-52 Stratofortress is still the backbone of U.S. long distance bomber squadrons.

B-52

Boeing took Americans high in Earth's atmosphere. The next vignette tells about Americans who went to the edge of eternity.

Life Principle

"Let perseverance be your engine and hope your fuel."

-H. Jackson Brown Jr.

The Defending of America

Topic 13
*Discoveries &
Explorations*

Chapter 11

Section Three
Topics 11-15

**SPACE—
THE NEW
FRONTIER**

VOCABULARY

Domain: an area
Inaccessible: impossible to get to, cannot access
Propulsion: a propelling force forward, a push
Lunar: having to do with the moon
Sputnik I: Russian satellite
Satellite: a man made object that orbits Earth
Meteorologist: one who studies Earth's atmosphere and weather conditions
Verified: to affirm, to prove correct
Meteorite: an object that enters Earth's atmosphere from outer space
Deploy: to send or let out

Discoveries at both the North and South Poles in the early 1900s failed to satisfy man's search for unexplored *domains*. For centuries, Earth's moon seemed *inaccessible* to scientists and lovers who gaped at the moon in wonder. Space exploration became man's new dream. Scientific discoveries led to the tools and technology needed for space travel. Rockets played the key role in pushing the first vehicles, and soon man himself, beyond the pull of gravity.

For years, solid fuel ignited in *propulsion* chambers on the ground had been used to blast rockets off the earth's surface. In 1926, American scientist Richard Goddard mixed liquid oxygen with gasoline and discovered a new fuel. He constructed a fuel tank and propulsion engine on board a rocket, and using his new liquid fuel, proved that rockets could travel with their own source of power. Goddard continued to design more powerful rockets until his death in 1945.

Rockets built during World War II were so powerful that scientists believed they could send a man to the moon. The problem was keeping a man alive after he arrived on the moon and getting him safely back to Earth. After World War II, Americans began to pay more attention to space. The U.S. government established the National Aeronautics and Space Administration (NASA). Within a few years NASA started scientific projects that captured world-wide attention. Goddard's brilliant work laid the foundation used by NASA scientists to develop space probes, space shuttles, *lunar* vehicles and later, guided attack missiles for warfare.

In October, 1957, Russia startled the free world by launching *Sputnik I* to orbit the earth. America was embarrassed that a communist country had successfully orbited Earth with a space *satellite*. The U.S. determined to gain the lead in space exploration. In 1960, the federal government paid Goddard's wife and sponsors over $1,000,000 for the rights to more than 200 patents covering basic rocketry inventions. NASA also named Goddard Space and Flight Center outside Washington, D.C. in honor of Richard Goddard. On May 25, 1961, President John F. Kennedy (JFK) authorized funds and promised that America would put a man on the moon before 1970. The National Aeronautics and Space Administration (NASA) was designated responsibility for fulfilling that promise. JFK's involvement was honored in naming Cape Canaveral the Kennedy Space Center.

Rocket power alone did not make space exploration possible. Whatever devices went into space needed to be controlled, guided, and returned safely to Earth. Dr. John Hager's knowledge of radio waves was foundational to the electronic control system that directed space flights. In the 1950s, Hager led the group of NASA scientists who set up a series of sensitive radio receivers extending from Maryland to Chile to South Africa to Australia. NASA's radio system successfully tracked space satellites and collected information from space capsule instruments. The system also proved beneficial for other scientific projects. Satellites, for example, carried equipment to photograph the earth's cloud cover. Weather reporters and *meteorologists* were given a perspective that increased their ability to predict weather accurately.

New technology was needed. Power needs had to be estimated accurately because excess fuel weight would reduce the range of a spacecraft. Magnetic compasses could not show directions in space due to the lack of gravity, so computers were needed to determine speed and location by measuring the location of stars. Temperatures on the moon and in space are extreme (possibly ranging from -250° F to +250° F), and gravity does not apply (everything floats in space), thus special spacesuit materials had to be designed to protect the men. A landing procedure to protect the returning craft was also essential.

Scientific theories had to be tested before men's lives would be endangered. First, NASA launched a rocket that became the first manmade object on the moon. That proved we could leave the gravity field of Earth and reach the moon. It also *verified* accuracy of calculated estimates about speed and fuel consumption.

Astronauts probed the frontiers of space with the same heroic qualities that guided the first daring pioneers of America's early history. Even though complicated machines and instruments performed remarkable tasks, astronauts conducted dangerous and daring experiments. The first astronaut, Alan Shepard, volunteered to face two challenges: the pull of gravity, which could crush his body as he tried to leave the Earth, and friction in the atmosphere which might turn the space vehicle into a blazing *meteorite* as it returned to Earth. American scientists were confident that nothing would go wrong. Each step of the exploration was carefully planned and tested. NASA was so confident of its procedure that officials were willing for the entire first space flight to be televised for the whole world to watch.

Alan Shepard

On May 5, 1961, a rocket with 82,000 pounds of thrust propelled America's first man into space. As he passed through the field of gravity, Shepard kept repeating *"okay . . . okay . . . okay"* so control engineers in Houston, Texas and people around the globe would know that Shepard was surviving. Within minutes, he was able to look back at the earth for a view no other man had ever seen. His spontaneous outburst of *"What a beautiful sight!"* showed how his emotions were touched by his pioneer journey into space.

Shepard's short flight lasted only 15 minutes. He reached an altitude of 117 miles and a speed of 5,036 miles per hour. Then he faced the fiery drop back through the burning friction of Earth's atmosphere. Everyone wondered if engineers had piled on enough layers of heat resistant tiles to protect the bell-shaped re-entry vehicle. The historic moment came when the scorched and blackened vehicle *deployed* its parachute and landed the first astronaut safely in the Atlantic Ocean 500 miles south of its launch site in Cape Canaveral, Florida. Today, Shepard's spacecraft is on display in the Smithsonian Air and Space Museum in Washington, D.C. Its name, *Freedom 7*, honors America and the pilots who became America's first astronauts.

Hundreds of scientists and engineers trained and tested the astronauts. Disconnecting or reconnecting spacecraft in space required skills performed outside the spaceship. The next flights let men practice walking outside the spaceship using tools in a weightless atmosphere. Step by step, new technology sent astronauts deeper and deeper into space. In 1962, John H. Glenn, Jr. took the risk of being the first American to go into orbit around the earth. Rocket power had grown to 360,000 pounds of thrust. Some people feared that such a powerful lift-off might propel Glenn into outer space from where he would never return. However, Glenn's flight of three successful orbits verified NASA's theories about orbit paths, and proved that men could control flights past the frontiers of space.

Gordon Cooper made history in 1963 by making 22 orbits around the earth. He demonstrated that *sustained* flight in space was possible for mankind. Before he returned to Earth, Cooper said a prayer that revealed his impressions about space and God. His words became the American Astronauts' Prayer. (You may read it at the end of this topic.)

NASA wanted American space capsules to carry a special message to the world. Names of spacecrafts were selected to reflect America: *Liberty Bell*, *Friendship*, *Eagle* and *Faith*. The names came out of

Freedom 7

VOCABULARY

Sustain: to continue to support for a length of time

Rendezvous: (rän dā voo)to meet or "get together"

Aeronautical: having to do with the physics of flying

Module: an individual unit on a spacecraft connected to more units that together make up the whole craft

Bickering: arguing, griping, complaining, blaming each other

Intriguing: fascinating, causing intense interest or curiosity

Genetics: the study of human genes and development

Forensic anthropologists: scientists who investigate crime scenes

America's past and stood for the country's best goals and ideals for the future.

In 1965, America's first space vehicle to carry two men stayed in orbit for 14 days. The mission was designed to join two teams to prove that space ships could *rendezvous* in space. Rocket problems caused delays in the first two attempts at lift-off. Time was running out for the scheduled meeting in space. When the third try was finally successful, Americans stayed beside their television sets. The newscaster said with a choke in his voice, *"The whole nation pushed that one up!"*

Americans again glued themselves to their TVs in 1969. They watched as two Americans descended to the surface of the moon. They heard Neil Armstrong say, *"The Eagle has landed."* America watched as Armstrong placed the first human footprints on the moon. Neil Armstrong, an *aeronautical* engineer, received the fame as the first man on the moon, but 400,000 people worked to get him there. They designed, built and tested the spaceship. They trained and monitored astronauts on earlier flights to prove every anticipated procedure.

Three men: Neil Armstrong, Michael Collins and Buzz Aldrin, were scheduled for that first trip to the moon. Each had flown in a previous test mission, but had never reached the moon. The spaceship, *Apollo 11*, was composed of three parts. The three astronauts would ride in the command *module*. A lunar capsule, *Eagle*, would leave the main ship and carry two men to land on the moon. The major part, a huge rocket, supplied power to launch the command module and capsule toward the moon.

Millions of people around the world watched by television as *Apollo 11* rockets fired, and the spacecraft lifted off the ground in Cape Canaveral, Florida at the Kennedy Space Center. NASA's Mission Control in Houston, Texas received and transmitted the astronauts' voices to Earth. Cameras aboard the command module transmitted live-action pictures of the trip. After reaching moon orbit, Collins remained in the command module while Armstrong and Aldrin descended in the *Eagle*

APOLLO 11

module to the moon's surface. On July 20, 1969, Neil Armstrong put his footprint on the moon as he broadcast a message to Earth, *"That's one small step for man, one giant leap for mankind."*

Gordon Cooper's prayer from space:

I must take this time to say a little prayer for all the people, including myself, who are involved in this operation.

I want to thank You,(God) for letting me fly this flight. Thank You for the privilege of being able to be in this position, to be in this wondrous place, seeing all these startling, wonderful things that You have created.

Help, guide, and direct all of us that we may shape our lives to be much better Christians so that we help one another and work with one another rather than fighting and bickering. Help us to complete this mission successfully.

Help us in future space endeavors to show the world that democracy really can compete and still is able to do things in a big way . . . able to do research, development, and to conduct new scientific and technical programs.

Be with all our families. Give us guidance and encouragement and let them know that everything will be OK. We ask in Thy name. Amen.

Transportation in America had progressed from men walking, to steam powered locomotives, to cars, jet aircraft, and finally to leaving foot prints on the moon! Free enterprise, integrity and courage had again opened doorways to another world that no one dared anticipate before. The next vignette is about your world.

W hile some men looked into the mysteries of space, other scientists tried to understand the

DNA AND WHY YOU LOOK THE WAY YOU DO

chemistry of the human body. The secrets to life were just as *intriguing* to some scientists as space was to astronauts. In 1942, a Canadian-born American, Robert Avery, made a basic experiment with material found inside a living cell. He wanted to find exactly what part of the cell carried the genetic material that decided how human shapes, color, height and gender are determined. He looked for the code, or pattern, that determined how cells created new shapes, sizes, and features when a new life was formed. What he found surprised everyone. The strongest part of the cell did not hold the secret. Instead, he studied the fluid surrounding the protein. The "sugar-coated molecules" known as Deoxyribonucleic Acid (DNA) determined human characteristics. Avery's discoveries sent ripples of excitement throughout the scientific world. *Genetics* and

DNA were relatively unexplored frontiers. They were waiting for adventurous scientists to probe and discover.

Robert Avery's discovery also started an emotionally loaded debate about the limits of science to apply DNA to human engineering—the changing of body characteristics through scientific research and application. Scientists wanted to know how DNA was put together. Once chemists discovered the pattern or *code* for living cells, scientists hoped to be able to change the natural order of human development. They anticipated being able to create new cells with selected features.

Some people did not want scientists to probe into the secrets of how life formed and changed. Many people had moral convictions against scientists attempting to alter the natural process of human development. Some people believed genetic engineering would lead to creating life artificially; they argued that artificial creation of humans would devalue life.

In the 1940s, six major conferences were held to discuss how scientists should do good and not evil with DNA science. Medical scientists expected their work to stop diseases and to enhance healthier bodies. *Forensic anthropologists* also anticipated discoveries in DNA to assist in identifying criminals and burn victims.

Scientists discovered that the stronger protein molecules bonded and formed a spiral chain. They also learned how the DNA molecules stayed together in pairs. However, *what* held them together to form their spiral pattern remained a secret.

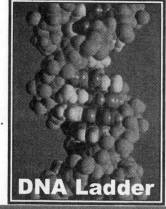
DNA Ladder

In 1953, James Watson from America and an Englishman, Francis Crick, tried to build a model to show how DNA held itself together. They studied the experiments of Maurice Wilkins in London, England whose work helped clarify the structure of DNA. Their combined research proved that the pairs of DNA molecules were supported by two outside structures. A model was built to describe the pattern; it looked like a ladder that was twisted. The scientists named the spiral shape the *double helix*.

The men had discovered how tiny changes came into being. If one of the pairs of molecules jumped apart, the entire spiral opened like a zipper. When it closed, new pairs were brought together. The men had found how the cell actually made changes that gave endless variety to life. In 1962, the Nobel Prize was awarded to Watson and Crick. Their work set off an explosion of new research into the mysteries of life itself. In the 1990s, other scientists conducted experiments based on Watson's and Crick's discoveries, to clone animals for use in medical research. Cloning is still a controversial subject today.

All these scientific successes seemed to put the United States on top of the world. But the next vignette tells how foreign oil almost brought American travel to a screeching halt.

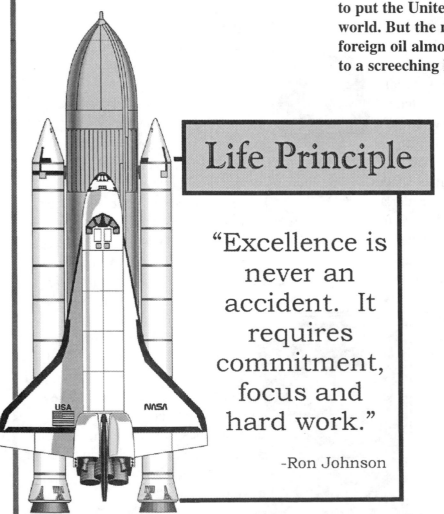

Life Principle

"Excellence is never an accident. It requires commitment, focus and hard work."

-Ron Johnson

The Defending of America

Topic 14
Light & Energy

Chapter 11

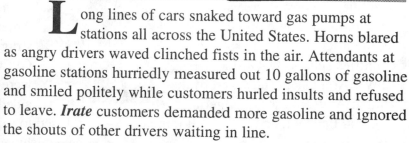

"NO MORE FUEL"

Section Three
Topics 11-15

Long lines of cars snaked toward gas pumps at stations all across the United States. Horns blared as angry drivers waved clinched fists in the air. Attendants at gasoline stations hurriedly measured out 10 gallons of gasoline and smiled politely while customers hurled insults and refused to leave. *Irate* customers demanded more gasoline and ignored the shouts of other drivers waiting in line.

The date was late 1973, and people were frustrated. Gasoline seemed to be one of those things that America would always have. Like sunlight or water, gasoline had been relatively inexpensive and always available. Now, prices soared, and the amount of fuel each station had was limited. Station managers posted signs, "No more fuel."

Fortunately, the worst part of the crisis was over in a few weeks. Because of the panic, motorists tried to purchase more gasoline than usual, but gasoline stations and transport truck companies were unprepared. New supplies soon arrived, and customers could buy all that they wanted—for a very high price. Even though the crisis passed, a long term problem confronted the United States: resources from which America received her energy were limited.

In the 1950s and 1960s, Americans consumed massive amounts of fossil fuels such as oil and gasoline. The cost of producing these resources had been dropping year after year. As a result, people did not worry about conservation or the controlled use of natural resources. Business owners allowed their factories to burn fossil fuels freely, automakers made cars that used large quantities of gasoline, and homebuilders constructed homes with materials that did not *insulate* well.

During this same time, most of America's energy came directly from within her own borders. In the years from 1950 to 1970, only 21.5% of oil was imported. While countries in the Middle East had an incredible amount of oil on the world market, the world wide price of oil was very low.

VOCABULARY

Irate: angry, upset, dissatisfied
Insulate: to keep out extreme temperatures (too hot; too cold)
Refineries: companies which produce gasoline
Procure: to obtain
Soundly: completely, without doubt
Maim: to cause severe bodily harm

On September 14, 1960, five countries—most in the Middle East—formed an alliance called the Organization of Petroleum Exporting Countries (OPEC). Iran, Iraq, Kuwait, Saudi Arabia and Venezuela realized that petroleum pumped in huge quantities created a world-wide surplus that caused gasoline to be very cheap and easy to buy. OPEC agreed to stop producing so much gasoline, thereby, decreasing the amount of available oil—driving up the price. Other oil producing countries such as Qatar, Indonesia, Libya, Abu Dhabi (now part of the United Arab Emirates), Algeria, Nigeria, Ecuador, and Gabon all joined OPEC by 1973.

Prices remained stable and OPEC was relatively ineffective at controlling world-wide oil prices. Then, two things happened to cause a world-wide fuel crisis and long lines of cars at gasoline stations. First, the U.S. Federal Government raised taxes on domestic oil companies and at the same time placed tough additional production regulations on U.S. *refineries*. The taxes and regulations made production much more costly and difficult for the U.S. to refine its own oil. Petroleum-producing states like Texas, Louisiana and California plunged into economic depression as their local refineries shut down production because they could not afford to comply with the government regulations. America then turned to foreign nations to *procure* oil.

Secondly, just as the United States was turning to these foreign countries to supply oil, OPEC nations allied themselves with Soviet Russia and refused to sell petroleum products to the United States. OPEC wanted to force America into negotiating with Arab nations. The Yom Kippur War of 1973 had just ended. In that war, Egyptian and Syrian forces attacked Israel, but were *soundly* defeated by Israeli forces. America had aided Israel in the struggle. The countries that made up OPEC hated the Jewish people and were angry that the United States aided Israel. The fact that OPEC refused to sell oil to the U.S. was designed as punishment and to be a warning not to assist Israel.

This led to the situation described earlier (long lines and irate customers), and Americans realized that dependence on OPEC oil was dangerous. Additionally, consumers acknowledged that continued use of large luxury automobiles was not economically wise. Not only did large sedans consume more fuel, the cost of manufacturing big vehicles was expensive. They required more metal, plastic, glass and fabric. Another factor affecting availability of raw materials was the Vietnam War, which had consumed vast quantities of copper, leather, fuel and other products. The combination of war, large vehicles and industrial growth had consumed millions of gallons of America's petroleum resources.

Smaller cars that consumed less fuel became popular. New homes were built with special insulation that conserved heat in winter months and reduced air conditioning bills during hot summer months.

Emergence of the Environmental Movement was another reason resources were used more cautiously. During the 1960s Americans had become increasingly alarmed at industrial damage to nature. Streams were  dirtied, forests destroyed, and the air polluted. Excessive use of gas, oil, and other fossil fuels damaged the environment and affected national safety—especially along coastlines and interior waterways. American manufacturers began to pay more attention to industrial techniques that would benefit the environment.

On April 22, 1970, the first Earth Day occurred. It was an anti-industry protest that focused national attention on environmental problems. It marked the true beginnings of the modern Environmental Movement. Government authority became increasingly more powerful and far reaching as federal agencies exercised unparalleled authority to restrict industrial development. Drastic efforts were introduced to clean up environmental damage.

Government regulations were not implemented without difficulties, however. Some changes demanded by environmentalists were extreme. While environmentalists had been successful in bringing to the forefront very realistic concerns, some members of the movement began advocating such drastic, and indeed sometimes violent, actions that the entire movement began to be seen as a radical anti-capitalism, anti-free enterprise movement.

For example, some protesters sabotaged lumber yards, or drove metal spikes into trees so that loggers who attempted to cut trees would snap chainsaws, killing or *maiming* the loggers. Other federally-backed environmental laws caused thousands of people in the lumber and manufacturing industries to lose their jobs. Many advocates of the Environmental Movement believed the world was overpopulated, and recommended letting unhealthy people die by cutting U.S. assistance to famine-stricken countries. The movement lost support in mainstream America as environmentalists championed more extreme positions to protect birds, snails and fish at the cost of human life, jobs and welfare.

In the decades following the first Earth Day, tough environmental problems had to be solved. Cleaning up the environment was costly, and Americans had to determine what a clean environment was worth. The cost of completely getting rid of cars was too high. However, the cost of manufacturing cars that produced a limited amount of pollution was a price worth paying. Throughout the 1990s, Americans sought new forms of transportation that were less damaging to the environment than conventional gasoline powered automobiles.

Several new sources of energy were being explored—sunlight, ocean water and easily obtainable recycled garbage. The main problem was that new sources were more expensive to produce and package for economical use than standard fossil fuels.

By the dawn of 2000, major improvements had been made in legislation and industrial production systems. Americans were conserving their resources and recycling more. New sources of energy were being explored— such as sunlight, ocean water and recycled garbage—and Congress had done away with some of the extreme environmental protection rules.

The Environmental Movement, civil rights issues and anti-Vietnam War sentiment represented a nation-wide debate over values and principles in America. The next lesson focuses on the national debate over religious issues.

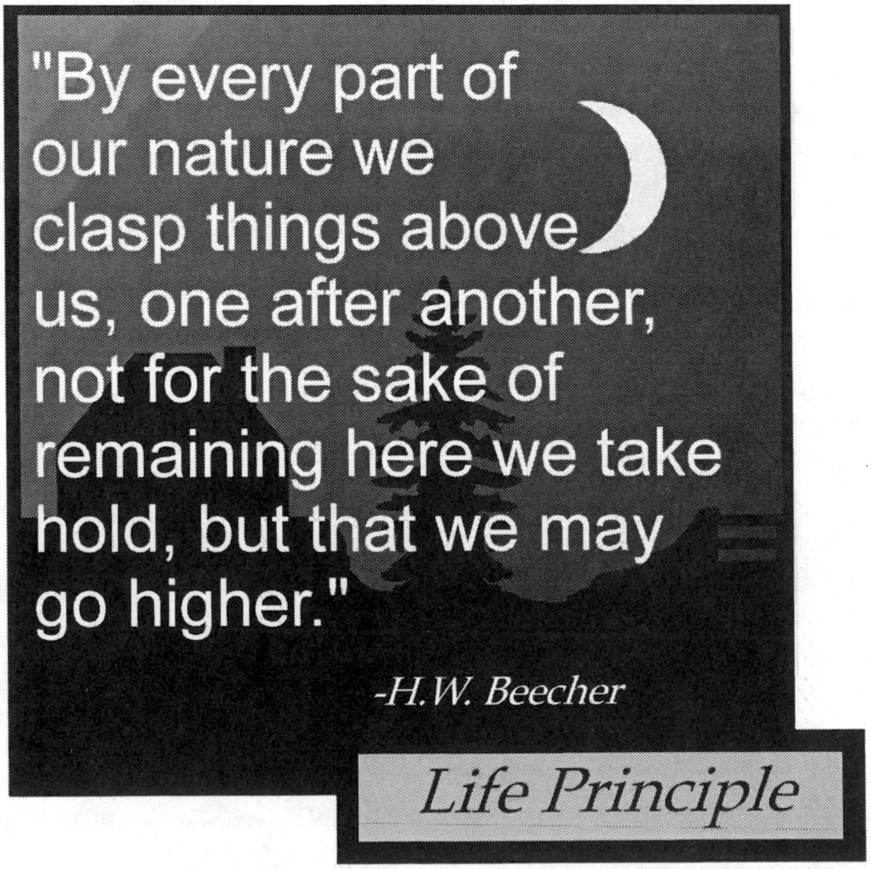

"By every part of our nature we clasp things above us, one after another, not for the sake of remaining here we take hold, but that we may go higher."

-H.W. Beecher

Life Principle

The Defending of America

Topic 15
*Religion &
Celebrations*

Chapter 11

Section Three
Topics 11-15

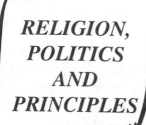

RELIGION,
POLITICS
AND
PRINCIPLES

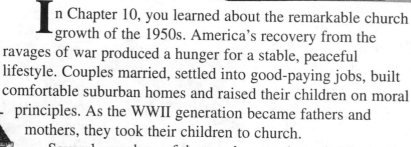

In Chapter 10, you learned about the remarkable church growth of the 1950s. America's recovery from the ravages of war produced a hunger for a stable, peaceful lifestyle. Couples married, settled into good-paying jobs, built comfortable suburban homes and raised their children on moral principles. As the WWII generation became fathers and mothers, they took their children to church.

Several preachers of that era became household names, *bolstering* the image of religion in America. Norman Vincent Peale, pastor of a large congregation in New York City, wrote a bestseller called *The Power of Positive Thinking* (1952). The book, which used Biblical verses to promote an optimistic outlook on life, reflected America's optimism of the 1950s. C.M. Ward, an Assembly of God preacher, pioneered radio broadcasting of sermons during the 1940s. Monsignor Fulton J. Sheen was a best-selling author with his *Peace of Soul* (1949). He also hosted a popular radio show called "The Catholic Hour." Other preachers who gained large audiences were Bob Jones, George W. Truett, John R. Rice, J. Vernon McGee, Jack Hyles, W.A. Criswell and Richard DeHaan.

The most well-known and respected preacher between 1950 and 2000 was Billy Graham. Born on a North Carolina farm in 1918, Graham embraced Christianity at the age of 16 and believed God had called him to become a minister. After seminary training, he was appointed campus evangelist for Youth for Christ, an organization that helped troubled teens build effective positive lifestyles through community activities. In 1949, Billy Graham held a tent revival in Los Angeles (L.A.), California. By that time, Graham had been recognized as an outstanding evangelist who presented a simple Biblical message with high energy.

Reporters called the young preacher *God's Machine Gun* because of his fast speaking pace. The results of Graham's *crusades* in changing lives from hopelessness to faith caught the

VOCABULARY

Bolster: to build up, to enhance
Crusade: a large gathering where a minister preaches
Recipient: one who receives something
Disillusioned: not knowing one's purpose in life due to beliefs or ideals being crushed
Turmoil: upheaval, violent disruption
Grope: to search for desperately
Relevance: meaning in life
Arrogant: proud, refusing to accept changes for the better
Cult: a religion that is considered extreme or false
Astrology: "reading" stars to tell the future

attention of publishing giant William Randolph Hearst, who instructed his reporters to *"puff Graham"*—a newspaper term meaning to promote Graham's message of new life through Bible principles. The L.A. revival proved to be the launching pad for Graham's international ministry. During the next five decades, Billy Graham's Crusades attracted millions of people in major U.S. cities and foreign countries around the world. More than 250,000 people jammed in New York's Central Park to hear Billy Graham. Some crusades extended six weeks as crowds were turned away each night for lack of seating room in England, Germany, Poland, Russia, Korea, Brazil and the Baltic regions.

Billy Graham's Crusades
Trafalgar Square in London 1954

Newspapers compared Billy Graham to America's famous preachers of the 1870s and 1890s—D.L. Moody and Billy Sunday. From the beginning of his career, Graham recognized the value of a popular new form of entertainment—television. His *Hour of Decision* show, featuring special guests, ran from 1951-1955. Later, portions of Graham's popular crusades appeared as both television and radio specials.

VOCABULARY

Mysticism: the belief that through meditation and occultic practices one unites spiritually with deity
Freewheeling: very enthusiastic, often perceived as shallow and careless
Savvy: intelligence, cleverness
Pluralistic: a society of various ethnic peoples

The innovative young preacher began to use motion pictures to evangelize mass audiences. The Billy Graham Evangelistic Film Ministry (later changed to World Wide Pictures) was formed to produce and market dozens of high quality films of American and Christian heroes and heroines.

Graham launched *Decision* magazine in 1958. The monthly publication contained Bible stories, Christian teaching, and articles about preaching crusades.

In a culture where public figures often disappeared as quickly as they attained fame, the decades only added to Billy Graham's popularity. He became *America's Preacher*, advising eight U.S. presidents, holding evangelistic campaigns in every major U.S. city, and effectively using the media to promote the Christian message. In addition, Graham tirelessly crisscrossed the globe. His high-profile crusades drew thousands—sometimes even millions. Graham's crusade in Seoul, Korea during 1973 attracted 1,100,000 people, which at that time stood as the largest religious gathering in the history of the world.

Billy Graham's name has appeared 37 times in Gallup's *Top-Ten Admired Men* annual poll. On May 3, 1996 the U.S. Congress awarded Billy Graham the Congressional Gold Medal, which had been presented only 114 times. The original *recipient* was George Washington. The first clergyman to receive the medal, Graham said with characteristic modesty, *"We know that someday, we will lay it at the feet of the One we seek to serve."* Graham's humility and grace earned respect and admiration for his organization.

In 1953, Graham took a bold stand against racial segregation. He announced that his Chattanooga, Tennessee crusade would be integrated. Graham himself let down the ropes that separated the black and white sections of the arena. Four years later, Graham integrated his staff by adding a young black pastor named Howard O. Jones. In that same year, Graham asked a black preacher named Martin Luther King (MLK) to lead prayer at the New York City crusade.

In 1963, Dr. King became a major figure in America's Civil Rights Movement after delivering his "I have a dream" speech to 200,000 civil rights activists in Washington, D.C. King called on black and whites to live together without hatred. When he accepted the Nobel Peace Prize on December 11, 1964, King stated, *"Nonviolence is the answer to the **crucial** political and moral questions of our time; the need for man to overcome oppression and violence without resorting to oppression and violence."*

The 1960s were characterized both by religious inquiry and rebellion against Bible principles. Young adults raised by babysitters or left alone during childhood rejected the morals and traditions of America's past. **Disillusioned** and angry youth experimented with drugs, marched in public protests and flaunted sex outside of marriage. In the **turmoil** of race riots, political assassinations, and the Vietnam War, religion seemed irrelevant to youth who had not been trained to embrace basic moral standards. After the U.S. Supreme Court removed prayer and Bible reading from public schools in 1962-63, moral values eroded as teen pregnancies, rape, sexually transmitted diseases (STDs), violent crimes and divorce began to rise. The cover of a 1966 issue of *Time* posed the question, *"Is God Dead?"*

The entire nation seemed to stumble and **grope** for **relevance**. Bumper stickers attempted to keep the nation focused. *"If your God is dead, try mine!"* and *"God isn't dead, I talked to Him this morning."* Throughout America, church attendance slumped in mainline denominations. Traditional pastors retreated from involvement in politics and social issues as the nation recoiled from **arrogant** disregard of basic moral principles.

Other religious groups edged into America's traditionally Christian arena as pastors retreated. In bold contradiction to Dr. King's nonviolent stand against racial segregation, the Nation of Islam, or Black Muslims, advocated social violence. Black Muslims adopted the Middle Eastern religion and principles of Islam, worshiping one God called Allah and revering the teachings of the ancient prophet Muhammad who violently opposed Christianity. Black Muslim leaders openly advocated that young blacks commit murder and violence against whites, as *"therapy against the ravages of the white-dominated hell called America."*

The chief spokesman of the Nation of Islam in the United States was Malcolm X, born Malcolm Little in 1925. At the age of 20, he committed robbery and was put in prison where he converted to the Black Muslim faith and changed his name. Later, Malcolm X softened his violent rhetoric and called for social reforms. Black gunmen, disillusioned with Malcolm's new stance, assassinated him in 1965.

By the mid 70s, Americans grew weary of drugs, violence and consequences of premarital sex. Scores of families turned back to the refuge of religion. Not all decided on Christianity. Some drifted into **cults**, **astrology** and Eastern **mysticism**. Christianity was far from forgotten, however. Christianity again became a dominant focus with the arrival of *The Jesus People*, a **freewheeling** movement that attracted disillusioned youth who turned to Christianity and witnessed their faith on the streets. On college campuses, students flocked to religious events. EXPLO '72, sponsored by Dr. Bill Bright's Campus Crusade for Christ, drew 80,000 participants to Dallas, Texas. InterVarsity Fellowship's convention in Urbana, Illinois challenged hundreds of college students to become missionaries.

Religion and the media enjoyed a successful union by the mid 70s. The so-called *Electronic Church* beamed hours of religious TV 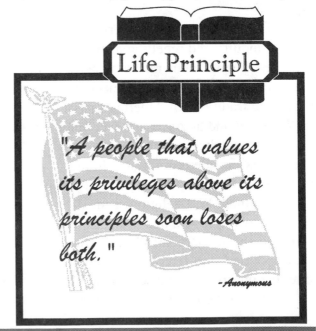 programming into American homes. Popular television evangelists reached millions with programs such as Jerry Falwell's *Old Time Gospel Hour*, Robert Schuller's *Hour of Power* and Pat Robertson's *700 Club*.

The public also gobbled up religious books. In 1971, Tyndale House published *The Living Bible*. More than 40,000,000 copies sold in Canada and the United States. *The Late, Great Planet Earth* by Hal Lindsey detailed Biblical prophecy. Lindey's book was a #1 New York Times bestseller and had sold over 27,000,000 copies by 1998. Through the dismal 1960s and 1970s, and into the new millennium, the Bible, in various translations, has remained the #1 best selling book in America and the world.

In 1976, religion was further showcased with the election of Jimmy Carter to the Presidency of the United States. Carter,

a former peanut farmer and Sunday School teacher in Georgia, was a self-described *"born-again Christian."*

Jimmy Carter

Because of Carter's election, and the new political clout that conservative Christians were wielding, *Time* Magazine called 1976 "The Year of the Evangelical." Religious involvement swept into the next decade as evangelicals strongly supported political candidates who opposed abortion, the prayer ban in public schools, and the exclusive teaching of Darwinian evolution in science textbooks. Most of these Christians were not "fightin' fundamentalists" or "right wing extremists;" they were young voters with political **savvy** and a burning desire to correct social ills through application of basic moral principles.

In the next chapter, you will explore the church-state clashes that occurred with increasing frequency in the 1980s and 1990s. You will also learn how religion changed its packaging to appeal to America's fast-paced, *pluralistic* society.

Life Principle

"A people that values its privileges above its principles soon loses both."

-Anonymous

The Defending of America
1945-2000

The People, Places and Principles of America

Chapter 12

CHAPTER 12
TABLE OF CONTENTS

Chapter 12
Time Line 1945-2000

Use this time line for referencing important dates throughout the chapter.

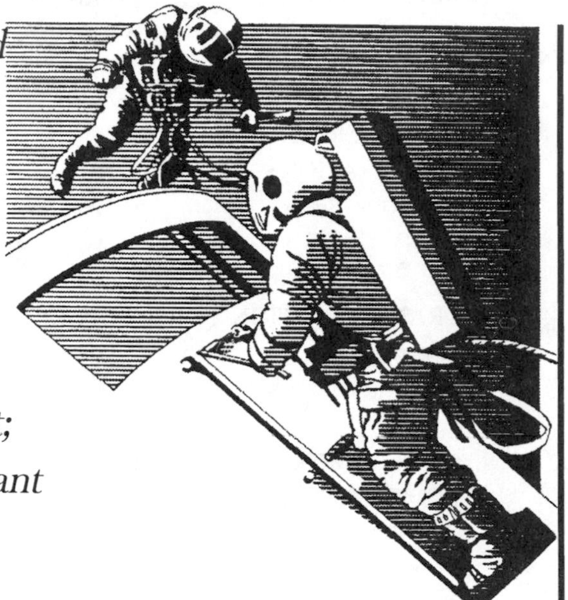

1945 Communist Troops Gained Control of Eastern Europe

1948 Berlin Airlift

1950 Korean War Began

1953 Vietnam War Began

1954 First Nuclear Power Plant; First McDonald's Restaurant

1958 First Plastic Money

1961-1989 Berlin Wall

1969 Armstrong Walked on the Moon

1973 Vietnam War "over"

1981 MS-DOS

1983 First Woman in Space

1991 Desert Storm (Gulf War)

1999 Impeachment Proceedings Against President Clinton

2000 Western Forest Fires

The Defending of America

Topic 1
Military

Chapter 12

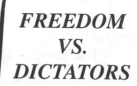

**FREEDOM
VS.
DICTATORS**

Section One
Topics 1-5

After World War II ended, the nations of the world were on edge. Atom bombs had been deployed over Hiroshima and Nagasaki. Even physicists in U.S. observation planes over Japan were surprised at the destruction and terrible magnitude of the atomic bomb, but the full realization of the extent of the bomb was still incomplete. Months later, doctors and scientists from the United States visited Hiroshima and were shocked at the devastating effects of the two bombs.

Japanese who were in the direct *vicinity* of the bomb's blast were, in a way, more fortunate than people a mile away. No one within half a mile of either bomb's center survived the explosion. Between half a mile and a mile from where the bomb hit, about nine out of ten people were killed instantly. Those who were not killed outright usually died slowly from burns or maimed bodies. For some, death took years as the radiation ate away at their bodies in the form of cancer. American use of the atomic bomb on Japan demonstrated the destructive capability of atomic weapons. Fortunately, the first atomic bomb was not available to Axis Powers. Otherwise the entire world today might be under bondage if the Japanese had used atomic bombs on Pearl Harbor, or Hitler had dropped an atomic bomb on London or Washington, D.C.

After World War II, most of Europe and much of the rest of the world came under direct or indirect control of the Allied victors. Unfortunately, U.S. President Franklin D. Roosevelt and British Prime Minister Winston Churchill allowed Communist Russia's leader, Joseph Stalin, to control countries in eastern Europe at the end of WWII. Soon all of Eastern Europe was under the iron grip of ruthless Communism. Eventually, the United States and the Soviet Union—also known as the Union

VOCABULARY

Vicinity: area, place
Virtually: in reality, basically
Adherents: those who follow specific teachings or doctrines
Espionage: spying to obtain information from another nation
Guerrilla warfare: small units of soldiers that sabotage enemy forces by sneak attack, hit-and-run methods

of Soviet Socialist Republics, or U.S.S.R.— emerged as the two primary military powers on the globe. They were referred to as the *superpowers*. However, their national government structures operated from entirely opposite beliefs.

The Soviet Union was ruled by a communist form of government. Communism is a government system in which industries, farms, businesses, and *virtually* any activity that makes money is owned and strictly controlled by communist rulers. Individuals in that system do not have freedom to make a profit. As in Fascism, few personal freedoms exist under Communism. Criticism of government policies is not allowed and earns severe punishment. Communism requires total allegiance of its citizens. People are not allowed to look to an outside source, such as to God, for help in solving their problems. For this reason, Christians, Jews and *adherents* of other religions are persecuted under a Communist regime. A comprehensive system of slave labor camps and prisons were set up in Russia, China, Cuba and East Germany to punish people who opposed or tried to escape from Communist control. The Soviet Union was committed to a policy of spreading Communism as rapidly as possible to every country on earth. In this effort, they cruelly attacked and conquered nearly one-third of the globe. Soviet rulers introduced *espionage* in the United States and *guerrilla warfare* in Africa, South America, Asia and Europe.

Americans, on the other hand, believed that a republic with free enterprise and private ownership was the best form of government. Americans, with their love of personal freedoms—such as freedom of speech, freedom of worship and freedom to defend their property—did not want other countries enslaved by Communism. Americans believed that if left *unchecked*, Soviet Leaders would eventually hold the entire world in the grip of Communism, and freedom world-wide would be lost. Soviet Communism exercised brutal tactics, especially in Asia, Africa and South America. Anyone who resisted Communism was tortured and/or executed. Soviet rulers held no regard for human life.

Some Countries controlled by Communism during the 1960s:	
Russia	China
North Korea	North Vietnam
Laos	Cambodia
Cuba	Angola
Tanzania	Congo
E. Germany	Romania
Algeria	Yugoslavia
Poland	Hungary
Estonia	Latvia
Lithuania	Nicaragua
Czechoslovakia	

After WWII, a 45-year-struggle emerged between America's ideals of freedom and Communism's determination to conquer and enslave. This struggle was known as the Cold War. The Soviets constantly engaged in espionage and scare tactics to intimidate allied forces. Soviet leader Nikita Kruschev pounded a table with his shoe at the United Nations and shouted, *"We will bury you!"* The U.S.S.R. developed a policy of *isolationism*, which kept tight restrictions on travel into or out of Communist controlled countries. Rigid censorship controlled information entering or leaving the Soviet Union, preventing open communication and the free exchange of ideas. After WWII, Sir Winston Churchill, Prime Minister of Great Britain, described Soviet policy as an *Iron Curtain* which had dropped across eastern Europe.

After World War II, Germany was divided among the United States, Great Britain, France and Russia. Berlin, which lay inside the borders of the Russian *sector* of Germany, had been the capital of Germany and was therefore also divided into four parts—one part belonging to each former WWII ally. Russia was not happy that an island of democracy was operating in her sea of Communism. Russia sought a way to drive out the Americans and other democratic Allies to show Berliners that American support for western Germany was not sincere. Thus, in June of 1948, Communists blocked all road, train and water traffic through East Germany leading into West Berlin. The Soviets hoped their blockade would persuade western powers, who held West Berlin, to desert the West Berliners who depended on Allied assistance. Instead, the Americans, French and British started the Berlin Airlift. For 11 months, Allied planes transported food and supplies to West Berlin.

Russia finally lifted the blockade, but increased its efforts to spread *atheistic* and *humanistic* Communism throughout the world. The U.S.S.R. implemented an extensive espionage system designed to destroy any government that opposed the Soviet plan for world domination. Soviet Communist spies obtained secret formulas for the atomic bomb from the United States and began to develop atomic bombs in Russia. Soviet leaders then began a world-wide scheme to use atomic bombs to conquer the United States and the entire world.

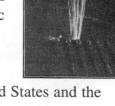

In 1950, ten democracies of western Europe, the United States, and Canada formed a mutual defense alliance called the North Atlantic Treaty Organization (NATO)

VOCABULARY

Unchecked: not stopped
Isolationism: not trading or engaging in activities with other countries
Sector: section
Atheistic: the belief that there is no God
Humanistic: the belief that mankind is the ultimate authority in the universe
Retaliate: to get revenge, to respond to an inappropriate action
Demoralized: removed the desire to continue fighting; removed hope
Morale: moral and mental courage to endure hardship
Confiscate: to take away property against the will of the rightful owners
Ultimatum: a final statement of warning in political negotiations
Obliterated: completely destroyed

in response to the threat of armed military attack by the U.S.S.R. NATO nations promised that if any member of NATO were attacked, the other members would defend the attacked nation. Russia could not attack one country without experiencing war with all the NATO countries. In 1955, the Communist countries of eastern Europe were forced to join a similar alliance called the Warsaw Pact, which included Russian-controlled countries such as Poland, Yugoslavia, Estonia, Latvia, Lithuania, Romania, Hungary and Albania.

During that time, other events escalated the Cold War. The U.S.S.R. built the Berlin Wall in 1961 separating East and West Berlin to prevent people from escaping Communism through Germany. In 1962, the U.S.S.R. placed missiles in Cuba—only 90 miles from Florida—from where the Communists could quickly strike targets in the nearby United States. President Kennedy threatened to *retaliate* with nuclear weapons, so the Soviets withdrew their missiles from Cuba.

Soviet and Chinese Communists united to spread atheistic Communism throughout Asia. Every nation that bordered Russia or China was deliberately attacked and brought under Communist control.

Following World War II, Russian and Chinese Communist forces occupied North Korea; South Korea was protected by American forces.

On June 15, 1950, North Korea invaded South Korea, beginning a military struggle between the Republic of South Korea and Communist North Korea. The United States supplied South Korea with reinforcement equipment and troops. Nineteen other nations joined the United States in providing troops to be placed under U.S. General Douglas MacArthur who commanded all United Nations forces. Ironically, all United Nations combat plans against North Korean troops had to be approved by the Soviets, who sat on the United Nations Security Council and constantly prohibited General MacArthur from defeating the Communist North Korean forces. In frustration, General MacArthur requested Congressional permission to attack Chinese supply trucks which were supporting North Korean forces. President Truman refused to endorse MacArthur's request and relieved MacArthur of his command as Director of United Nations forces. General Dwight Eisenhower was appointed to direct United Nations forces, but he, too, was prohibited from winning the war. After three years of fighting, a truce was signed, allowing South Korea to remain a free country. Communist aggression had been stopped but not defeated. Communists then changed their attention from Korea to Vietnam.

The Vietnam War was a tragic chapter in the U.S. battle against Communism's expansion. The war began in 1952 when China and the U.S.S.R. equipped North Vietnamese Communists (called Vietcong) to overthrow South Vietnam. The United States, France, England and Australia supported South Vietnam by providing troops and ammunition through the United Nations.

General Eisenhower was elected President of the United States and began the policy of sending American troops into South Vietnam. Presidents Kennedy, Johnson and

Nixon all continued this policy, believing that if one Southeast Asian country fell into the hands of the Communists, all Asian countries would fall like a row of dominoes. The undeclared Vietnam War cost Americans $25,000,000,000 per year between 1953-1973. Tragically, during the Vietnam War more than 57,000 U.S. soldiers lost their lives, and 150,000 more were wounded. As in the Korean conflict, the United States was not permitted to conduct its military campaign without United Nations approval, and the Soviets used their power in the U.N. Security Council to prevent America from defeating the Communist aggressors. U.S. involvement in the Vietnam War **demoralized** Americans as fighting dragged on for two decades. *Morale* among and respect for U.S. fighting men dropped to an all time low.

In 1973, the North Vietnamese government and the Vietcong signed a cease-fire agreement with the South Vietnamese. The agreement required United States troops to leave in 60 days, and the 145,000 North Vietnamese troops would be allowed to stay in South Vietnam, but were not allowed to increase troops and supplies. As with all Communist agreements, the Vietnam treaty was broken, and by March of 1975, North Vietnam had conquered South Vietnam. Other parts of Southeast Asia soon came under brutal Communist rule. World maps in 1975 revealed that Communism was indeed swallowing the world. Communist dictators controlled Cuba, Nicaragua, China, Eastern Europe, Central Africa, Southeast Asia and parts of the Middle East.

Back in the 1950s and 1960s, both Russians and Americans developed space programs, putting satellites into orbit with the ultimate goal of using space to project missiles against hostile nations. Both countries channeled resources into developing space programs that would demonstrate superior military capability.

In 1973, both the U.S.S.R. and the United States agreed to slow their production of nuclear arms. This gradual lessening of tensions between the super powers was called *detente* (pronounced "day-taunt"). In 1985, U.S. President Ronald Reagan called Russia *"the evil empire"* and vowed to use space technology to protect freedom even if the United States had to *"strike the Soviets from space."* Reagan's forcefulness convinced Soviet President Mikhail Gorbachev to decrease Soviet presence in European countries and to tear down the Berlin wall.

Meanwhile, the Soviet Union maintained a strong military power sustained by slave labor, but the economic and moral failure of communism weakened the U.S.S.R. In 1989 the Communist party lost power in Russia and Europe, the Berlin Wall came down, and free elections were held in most of the previously Communist countries. The Cold War ended. The world was free of Soviet Russia's domination. However, the Communist governments of China, Vietnam, North Korea and Cuba refused to free their people. In 2000 those countries were still ruled by Communism's ruthless iron grip.

A significant factor in the collapse of Communism was the religious growth behind the Iron Curtain during the 1960s and '80s. Billy Graham Crusades attracted thousands of people in Hungary, Poland, Moscow and the Baltic region. Within the jaws of Communism were Christian people who prayed daily for the fall of Communism. It crumbled under the pressure of internal moral and political corruption and relentless effort by its people to obtain their freedom. Afterward, the United States adopted a forgive and forget policy toward Russia. Diplomatic relationships became friendly.

Even though the Cold War had ended, other battles had to be fought. During the 1980s President Reagan opposed pro-communist leaders in Nicaragua, Granada and Lybia. Reagan's decisive military action sent a clear message to dictators that the United States would not tolerate hostile aggression against America, its people or interests.

Early in 1990, Iraq's leader, Saddam Hussein built up a large debt from his war with Iran. Hussein decided to *confiscate* the oil fields, refineries and shipping ports in nearby Kuwait to finance Iraq's war debt. Under Hussein's leadership, Iraqi troops captured Kuwait's oil facilities and 11,100 hostages, of whom 3,100 were Americans. Hussein's 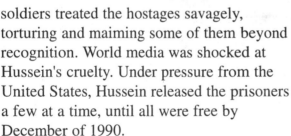 soldiers treated the hostages savagely, torturing and maiming some of them beyond recognition. World media was shocked at Hussein's cruelty. Under pressure from the United States, Hussein released the prisoners a few at a time, until all were free by December of 1990.

Hussein was given an *ultimatum* by the United States and backed by the U.N. Security Council to be out of Kuwait by January 15, 1991. On January 12, 1991, the U.S. Congress narrowly granted President Bush permission to use military force if Hussein refused to leave Kuwait. American forces, joined by troops from nearly two dozen other countries, stationed war ships

in the Persian Gulf region to defend Kuwait's oil fields. For 37 days, the united military forces, called Operation Desert Storm (Gulf War) did indeed "storm" Hussein's forces.

On February 23, 1991, the United States began a four day ground, naval and air offensive. Iraq's roads, bridges, water plants and airports were destroyed. Many of the surviving Iraqi troops surrendered by the tens of thousands. On February 27, Iraq surrendered and agreed to withdraw from Kuwait. U.S. forces reclaimed Kuwait for the Kuwaiti citizens, who expressed their gratitude by hugging American soldiers.

Desert Storm elevated world-wide respect for U.S. military technology. The use of precision camera-guided missiles startled the world. Under the decisive leadership of Secretary of Defense Chaney and General Schwarzkopf, U.S. forces *obliterated* Iraq's army and air force, rendering Iraq defenseless. The message was clearly understood by aggressors—President Bush had the courage and capability to defend freedom anywhere in the world.

Under President Clinton, U.S. troops were again placed under United Nations authority in Bosnia to attempt to stop fighting among ethnic groups. In February 1998, President Clinton deployed U.S. troops to the Middle East to force Iraq to submit to U.N. inspection teams. Hussein was suspected of manufacturing lethal germ warfare weapons which he allegedly planned to use against Israel and western nations. In August 1998, President Clinton authorized U.S. missile attacks on suspected terrorist sites in Afghanistan and Sudan. During December of 1998—at the height of impeachment proceedings—President Clinton ordered U.S. fighter planes to bomb Iraq military sites and to shoot down Iraq planes which attacked U.S.

aircraft or ground forces. In the fall of 2000, more than 48 nations were still engaged in some form of military conflict, causing thousands of American military forces to remain on active duty throughout the world.

In March 2000 President Clinton sent 900 U.S. soldiers to help flood victims in Mozambique, Africa. In October, 2000 more than 5,300 U.S. military troops were still stationed in Kosovo to assist the United Nations with peace keeping efforts between Serbians and Albanians.

Throughout the late 1990s and into the 21st century, U.S. military leaders were attempting to upgrade military preparedness and strike capability by modifying tanks, airplanes, missiles and ships with computer enhanced laser-directed technology. Military strategists recognized the demand for "smart" weapons not too different than those seen on the popular space movie *Star Wars*.

Other significant events were occurring world wide. No more unexplored countries on Earth remained, but explorations continue in non-geographic areas, as you will discover in the next vignette.

Life Principle

"*Humility must always be the portion of any man who receives acclaim earned by the...sacrifices of his friends.*"

-General Dwight D. Eisenhower

The Defending of America

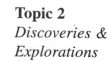

Topic 2
*Discoveries &
Explorations*

Chapter 12

Section One
Topics 1-5

**WHAT IS
LEFT TO
EXPLORE?**

Sending a letter home from outer space was still science fiction when Shannon Lucid was in high school. Much later in her life, on June 16, 1996, Astronaut Lucid transmitted a letter from 245 miles above the Earth where she was traveling at 17,500 mph. Her letter was *downloaded* on a laptop computer and beamed on the Internet to her family. She was on her fifth trip into space traveling on the Russian Mir Space Station with two Russian scientists. Computer technological discoveries enabled her to exchange E-mail messages with her family.

In 1985, Dr. Lucid realized her life-long dream of becoming an astronaut. Eleven years later she made her fifth trip into space and accumulated more time in orbit than any other man or woman. Self-discipline to be patient helped Dr. Lucid adjust to difficult and unusual situations to which she responded with a positive attitude. For example, once while she made repairs to the space station, she was suddenly surrounded by pieces of floating scrap metal that banged into each other, creating an awful racket. Instead of being annoyed, Dr. Lucid's response was simply to think of the metallic tones as if they were music from *cathedral* bells.

Dr. Lucid engaged in complex scientific work during her extended stay on the Mir Space station, but maintained focus on the life principles which had formed her character. One Sunday, at her request, a Southern Baptist pastor in Fort Worth, Texas transmitted his sermon to Dr. Lucid in space through a satellite communication system.

Computer technology had also reached the point of making dreams come true for medical doctors. In 1975, Dr. Mark Carol, a *neurosurgeon*, discovered a plan for treating *malignant* tumors. He knew that radiation beams needed to be molded to fit exactly the shape of the tumor. At that time, computers were too primitive to carry out his plan.

VOCABULARY

Download: electronic transfer of data (information)
Cathedral: a large church
Neurosurgeon: a doctor who operates on brains
Malignant: deadly
Gallant: brave, noble, heroic
Cofferdam: a body of water that is pumped dry
Interlocking: connecting, joining
Excavation: an uncovered and exposed historical site

In 1992, Dr. Carol worked closely with computer scientists at Carnegie Mellon University in Pittsburgh, Pennsylvania to create the Peacock system. It enabled doctors to gather data from a three-dimensional image of tissue growth. It arranged thousands of tiny beams of radiation to fit the exact shape of the tumor.

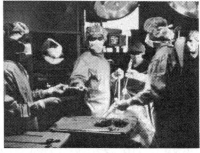

Surgeons could program the computer to avoid healthy tissue areas which could be damaged by radiation.

Bold, new scientific equipment probed the future and helped scientists uncover treasures from the past. In 1985, Dr. Robert Ballard used modern computer technology to discover the remains of the *Titanic*. As you learned in an earlier chapter, the "unsinkable" *Titanic* struck an iceberg on its very first voyage from England to New York in 1912. The gigantic floating city disappeared into the cold blackness of the North Atlantic and settled to the ocean floor two miles down. The exact location remained a secret between 1985 and 1995 to prevent souvenir hunters from interfering with salvage efforts.

In 1995, sonic technology swept the Atlantic Ocean floor to give the world a view of the *Titanic* wreckage. Afterward,

technology helped researchers piece together accounts of the *Titanic* and to produce a second dynamic film of the disaster. In 1997, U.S. film makers spent $120 million to produce the movie *Titanic*. Producers applied the very latest computer graphic technology to create realistic re-enactments of the tragic event of 1912.

Sensitive equipment also picked up magnetic signals coming from iron buried in thick mud on the Texas coast. In 1995, marine archaeologist Barto Arnold located a small wooden French ship buried for more than 300 years. History records La Salle's bold expedition to start a settlement at the mouth of the Mississippi River in 1682. La Salle's **gallant** effort to locate the Mississippi River ended when his ship, the *Belle*, sank into the waters of Matagorda Bay, Texas.

The boat resting in only a dozen feet of water held the story of sailors at work before their death. The Texas Historical Society, in charge of the recovery, built a 1.4 million dollar **cofferdam** surrounding the small ship. Sand and gravel filled the space between two walls of **interlocking** steel plates sunk 40 feet below the surface and rising 6 feet above sea level. Water was pumped out to make a pit which revealed the oak ribs on the ship poking through the gray mud. That was the first dry-land **excavation** of a wreck in this hemisphere. The ship which measured 51 feet long and 14 feet wide, was pieced back together at Texas A&M University. The muck along the bottom of the bay preserved objects such as ropes, barrels, a leather shoe, bowls, lead shots, and glass trade beads. The identifying object that associated La Salle with the ship was a cannon containing the markings of the French admiral.

In July 2000 Ballard's equipment located an ancient village of the Black Sea supporting the theory of a global flood, thousands of years ago.

In the next vignette, you will learn of the hopes of two women to travel from Houston, Texas to the edge of the universe.

Life Principle

"Discoveries and inventions result when men become dissatisfied with mediocrity, discomfort or pain."

-Ronald Johnson

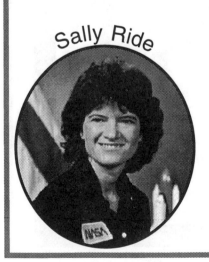
Sally Ride

The Defending of America

Topic 3
Transportation

Chapter 12

COMMUTING TO WORK

Section One
Topics 1-5

Would you rather play tennis or be whirled into orbit around planet Earth? Sally Ride did both. A physics teacher challenged Sally to set high goals so she balanced studies in math and science with exercise on the tennis court. At college, Ride excelled in academics, but found time to continue sports and was among the top female tennis players in the Eastern United States. After graduation, she chose to continue studies in *astrophysics*.

When Neil Armstrong walked on the moon in 1969, only male test pilots were *eligible* to be astronauts. As the duties of astronauts changed, qualifications were adjusted to admit scientists and other professionals of both genders. Sally Ride was in the first group of women to be trained as U.S. astronauts.

On June 18, 1983, Sally Ride became the first American woman in space. At 32, she was also the youngest astronaut. Her mission was to help launch and receive a satellite that would gather important scientific data. From inside the spaceship capsule, Sally controlled mechanical arms that assisted other astronauts in recapturing the orbiting satellite.

Joining NASA in the same group with Sally Ride was Shannon Lucid. She had a childhood environment much different from Ride's. Lucid, daughter of American Christian missionaries, was born in China during WWII. The first year of her life was spent in a Japanese prison camp.

She trained as a pilot and *biochemist* before entering the space program. Her first trip in space was aboard the space ship *Discovery* in June, 1985. Her talents were focused on determining and measuring effects of space travel on human health.

Commuting to work by space rocket is limited to astronauts, such as Lucid, Ride and Armstrong. Most employees who work on planet Earth either walk to work, peddle bikes,

VOCABULARY

Astrophysics: the study of proportions of stars and planets
Eligible: able to be accepted
Biochemist: one who studies the chemistry of plants and animals
Commute: to travel between home and work or school on a regular basis
Metropolitan: cities
Sophisticated: highly complex, advanced technology

ride in cars, buses or trains or fly in airplanes.

Few Americans commuted to work by plane in 1945, but in 2000, 40% of commercial air travel was for business purposes. Private planes also became popular after WWII.

Two companies, Piper and Cessna, began to manufacture small single and twin engine planes for private use by ranchers, corporate executives and businessmen. During the 1960s and 1970s, hundreds of small airports were opened to accommodate private planes.

Commuter trains were another popular means of transportation in large *metropolitan* areas during the 1950s. New York City's suburban trains connected with three levels of underground subway tunnels. Chicago's system of elevated train tracks for electric powered cars evolved from simple slow moving coaches to *sophisticated* computer scheduled trains that transported thousands of employees to and from their jobs.

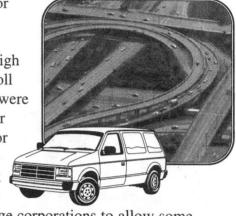

Modern day diesel-powered buses provide transportation among suburbs and inner city stations. Extensive concrete and steel freeway systems criss-cross America's metropolitan areas, providing an efficient highway network on which people commute to and from work sites.

Since 1948, automobiles have carried most employees to their jobs. By 1990, High Occupancy Vehicle (HOV) lanes were designed during rush hours for cars containing 2 or more people. Another innovation, High Occupancy Toll (HOT) roads were established for autos with 3 or more riders. Flexible work hours became popular in large corporations to allow some employees to avoid rush hour traffic. Taxi cabs have operated in highly populated areas such as New York City, Chicago, Los Angeles, Dallas, Denver and Washington for several decades and remain primary sources of transportation for local and out-of-town executives and businessmen who conduct work assignments in metropolitan areas.

The previous 30 years brought major changes in American government involvement in the lives of private citizens and businesses. The next vignette will help you understand how your life will be affected by those changes.

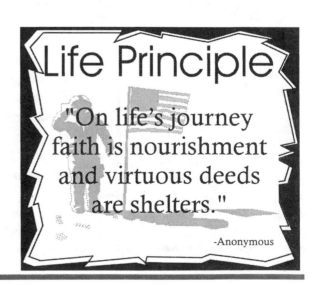

Life Principle

"On life's journey faith is nourishment and virtuous deeds are shelters."

-Anonymous

186

The Defending of America

Topic 4
*Government
& Economics*

Chapter 12

FREE ENTERPRISE VS. BIG GOVERNMENT

Section One
Topics 1-5

Alaska pipe line

The 1970s produced an explosion of political *activism* and government agencies. Post-WWII prosperity ended in the early 1970s. The stage had been set by massive amounts of environmental legislation which crippled the American oil industry and left the U.S. dependent on imported oil.

In response to American support for Israel during the Yom Kippur War, Saudi Arabia cut oil supplies to the U.S. in October of 1973. The effects were devastating. As prices for gasoline and *utility bills* increased, Americans had little income to spend on items other than necessities. Businesses failed, and America fell into the worst economic recession since WWII.

President Nixon responded by imposing the first peacetime *price controls* on oil and gasoline in American history. Price controls were usually reserved for war time emergencies and had not been enacted in the United States since WWII. Gasoline station owners soon lost customers and had to lay off workers and cut back hours of operation.

Legislators debated on how to solve the crisis. Liberals wanted to continue price controls. They encouraged home insulation, gasoline rationing, and lower speed limits to conserve fuel. Conservatives recommended removing price controls to encourage oil drilling and developing other sources of energy from coal, nuclear reactors, and solar power.

Ultimately, the conflict focused on environmental issues. Environmentalists opposed Nixon's successor, President Gerald Ford, who planned to build a pipeline across Alaska. The pipeline would tap into Alaska's huge oil reserves, providing America with over 2,000,000 barrels of oil a day—reducing U.S. dependency on hostile Saudi Arabians. On November 13, 1973, Ford's plan was approved. Reduced environmental legislation soon led to more oil drilling in Texas, Oklahoma, Louisiana and other states.

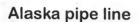

VOCABULARY

Activism: aggressive action toward an agenda
Utility bills: payments for electricity (phone, lights, water, heating/cooling, etc.)
Price controls: government set price levels on goods and services
Reincarnation: the belief that after physical death, life reappears in another form (i.e. a bug, cow, fish, or another human in a different historical era)
Intrusive: restrictive, forceful
Bureaucrats: people who work for government agencies

The Environmentalist Movement produced the Environmental Protection Agency (EPA) and the Clean Air Act in 1970 and the Endangered Species Act in 1973. During the 1980s, the Environmentalist Movement revived, largely by its connection with the New Age religious movement which embraced the concept of *reincarnation*.

Safety and consumer rights movements produced the Occupational Safety and Health Administration (OSHA) in 1970 and the Consumer Product Safety Administration (CPSA) in 1970.

The 1970s also introduced the Federal Energy Administration (1974), the Department of Energy (1977), and the Department of Education(1979).

Altogether, the number of federal agencies with their *intrusive* regulations doubled from 1960 to 1980. The wave of regulations took its toll on the economy. American production slowed and even declined as businesses suffered under stringent federal government controls. The growth of government agencies, coupled with judicial activism, transferred power from elected officials to appointed *bureaucrats* who used their positions and authority to force businesses to comply with tedious federal regulations that hurt companies and their employees.

In 1978 Iran's Ayatollah Khomeini raised prices on exported crude oil. Iran's control over oil revealed American

vulnerability to the rest of the world. Inflation and unemployment in America that resulted from the oil crisis were dominant issues during the 1980 presidential election.

Ronald Reagan wanted to reverse the trend of government expansion. He cut tax rates and struggled to free business from the shackles of government regulations. The size of the *Federal Register*, which gives information about every governmental agency nationwide, had risen during the Johnson and Nixon administrations, fallen under Ford, and risen again under Carter.

President Ford

When Reagan entered office, the *Federal Register* was at its all-time peak, close to 90,000 pages of stringent regulations on businesses. Over the next eight years, Reagan cut the size of the register in half, a testimony to his efforts to reduce government intrusion in the economy and in Americans' lives. By emphasizing the principles that made America great, Reagan reminded Americans of the benefits of the free enterprise system. Under Presidents Bush and Clinton, however, the *Federal Register* began to grow again.

Reagan's tax-cutting was the economic debate of the 1980s. He believed that cutting tax rates would result in economic growth and ultimately increase *tax revenue*. The Economic Recovery Act (1983) included an across-the-board 25% cut in tax rates. Consequently, the revived economy produced record tax revenues throughout the '80s. In addition, inflation, interest rates and unemployment all declined during the Reagan presidency.

Reagan also wanted to cut government spending, but his efforts were

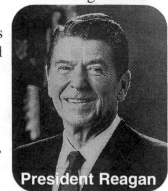

President Reagan

blocked by a Democratic congress, leading to massive government debts. Reagan's efforts to restrict abortion and allow prayer in public schools were also unsuccessful.

Reagan's successor, George Bush, was not able to sustain many of Reagan's policies. Bush accepted tax increases, made **concessions** to environmentalists, and enacted a new Civil Rights Act—which required employers to prove they were not discriminating. Such policies forced many companies out of

President Bush

business because they could not comply with more government regulations. Conservatives became **alienated** from the Republican party and offered little support for Bush. Without strong **grass roots** support, especially from evangelical Christians, Bush lost the 1992 Presidential election to Bill Clinton.

VOCABULARY

Vulnerability: openness to danger or harm
Tax revenue: money collected from people through taxes
Concessions: giving in, not standing up against
Alienate: to withdraw from and no longer be associated with someone
Grass roots: local citizens involved in politics
Proponent: one who supports and advocates
Materialistic Socialism: economic policies based on government ownership of businesses with no regard for moral principles
Restitution: payment to victims
Expansionism: expanding government intrusion into private business through regulations
Lack luster: without excitement

Bill Clinton claimed to be a "new Democrat" who wanted to reduce government intrusion in the economy. The North American Free Trade Agreement (NAFTA) in 1993, which opened trade with Canada and Mexico, seemed to support his claim.

Clinton's other policies, however, proved him to be a **proponent** of **materialistic socialism**. The Family and Medical Leave Act (1993) required employers to guarantee a job for employees absent for child birth, placing further burdens on employers. In 1994, Clinton pushed for a crime bill that emphasized compassion and comfort for criminals rather than **restitution** to crime victims.

Clinton's big government agenda was evident with his accommodation of gay rights activists, his reluctance to reduce dependency on welfare and his attempt to nationalize medical service—which would have made private doctors government employees and greatly reduced patient choices for medical care. His opposition to a strong military concerned voters. In 1994, Americans elected a Republican congress to combat Clinton's liberal socialistic **expansionism.**

The Republicans, led by Newt Gingrich, Dick Armey and Trent Lott, won a majority in both the House and the Senate by emphasizing the *Contract With America*, a ten-point agenda designed to restore the free enterprise system and mend the fractured American family. The years of 1995 and 1996 were devoted largely to legislative battles over the Contract. The pressure of an upcoming election helped the Republicans push some of their plans past Clinton's opposition. Republican candidate Bob Dole conducted a *lack*

luster campaign. He was no match for Clinton's appealing strategy of promises of economic benefits to middle class voters. Clinton won the presidency again in 1996. Republicans retained control of the U.S. Senate and House of Representatives.

The Republican congress succeeded in requiring federal agencies to abide by the same laws required of private businesses. They required a three-fifths majority vote for tax increases and gave the president a *line-item veto* to ease legislative battles. However, the line-item veto was ruled unconstitutional by the U.S. Supreme Court in June, 1998. Congress enacted legislation to reduce *frivolous* lawsuits and forbid the Internal Revenue Service (IRS) to force businesses to defend themselves against bureaucratic controls and *opportunistic* legal firms.

Other Congressional legislation included tax credits for adoption, stricter penalties for *pedophiles*, and punitive action against *deadbeat dads* who failed to accept moral and financial responsibility for the children they produced.

Republicans were not able to persuade Democrats to support an amendment requiring a balanced budget. Congress also failed to impose term limits that would have ended the era of career politicians.

In 1996, Republicans persuaded Clinton to sign the Welfare Reform Bill which was the first step toward dismantling the failed federal welfare system. Congress authorized individual states to set up their own welfare policies to prohibit people from receiving welfare payments for more than two consecutive years or for more than five total years during a lifetime, and to encourage people to regain their dignity through employment.

The 1996 re-elections of Clinton and the Republican Congress foreshadowed more legislative battles and changes in American culture. Political campaign issues during the 1998 election focused on tax reform, school *vouchers* and *deficit* spending.

However, other important economic events were also happening during the 1980s and 1990s. One important factor was the

VOCABULARY

Line-item veto: the right of a president to disapprove selected parts in a bill passed by Congress

Frivolous: silly, shallow, unimportant, not critical

Opportunistic: efforts by lawyers to encourage people to sue one another

Pedophiles: adults (usually men) who molest children (usually boys)

Deadbeat dads: fathers who do not pay child support or share the responsibilities of raising their children

Vouchers: government payment for students to attend private schools

Deficit: a shortage of government money due to greater spending than tax collecting

Microprocessor: the central "brain" of a computer; the central control unit

Implementing: putting into action

Centralized government: a government that promotes excessive regulations

Precedence: superior; to be of more importance

booming information industry which owed its success largely to one man, Intel engineer Ted Hoff, who invented the *microprocessor* in 1971. As microprocessors became more powerful and smaller, they were used in products like video games, digital watches and microwave ovens. Most importantly, the microprocessor was the technology behind development of the personal computer (PC)—which led to startling changes in the way Americans processed information.

The undisputed king of the information age was Bill Gates who built a fortune by staying one step ahead of the developing computer industry. In 1976, Gates co-founded Microsoft which began marketing computer languages and software programs. In 1995, his Windows 95 operating system led to a feeding frenzy of purchases that made news worldwide. In 1998, Microsoft *implemented* a comprehensive plan to integrate Windows 98 with Internet Explorer, an Internet document viewer or browser. The U.S. Department of Justice filed suit against Gates to restrict Microsoft's marketing plan for Windows 98.

Other business enterprises of the 1970s and 1980s related to Asian immigrants. Foreign born professionals made crucial contributions to high-technology areas like telecommunications, biotechnology, chemicals and computers.

Immigrants from India became physicians, dentists, engineers and motel owners. A wave of Filipino immigrants made contributions to science, engineering and medicine. When South Korean officials imposed oppressive price controls on citizens of Korea, thousands of Koreans came to America and purchased or opened new retail stores, gasoline stations, restaurants and grocery stores.

When Saigon, South Vietnam fell to the Communists in 1975, about 130,000 Vietnamese fled to America. As the communist regime became more oppressive, Vietnamese people resorted to desperate measures to escape their own country. More than 277,500 families packed into leaky boats and braved the Pacific Ocean between 1977 and 1979 to begin new lives in America. They proved to be productive citizens—becoming doctors, dentists, restaurateurs and store owners.

The new Asian-Americans did not allow language barriers, racism or strict licensing laws to crush pursuit of the American Dream. As Korean-American restaurant owner Choi Deckchun explained, *"In Korea, money and politics determine everything. Here* (in America) *it's the land of opportunity."*

The American dream has been achieved by millions of people who faced difficult challenges. The story of Kenilworth-Parkside is an example of how one man can make a difference in life.

Kenilworth-Parkside was a 464-unit public housing project in Washington, D.C.—overflowing with crime, teen pregnancy, vandalism and welfare checks. The bureaucracy that operated the project was so dysfunctional that for two years residents had gone without heat or hot water.

Robert Woodson had abandoned the Civil Rights Movement as its emphasis shifted from emphasizing racial equality to enhancing *centralized government*. In 1981, Woodson founded the National Center for Neighborhood Enterprise (NCNE). He wanted to offer urban Americans a capitalistic alternative to welfare and government dependency.

Woodson's NCNE helped Kenilworth residents learn to administer the housing project themselves. NCNE offered the residents legal counsel, fund-raising assistance, public relations help and economic analysis to measure the project's progress. Residents took responsibility for collecting rent and performing maintenance. A neighborhood watch kept drug dealers away and encouraged personal and parental responsibility. For example, when a child vandalized the laundry room, that child's mother was assigned to supervise the laundry room. Laundry room vandalism stopped.

Some residents began opening private businesses in the project. A barber shop, a daycare center, a snack bar and a thrift store appeared. These businesses employed project residents.

After two years of resident management, Kenilworth showed great progress. Teen pregnancy had been reduced 50%. The rate of welfare dependency had declined from 85% to 35%. Crime fell 75%. Kenilworth residents gained self respect, and taxpayers saved money.

In 1985, Coca-Cola learned a tough lesson in free enterprise. Coke replaced its 99-year-old Coke formula with a sweeter tasting *New Coke*. Even after a massive advertising campaign, consumers refused to buy the new product. Sales plummeted. Coca-Cola lost $35,000,000 in just 77 days. The old Coca-Cola Classic formula quickly reappeared on the shelves. Consumers made a statement: buyer demand takes **precedence** over supplier advertisements.

Although critics argue that the free enterprise system allows big businesses to "control" consumer behavior through mass advertising, the *New Coke* failure was clear evidence that consumers make their own decisions. In the American free enterprise system, the consumer is boss. The *New Coke* experiment also showed how free enterprise forces businesses to surrender to reality. When sales plummeted, Coke immediately realized and corrected its mistake.

Computers and the information age made a major impact on American society during the 1990s. Knowledgeable and informed entrepreneurs can wear bathrobes while seated before computer screens in homes and cruise the Internet while transacting business.

Thanks to personal computers, thousands of Americans started their own businesses. The old adage, *It takes money to make money*, may be replaced by, *It takes computer skills to make money*. Employees with computer skills are twice as employable as people who do not know how to process information on computers.

In the information age, education—ongoing education—is essential to business success and preservation of capitalism. The American Dream is literally at the fingertips of anyone who has a dream and personal character to work until his or her dream comes true.

Computers changed the way Americans communicated and made financial exchanges. Businessmen were given special purchasing power in 1958 when American Express and other companies provided "plastic money"—credit cards. By the late 1960s, computers enabled American Express, MasterCard, Visa, Discover, JC Penney, Sears, Montgomery Ward and other retail stores to offer "plastic money" to customers who wanted to make purchases on credit.

Americans learned quickly how to say "charge it." Personal debt soared as buyers used "plastic money" on a promise to pay later when their computer generated invoices arrived in the mail. Credits were too easy for some users, consequently they became deeply in debt. Wise card users learned to buy only for convenience and then items which could be paid off within 30 days to avoid interest and accumulated debt. Even so, credit card debt reached $425 billion by March of 2000.

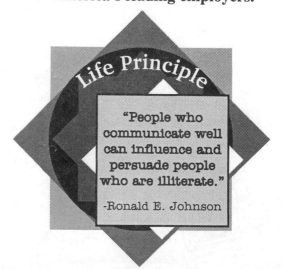

Computers also impacted the stock market in the 1980s and 1990s. Stock is a term used to identify shares or portions of ownership of companies. A company is financed by stock owned by people who invest in the company. The amount of ownership is determined by the number or quantity of stock owned. For example, a man who owns 100% of a company would own 100% of the shares of stock. A person who owns 50% of a company would own 50% of the stock.

Company stock is bought and sold for company investors through the use of computers in investment companies. Investment companies operate simply as a convenience for share holders to buy or sell company stock.

In the 1980s and '90s, investment companies programmed their computers to buy and sell investors' stock to earn the highest profit for investors. A problem developed when investment company computers automatically sold or bought large quantities of stock, causing the entire stock market to experience dramatic profits and losses for investors. Investors had to learn to use computers, but not allow them to make decisions for investors.

The term "Y2K bug" became popular as people realized that the year 2000 would affect computers. "Y2K" represents the "Year 2000" (K represents 1000). The "Bug" in some computers resulted when only two program spaces were allowed for the year (for example instead of 1999, the number 99 was used to indicate the year). Both computers and software programs that relied only on two digits would interpret the year 2000 indicated with two zeros (00) as 1900 (00). American businesses spent more than $400 billion to prevent computer systems from failing when their computers' clocks rolled over to the year 2000. January 1, 2000 rolled over with hardly a "hiccup." People throughout the world celebrated the new millennium with optimism and confidence

Major economic changes in our country were brought about by entrepreneurs who knew what they wanted. The next lesson introduces you to some of America's leading employers.

Life Principle

"People who communicate well can influence and persuade people who are illiterate."

-Ronald E. Johnson

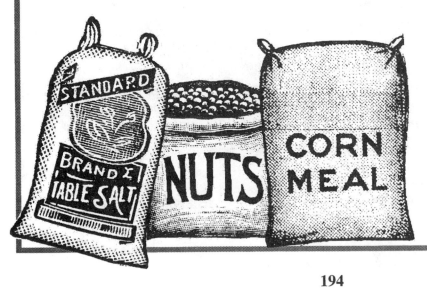

The Defending of America

Topic 5
*Industry &
Medicine*

Chapter 12

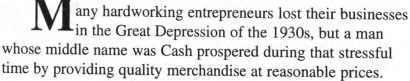

DRY GOODS, SOAP AND COMPUTER CHIPS

Section One
Topics 1-5

Many hardworking entrepreneurs lost their businesses in the Great Depression of the 1930s, but a man whose middle name was Cash prospered during that stressful time by providing quality merchandise at reasonable prices.

In 1897, J. Cash Penney started his remarkable career as a clerk for the Golden Rule Company in Longmont, Colorado. Five years later, he purchased one-third interest in the company and established his own store in the mining town of Kemmerer, Wyoming. Penney studied the community and the needs of its people before opening the new store. Local entrepreneurs scoffed when Penney decided not to extend credit and to charge everyone regardless of social status, the same price for products. The townspeople, however, were delighted with Penney's policies, merchandise and service, making the store an immediate success.

In 1907, Penney bought out his partners and launched his own chain of Golden Rule stores. He employed good people, called associates, and offered high quality merchandise at low prices. Basic to all his business decisions were the religious and philosophical beliefs Penney inherited from his minister father. Penney managed his company according to the Golden Rule— *"Do to others as you would have them do to you."*

By 1912, Cash Penney owned 34 stores. One year later, J.C. Penney Co., Inc. was established. Penney pioneered the practice of *profit sharing*. In 1920, with headquarters in New York City and 197 stores operating coast to coast, J.C. Penney's profit-sharing practice became "a nationwide institution." Annual revenues grew to $43,000,000 and were shared with Penney associates.

In the decade preceding 1930, J.C. Penney opened more than 1,250 stores. During the depression years of the 1930s, the J.C. Penney Company grew to 1,586 stores with annual sales more than $300,000,000. J.C. Penney Company became a large stock-holder owned company and continued its growth through

VOCABULARY

Profit sharing: company profits shared with employees
Acquisition: gaining ownership
Pharmaceutical: pertaining to prescription medicine
Chains: network of stores under the same ownership
Biodegradable: capable of decomposing naturally
Independent distributor: person who sells out of his/her home
Credibility: public confidence in a company or person
Mainframe: the large central control unit for a network of smaller computers

acquisition of several *pharmaceutical* drug *chains* in the mid 1990s. Penney's attention to consumer buying patterns kept the company among the top retail stores in America.

Integrity and good deeds were not confined to American-born citizens like Penney. John Tu and David Sun were the co-founders of Kingston Technology Corp., a California computer software company. These immigrants from Taiwan were described by their employees as models of generosity, compassion and fairness. In the 1990s, Mr. Tu and Mr. Sun often surprised employees by paying for funeral expenses for relatives and providing unexpected gifts. Mr. Sun gave his Jaguar to one amazed employee when she casually mentioned her childhood dream of owning one. The extent of their generosity was realized in December, 1996, when Kingston Technology Corp. announced an astonishing $100,000,000 bonus for their 523 employees. The owners described it as the workers' share of $1,500,000,000 they received for selling 80% of their company.

According to *Forbes Magazine*, Mr. Sun and Mr. Tu were worth more than $900,000,000 each, but their success did not come easily. Mr. Sun's father abandoned his family when David was only five. His mother, a high school biology teacher, encouraged young David to *"Treat people right, then they will help you when you need it."* Mr. Tu's family fled to Taiwan when civil war broke out in China. After immigrating to America, Tu remembers his mother saying *"Don't bring flowers to those who have plenty—bring coal to people when they need heat in winter."* Kingston employees were better human beings because of their association with Mr. Tu and Mr. Sun—two generous businessmen who also practiced the Golden Rule.

Two other entrepreneurs in Michigan built the world's largest multi-level marketing organization. The next vignette tells how thousands of people are achieving their economic dreams because of two men who began a business in a bath tub.

Two young entrepreneurs, Jay Van Andel and Rich DeVos, co-founded the Amway company because of a dream to own a business built on four concepts: freedom, family, hope and rewards.

AMAZING AMWAY

According to Jay Van Andel, *"Amway is built on the desire of people to seize opportunities and achieve their dreams."* Amway Corporation allows people known as distributors to purchase *starter kits* to establish their own Amway businesses. Income is derived from personal sales and a percentage of sales made by recruits who come into the organization through the distributors' efforts. Rich DeVos stated, *"The heart of Amway is helping people to help themselves."*

The Amway Corporation began in 1959 with L.O.C., a *biodegradable* multipurpose cleaner developed in a basement bath tub. By 2000, Amway catalogs featured more than 400 products for skin and hair care and nutrition. Water treatments, cooking utensils, and home care products were also available through Amway.

More than 2,500,000 *independent distributors* have sold in excess of $6,800,000,000 worth of merchandise. As the world's largest multi-level marketing organization, Amway sets the standard for other companies that employ a direct sales approach.

A 380 acre site in Ada, Michigan is home to their World Headquarters, but Amway markets stretch to more than 80 countries and territories. The principles by which Amway operates set the organization apart: emphasis on sales, integrity and environmental awareness in every phase of operations including manufacturing, research and development, marketing and public education.

Amway executives stated, *"Integrity is essential to our business success. . . . Amway success is measured not only in economic terms, but by the respect, trust, and credibility we earn. . . .Each individual is responsible and accountable for achieving personal goals, as well as giving 100% effort in helping achieve corporate or team goals. We also*

have a responsibility to be good citizens in the communities where we live and work."

The theme of "Helping Others Help Themselves" is reflected in Amway's outreach to people in need. The corporation and its independent distributors contribute to the National Easter Seal Society, Toys for Tots, Children's Miracle Network, Junior Achievement, and the United Negro College Fund. Through their unique "Look Good . . . Feel Better" program in Australia and Canada, Amway donates cosmetics and skin care products to female cancer patients.

Perhaps the bottom line is not the financial success of the company or even the assistance Amway gives to others, but the principles stated by the co-founders and their family members who serve on the Policy Board. According to Amway's Founders' Fundamentals, *"Freedom is our natural state and most conducive environment. . . . It* [freedom] *allows for our belief in God and for the opportunity to build a meaningful, purposeful life."* Another Fundamental states, *"We are proud advocates of freedom and free enterprise. Human economic advancement is clearly proven to be best achieved in a free market economy."*

The next vignette tells how Bill Gates changed the way America processed information.

VOCABULARY

Retailer: one who sells products to walk-in customers

Share: a percentage of ownership of a business

Operation: a business

Charitable contributions: financial support for organizations that benefit society—such as churches, Boy Scouts and the Salvation Army

Civic affairs: important issues that concern a local community

Eradicated: gotten rid of, destroyed

Landmark: well known and important to history

BILL GATES AND MICROSOFT

Bill Gates was 19 years old when he and a high school friend, Paul Allen, founded Microsoft Corporation. Gates became a billionaire before his 30th birthday. In 1975, he and Allen developed the BASIC programming language for the first personal computer (PC). Gates and his company introduced Microsoft Disk Operating System (MS-DOS) in 1981. *MS-DOS* is codes and commands necessary to operate computers. Gates' software program enabled the original International Business Machine (IBM) desktop PC to operate as efficiently as a ***mainframe*** computer. In the mid 1980s, Gates' Microsoft Company introduced *Windows*—a sophisticated system that allows computer users to select icons (symbols, graphics, pictures) to command computers to start various programs. With the successful introduction of BASIC, MS-DOS and Windows, Microsoft and IBM took firm command of the emerging PC market.

According to Gates, he founded Microsoft Windows on his *"vision of a personal computer on every desk and in every home."* Gates' creative and technical aptitude transformed information systems in the business world. His genius, brilliance and entrepreneurial spirit gave millions of ordinary people access to the world of computers, fulfilling his vision.

Bill Gates was not the only individual who affected American business. A hometown boy from Rogers, Arkansas really made it big. The next vignette tells how he built Wal-Mart by selling tools, towels, toasters and hundreds of other household items at fair prices.

Sam Walton established Wal-Mart's three basic principles: customer service, respect for the individual and corporate excellence. These simple principles made

THE WONDER OF WAL-MART

Wal-Mart company the world's number one ***retailer***.

Sam Walton and his brother, Bud, opened the first Wal-Mart Discount City in Rogers, Arkansas in 1962. Local people liked the hometown identity and the friendly faces of Wal-Mart associates. The quality and variety of merchandise was good, and prices were low. Neighbor told neighbor, and before long Wal-Mart stores began to multiply. In 1969, the company incorporated as Wal-Mart Stores, Inc., with 18 Wal-Marts and 15 Ben Franklin Department Stores in four states— creating hundreds of jobs for local residents.

Three years later, Wal-Mart listed its stock on the New York Stock Exchange at $16.50 per ***share***. Going public provided investment capital needed for expansion. It also gave other Americans the opportunity to make money right along with the company. One hundred shares purchased in 1970 for a total of $1,650 was worth $6.5 million in 1993.

By 1979, Wal-Mart stores had expanded to 276 ***operations*** in 11 states with annual sales of $1,250,000,000. Most stores were in towns of less than 25,000 population. In 1988, the first Wal-Mart Supercenter, which combined groceries and general merchandise, opened in Missouri. Bud's Warehouse Outlets followed, along with international expansion. The company's 2000 Annual Report listed 2373 Wal-Mart discount stores, 1,104 Wal-Mart Supercenters, 512 SAM'S Warehouse Clubs and approximately 1,000,000 employees. Record sales established Wal-Mart as the second largest company in the United States and the second largest in the world.

Why are customers so loyal to *"the store that Sam built"*? Maybe it is the People Greeters who welcome each customer—or the college scholarships Wal-Mart awards to local high school seniors every year. Perhaps customer loyalty is based on the corporation's Support American Made (SAM) program, that promotes American-made merchandise and creates thousands of new jobs in America. Or maybe it was Mr. Sam Walton himself, who drove from store to store in his old pickup truck, encouraging Wal-Mart associates and shaking hands with customers.

Wal-Mart associates in each community decide how their *charitable contributions* should be spent. Wal-Mart and its associates support the United Way, the United Negro College Fund, the Children's Miracle Network Telethon (CMNT), and various local environmental efforts, educational programs and organizations. People of every race, religion, and nationality are represented among Wal-Mart's associates and the 90,000,000 customers each week.

Sam Walton died in 1992, shortly after President George Bush honored the entrepreneur with the Medal of Freedom, but the principles by which Walton personally lived, founded and operated his company are still noticeable in the Wal-Mart company. For example, Wal-Mart, top seller of recorded music in the U.S., announced in 1996 that it would no longer sell musical recordings that required industry warning labels due to explicit sexual or violent contents.

Sam Walton applied to his business intelligence, friendliness and basic American principles. He combined the three and built one of the most successful retail businesses in this nation's history. He understood what America wanted. He was fond of saying *"If people believe in themselves, it's truly amazing what they can accomplish."*

People who manage their own businesses have to believe in themselves and the American free enterprise system. In the next vignette you will learn about Rotary International and how it helps businessmen and youth.

ROTARY CLUB AND BUSINESS

Men and women in private business have been the backbone of America's economy since Jamestown (America's first permanent colony). Most large corporations began with one person's idea or product: Amway, Wal-Mart, Nike, Mary Kay and Microsoft. Thousands of small businesses are built on the free enterprise economic base on which America operates.

In 1905, a group of Chicago businessmen organized a club for professionals and businessmen. That club became Rotary International, where members represent a cross section of the business and professional services of communities around the world. Local clubs meet weekly to discuss *civic affairs* and to engage in projects designed to make communities better places for families and businesses. Local Rotary members contribute time and money from their businesses to improve health, education and the general welfare of America and the world. The objective of Rotary is to encourage private enterprise to meet human needs world wide. Rotary International was one of the main avenues through which polio was *eradicated* worldwide. Rotary clubs work closely with schools, Boy and Girl Scouts, Future Farmers of America and 4-H Clubs to encourage development of moral character and personal responsibility among youth. Members of Rotary Clubs practice four principles stated in the form of questions about which members think, say and do in their private lives and professions:

1. Is it the truth?
2. Is it fair to all concerned?
3. Will it build goodwill and better friendships?
4. Will it be beneficial to all concerned?

America's *landmark* corporations and organizations are successful because they apply principles of the American work ethic. The story of McDonald's is another vignette about free enterprise in America. Read about it next.

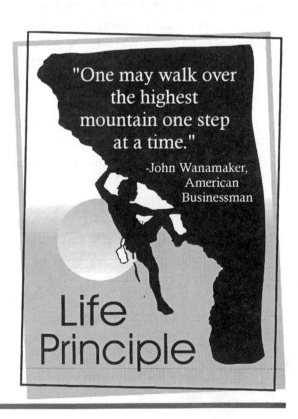

"One may walk over the highest mountain one step at a time."

-John Wanamaker, American Businessman

Life Principle

The Defending of America

Topic 6
Food

Chapter 12

Section Two
Topics 6-10

MAY I TAKE YOUR ORDER, PLEASE?

When milkshake machine salesman Ray Kroc went out of his way one day in 1954 to visit a restaurant customer in San Bernardino, California an idea was born—one that would change American food culture forever. Kroc was curious about a small operation owned by brothers Mac and Dick McDonald, which somehow managed to keep eight milkshake machines busy producing 20,000 shakes each month.

One visit convinced Kroc that he had stumbled onto something potentially very lucrative. What he observed was lines of customers ready to purchase small, 15 cent hamburgers (half the price of area competitors), bags of french fries, soft drinks and milkshakes. The unquestionably limited menu of cheap, quick food seemed to be just what many customers desired. *"This will go anyplace,"* thought Kroc . . . and he was right.

Within one year, after agreeing on a business relationship with the McDonald brothers, Kroc established his first franchise McDonald's restaurant in Des Plaines, Illinois. There, he refined the original concept by incorporating a food preparation assembly line system. Within two years, 14 McDonald's franchises were reporting $1,200,000 in sales.

"Don't worry about making money," Kroc told employees and franchise owners. *"Love what you're doing and always put the customer first!"* Four years later, 228 restaurants were earning $37,600,000 in sales. And so American fast food was born.

Today, the successful McDonald's Corporation includes 26,000 restaurants in 119 countries world wide. Thirty million customers each day result in annual sales of $38,491,000,000. Ray Kroc applied a simple American business principle: find a public need and fill it. He organized the McDonald brother's concept into an efficiently operated business that still provides what customers want to buy.

VOCABULARY

Preservatives: chemicals added to food to prevent spoiling

Additives: chemicals added to food to make it look appealing to customers

Vitamins: organic substances found in natural foods essential for normal bodily functions

Minerals: elements processed from soil and rocks to improve health

Herbs: plants used as medicines, seasonings or food

Consumer demand for fast food encouraged other food chains to begin selling their versions of the ever-popular hamburger and cheeseburger in malls. Chick-fil-A opened in 1967 in Atlanta's Greenbriar Mall. Chick-fil-A featured a pressure-cooked chicken breast sandwich created by founder and owner Truett Cathy. Said Cathy, *"It was a hamburger world. I thought, why not treat chicken like hamburger and place it between two pieces of toasted, buttered bread?"*

By 2000, about 1,000 Chick-fil-A stores operated in 35 states in the United States and other countries around the globe with sales of over one billion dollars. Chick-fil-A restaurants are closed on Sundays even during holidays and special events in order to allow employees to attend their local churches. Mr. Cathy established Winshape Foster Care which enables poor children to prepare for college and employment. A common statement by Mr. Cathy is, *"It's easier to build boys and girls than to mend men and women."* The corporate purpose is, *"To glorify God by being a faithful steward of all that is entrusted to us and to have a positive influence on other people who came in contact with Chick-fil-A."*

Today, Americans can choose from a large variety of fast food options like Godfathers Pizza, Jack In the Box, Wendy's, Arby's, Dairy Queen, Kentucky Fried Chicken and Burger King. In metropolitan areas where lives are busy and schedules are tight, fast food is almost a necessity. Many children begin reading by recognizing the signs and symbols of their favorite local restaurants. Over the past several decades, advertising jingles such as "Hold the pickles, hold the lettuce, special orders don't upset us . . . " and "You deserve a break today . . . " are often repeated phrases. While the menus of fast food restaurants have remained relatively small, the offerings have changed over the years to include food passions and interests of a more health conscious American public. Food chains which began with only hamburgers and french fries now also offer such selections as chicken, salads, tacos and stuffed jalapeños.

Variety and choice have been the key, not just in the fast food realm, but in other American food offerings such as barbecue, pizza, seafood, Cajun, soul food, yogurt and sandwiches. Traveling across America can be a taste-bud adventure. Eating at restaurants became a favorite form of American entertainment. Fast foods, while attractive and convenient, were not eaten without consequences. Processed foods preserved with man made chemicals, colorants, *preservatives* and other *additives* have contributed to skyrocketing medical bills, and sent a large percentage of the public on a quest for low fat, preservative-free "real food."

Along with a rising market for traditional food, the health food market also enjoyed a very steady growth. In response to these consumer demands, market providers began to offer dietary supplements such as *vitamins, minerals* and *herbs*. In 2000, health food stores were operating in most American communities.

Effective marketing and customer service enhanced a food-buying American public—whether in the form of restaurant choices dotting the highways, or in thousands of food ingredients lining supermarket shelves.

With changes in the way Americans ate, changes also had to occur in the way food was grown. Next learn how farming techniques changed during recent decades.

"Let your imagination release your imprisoned possibilities."

—Robert H. Schuller

Life Principle

The Defending of America

Topic 7
Agriculture

Chapter 12

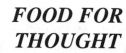

FOOD FOR THOUGHT

Section Two

Topics 6-10

From the time of the handheld *sickle* to computerized farming of today, agriculture has been constantly changing. Seldom bound by tradition, Americans were able to overcome obstacles and find new solutions to problems. As the world entered the 21st century, agriculture kept pace with population changes and market demands. Farmers became *diversified* and more skilled at using technology and chemistry. Farmers had sold hay, repaired tractors, processed feed and leased equipment for many years; but being able to farm successfully in the late 20th and early 21st centuries required more skill and education than just knowing how to plant and harvest crops.

As farming became more scientific, farmers learned to utilize *precision* farming techniques. With the use of computers, farmers gathered information such as where the soil was healthy, where it needed fertilizing, and the balance of fertilizers needed for maximum crop yield.

In 2000, specialized precision farming companies were purchasing satellite pictures of certain geographic areas and using computer programs to interpret agricultural *data*. Conditions of each acre were measured, analyzed and put on computer disks. Local agricultural cooperatives provided information to farmers who used the data to make wise decisions about crop selection, fertilizers and irrigation. Yesterday's farmers used horse-drawn plows. Contemporary commercial farmers ride in air-conditioned tractors, sit in air conditioned offices, and use precision computer programs to monitor soil conditions, moisture content and production yields.

Even though large commercial farms supply much of America's fresh produce, small family-owned farms raise

VOCABULARY

Sickle: a tool for cutting grain
Diversified: being educated and skilled in various related businesses
Precision: precise (exact) methods, no errors
Data: information
Cultivate: to prepare plants for harvest
Combines: tractors for harvesting grain
Contention: disagreement

thousands of bushels of fruit and vegetables for home tables. Each spring farmers climb aboard tractors before sun up and begin 10 to 12 hour days of plowing and planting.  During summer, farmers *cultivate* crops. In the fall, farmers guide large *combines* through acres of corn, wheat and maize from sun up to sunset to harvest grain that will be processed into bread, pizza crust, hamburger buns, tortillas, cereal and bagels. America is called the "breadbasket" of the world because tons of wheat and corn are raised in the United States and exported world wide. Much of the grain is raised on family owned farms.

Almost daily, huge ships loaded with American-grown grain set sail for ports in Europe, South America, Africa and Asia. The American farmer has become so efficient that he feeds himself and more than 80 other people. A combination of technology, chemistry, free enterprise and hard work enables individual American farmers to do the work that a half century ago required 50 to 80 workers. Whereas developing countries still hire workers to hand pick vegetables, nuts or berries, American farm equipment does the work in a fraction of the time. Automatic pickers, sorters and processors gather vegetables right in the field and have the products boxed and labeled for stores before being loaded  on trucks. America's free enterprise system and the spirit of the U.S. farmer combine to deliver tons of food to homes, schools, restaurants, military bases, hospitals and prisons around the world.

A significant part of American farming is the dairy industry. Each day before sun up thousands of cows are herded into milking barns. Workers hook up mechanical feeders and milking machines. While the cows eat vitamin-enriched grain, electrical-powered milking machines collect  milk. Stainless steel holding tanks keep the milk at precise temperatures until 18 wheeler trucks haul the milk to processing plants where milk is bottled and packaged for grocery stores or converted into buttermilk, cheese or yogurt. Dairy herds of 80 to 100 cows in Wisconsin are smaller than the huge Texas herds of over a thousand cows. Wisconsin cheese is well known for its quality, but Texas-size herds supply thousands of gallons of milk for America's breakfast cereal each morning. Other states like California, Nebraska and Florida also host large  dairy herds. Dairy farms operate in almost every state. Some farms produce milk for specialty products like ice cream, butter or cheese.

In recent times, dairy farmers have had to comply with stringent government regulations to protect the consumer from milk-related diseases, and to protect the environment (soil, water and air) from contaminated waste products. Responsible dairy farmers do not offer polluted products to the public, nor do they dispose of waste in rivers. A point of *contention* between farmers and environmentalists is how to operate dairies without polluting the environment.

Farmers and environmental activists constantly appear before legislative committees to advocate favorable legislation. Farmers desire the freedom to operate dairies without government intrusion and control. Environmentalists desire regulations that will force dairies to protect the environment. A dairy crisis occurred between 1995 and 1998 when the government imposed stringent regulations. Small dairy farms were unable to comply, and many farmers lost their jobs when dairies were forced to close down, consequently the prices for butter and milk became very high for consumers. Legislators, government agencies and farmers constantly struggle to address environmental concerns while meeting consumer demands for dairy products. Farmers work hard to supply market demands. The task is not easy under restrictions and government regulations designed to protect the environment.

Labor saving devices are an everyday part of American life, but all of them need a fuel source. The next vignette shows that sometimes getting that fuel is a problem.

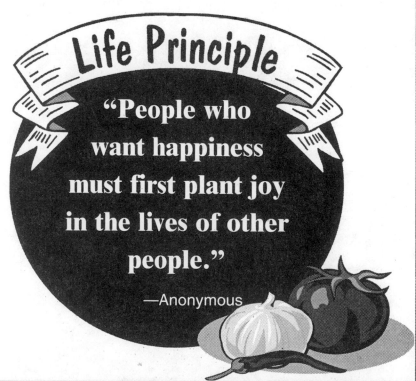

Life Principle

"People who want happiness must first plant joy in the lives of other people."

—Anonymous

The Defending of America

Topic 8
Light & Energy

Chapter 12

Section Two
Topics 6-10

HOW WARM MY HOUSE, HOW HIGH MY UTILITY BILL

American lifestyles have been dramatically altered by modern conveniences. With the flip of a switch, light floods a dairy barn, hospital or department store. With the push of a button, music replaces silence. People communicate around the world instantly by computer, radio, television and telephone. When hunger *pangs* strike, the refrigerator offers safely preserved food. If the food needs heating, the microwave heats it in minutes. Automatic washers and dryers hum and whirl in most homes. When the carpet is dirty, the vacuum cleaner picks up dust and dirt. The tasks which occupied most of the day for early Americans are now done in a fraction of the time.

Seldom, though, do consumers look outside their houses or apartments at electric meters that speed along tracking how much electricity has been consumed. Seldom do consumers think about the source of electricity, and how life would be without electrical power.

Electricity is produced by generators, batteries or solar cells. Some generators run on petroleum-powered steam turbines, others are powered by nuclear reactors. Many generators run on power provided by hydroelectric dams. Batteries turn chemical energy into electrical energy, and solar cells turn sunlight into electricity.

Most of America's energy needs are supplied by fossil fuels. Roughly 50% is supplied by petroleum, 20% by coal, and 25% by natural gas. Wood, water, solar power, nuclear energy and all other energy sources supply only 5%.

The country's demand for energy is obviously *depleting* supplies of fossil fuels. American scientists, aware of potential shortages, are researching conservation methods and alternative fuels.

VOCABULARY

Pang: sudden sharp pain
Depleting: using up
Off-peak: a time when most families are not using their heaters or air conditioners
Landfill: where garbage and waste are buried
Parabolic: involves a certain kind of curve

One alternative conservation method is the use of higher efficiency appliances which require less energy. Consumers are learning how to take advantage of *off-peak* times to use appliances such as electric ovens, dryers and hot water heaters in order to make more efficient use of heat pumps and air conditioners. Home owners are also encouraged to use a window film which blocks out 98% of harmful ultraviolet radiation, reflects 80% of the heat and allows visible light. A window film reduces heat from entering the home and helps reduce indoor heat loss during winter.

One widely studied alternative source of power is solar energy. In recent years, especially after the energy shortages of the 1970s, much research was conducted to find ways to harness the sun's energy. A solar unit, which converts the sun's energy to usable heat, has a metal plate painted black to absorb heat from the sun. Fastened to the back of the metal plate are tubes containing a liquid, usually water, that transfers and circulates the absorbed heat throughout the area to be heated. The metal plate is covered with several layers of glass and has fiberglass insulation below it. Such a system can be used as a water heater or to heat entire homes, barns or office complexes.

Solar Heated Barn

The solar furnace concentrates the sun's heat onto a small area in front of a *parabolic* mirror. Such solar furnaces can create temperatures up to 4,900 degrees Fahrenheit.

Solar energy provides electric power for nearly all man-made satellites. The collected energy is sent through solar cells made of silicon or other semiconductor materials to provide electricity. Solar cells provide the satellite with a reliable electricity source for many years.

Electrical power companies are experimenting with wind turbines to provide supplemental energy sources. Wind turbines catch the wind, powering turbines to turn generators and produce electricity. Windmills, too, remain a source of power in agriculture areas. During the energy crisis of the 1970s, Governor Brown promoted installation of hundreds of wind-powered generators to provide electrical power for California communities. The project did not prove to be efficient, but demonstrated the feasibility of such a source of energy.

Engineers in the solid waste industry can now create an alternative energy source from garbage buried in *landfills*. The natural decaying process produces methane gas. The methane gas is collected as a fuel to produce electricity. Waste management companies operate such plants nation-wide. A typical landfill gas-to-electricity plant generates enough energy to provide electrical power to 10,000 homes. Steam turbines generate about 20% of America's electricity.

The first Nuclear power plants were constructed in 1954 in Pennsylvania to produce vast quantities of electrical power. Nuclear fission of radioactive materials, such as uranium, produces heat used to convert water into steam. The Comanche Peak Nuclear Power Plant in Glen Rose, Texas produces enough electrical power to supply communities throughout central and northern Texas areas.

Drought and forest fires devastated more than one million acres of forest land in 13 western states during the summer of 2000. Texas experienced the worst drought in more than 50 years; many regions felt summer temperatures near 100 degrees for three months and the absence of rain for more than 85 days. Ranchers had to sell cattle, goats and sheep because watering tanks became dry. Numerous communities implemented water rationing programs and issued severe fines to people who violated water conservation policies. Utility companies operated at emergency capacity to provide power for overworked air conditioners in major cities like Dallas, Los Angeles and Phoenix.

As Americans became accustomed to conveniences, clothing styles reflected consumer demand for creative attire as you will see in the next vignette.

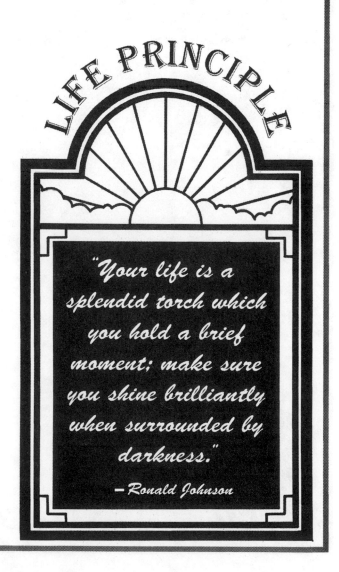

LIFE PRINCIPLE

"*Your life is a splendid torch which you hold a brief moment; make sure you shine brilliantly when surrounded by darkness.*"

— Ronald Johnson

The Defending of America

Topic 9
*Art,
Architecture,
Fashions & Furniture*

Chapter 12

Section Two

Topics 6-10

AMERICAN
STYLES
FROM THE
1960s
TO 2000

While Americans in the 1950s tended to prefer definite styles for fashion, furniture, and architecture, the next decade exploded with irregular shapes, colors, contrasts and styles. In contrast to the ordinariness of the 1950s, the 1960s marked a virtual revolution in thoughts and ideals. It was the dawning of the space age and "way out" fashions.

During the 1960s, trend-setters for fashion were not famous designers, but everyday people, mostly the younger generation. Pop art and pop culture dictated trends which, reflected an "anything goes" mentality, and set the '60s apart from any other decade. Marketing schemes for everything from hairstyles to moral choices were directed at youth. Tradition crumbled, and the *generation gap* hit like a hurricane. The *new morality* set in. Americans were changing radically, and so were personal life styles. The decline in moral values brought a move away from modest clothing fashions of the past.

The most dramatic change in women's clothing of the 1960s was the miniskirt. Introduced by London designer Mary Quant in 1955, the miniskirt ascended to upper thigh level by 1966. It was designed to encourage girls to use their bodies to flaunt traditional moral values. Hair styles also changed and challenged traditions.

Women of the 1960s wore their hair long and straight or cut short into a bob or wedge. Girls with naturally curly hair went to great lengths to torture curl out of their *tresses*. Some ironed their long hair on ironing boards; others used harsh straightening solutions. Determined girls even slept with their hair rolled around metal fruit juice cans. This drastic measure straightened hair, but wreaked *havoc* on sleep.

VOCABULARY

Generation gap: lack of appreciation of life styles between older and younger people
New morality: standards of right and wrong based on emotions and popularity
Tresses: strands of long hair
Havoc: destruction
Caftan: a long loose fitting Turkish style robe
Espadrille: a sandal with a rope or rubber sole with cloth upper part

Knee-high leather or plastic boots, sometimes called "go-go boots," accompanied the miniskirt. Facial cosmetics also changed to accommodate the space age look. Eyes were lined with bold black eyeliner and shadowed with bright green and blue. Women often wore pantsuits, disc earrings, hairpieces, wigs, and silver, lace or fishnet tights to capture male attention or be at the cutting edge of fashion.

By the late 1960s, a romantic trend moved to the forefront of fashion. Gypsy dresses, *caftans*, loose Oriental trousers, Levis, Indian leather fringing, and headbands became popular among the under-30 age group. Scarves, beads, tassels, and long straight hair or hair worn in ringlets struck a chord that pushed aside the pop and space fashions.

By 1969, fashion focused on individual preferences, drawing from styles and accessories all over the world. Rather than following definite fads, women chose clothing to express their personalities. Skirts in the early 1970s ranged from mini, to knee or mid-calf length, to maxi (floor-length). Antique clothing markets became a thriving industry. Women displayed layered combinations of blouses or jackets worn over turtleneck sweaters. Both men and women wore trousers that were wide at the cuff and tight fitting at the waist. These pants were first called *flares*, then referred to as *bell bottoms*. Shoes were high with thick *platforms* (heels). *Espadrilles* in bright colors or rope-soled shoes that laced up the leg were also popular. Hair was styled in layers.

The *maxi coat* made a romantic fashion statement in the mid 1970s. It was usually accessorized with a scarf and a *beret*.

In 1971, Ralph Lauren introduced his *Polo* shirts for men and produced tailored suits for women. Calvin Klein also created stylish clothes for both men and women. His marketing techniques focused on sensual arousal.

Toward the late 1970s, an emphasis on health and personal fitness influenced America's fashion frenzy. With dance studios and health gyms springing up throughout Europe and North America, specialized clothing for dancers and athletes became an integral part of the fashion trend.

In 1975, American designer Norma Kamali brought sportswear into the mainstream by introducing sweatshirts, bandeau tops, leotards, and leggings. Stretchy Lycra, developed by the DuPont Company in 1959, became a popular fabric for sportswear.

Two young men snatched a major part of the sports attire market by producing a durable designer athletic shoe. Phil Knight and Bill Bowerman each put up $500 to buy some light weight athletic shoes from an Asian manufacturer in 1964. The shoes were sold at a profit in the U.S. Using their profits, the two men reinvested in more running shoes. By 1969, the new company, BRS employed 20 people and had *revenues* of $300,000. In 1971, the Swoosh Design and NIKE name were created. Sales skyrocketed to $1.96 million.

Through cutting edge marketing techniques, astute awareness of customer life styles and production of an excellent product, the NIKE company shot to the top among shoe retailers. Production ads included prominent world-class athletes. The market technique was designed to appeal to

214

young athletes who aspired to athletic prominency like NIKE's famous sports figures—Michael Jordan, John McEnroe, Alberto Salazar and others. In 2000, NIKE revenues exceeded $5 billion.

NIKE shoes retailed at the $100 level, causing the shoe to be a status symbol among teenagers. Tragically, street thugs began to rob and kill youth to obtain the expensive NIKE shoes.

By the early 1980s, both men and women were choosing track suits and training shoes for comfortable leisure wear. Styles remained short and fitted or layered with wrap coats.

The term ***power-dressing*** made an impact on the business world by 1982. Corporate men wore classic pinstripe suits with straight leg trousers. Women in the office were expected to wear no-nonsense suits—jackets with padded shoulders over trousers or skirts. Power-dressing became required wear for climbing the ***corporate ladder***.

VOCABULARY

Maxi coat: an ankle length overcoat
Beret: a soft cloth hat with no brim or bill
Revenue: income
Power-dressing: dressing for success, business attire
Corporate ladder: the path to becoming a manager or executive
Retro: popular in previous years
Rekindle: to bring back
Nostalgia: places or objects of antique value that rekindle pleasant memories of past decades and eras
Rustic: southwestern (Spanish or American Indian) design for homes

Both men and women returned to a more traditional look in the '80s. Preppy college styles like tucked-in shirts, blazers and pleated pants with belts were popular casual and office wear.

By the late 1980s, blue jeans and denim jackets were often seen with embroidery, beadwork and decorative buttons. Hair was sometimes braided or beaded, especially among African-American women.

America's 1990s brought a wider spectrum of fashion choices. The first half of the decade reintroduced '60s styles, whereas the last half, inspired by the '70s, brought in the ***retro*** look. Individual fashions from the '50s and '60s usually reflected the work of one designer, with a total look from top to toe, including accessories. In contrast, stylists of 1998 combined high fashion clothes with street and ethnic styles. The '90s reflected the full spectrum of the fashion world, and few people conformed to one prevailing style.

Home interiors and furnishings of the 1960s reflected cluttered, chaotic pop art furniture that stressed leather rather than vinyl covered couches and chairs. Pop art culture inspired steel furniture, silvery pillow covers, white wood furniture, fold-away beds and lava lamps. Chairs made of polystyrene granules, or the ***bean bag*** chair, were popular.

Home interiors in the 1970s featured antiques, carvings and a ***rekindled*** interest in fine woods. A major influence on this return to simplicity and handcrafted furniture was Laura Ashley designs. Small floral prints, use

of country colors and ***nostalgia*** for Victorian antiques helped create the Laura Ashley style. Using cotton dress fabrics of the

19th century, Ashley made dresses, wall coverings and upholstery fabrics to reflect the return to country living. The country look gave homes a *rustic* touch of friendliness and romance.

Most households of 1998 included an assortment of furnishings from various sources including new, secondhand or antique selections reminiscent of southwestern, *Victorian* or traditional classical designs. Architects, since the early 1960s, attempted to create a new style called *postmodern* architecture. Post modern styles included Builder's Contemporary, Mansard, Neo-shingle, Neo-Classical Revival, Neo-Tudor, Neo-French *eclectic*, Neo-Mediterranean, Deconstructionist, Neo-Victorian and American Vernacular Revival. The wide range of styles reflected America's independent spirit among homeowners.

The Builder's Contemporary style utilized vertical siding with natural stained wood, large windows and numerous skylights. The Mansard style featured a French roof with smooth *stucco* walls, double front doors and arched windows. Neo-Shingle was a type of house which primarily used shingles and also had diagonal roofs.

Imitating George Washington's *portico* at Mount Vernon, Neo-Classical Revival homes included two-story porticos. The Neo-Tudor was a front-*gabled* house style with a steeply pitched roof. This style also featured a prominent chimney and fake timber beams. With arches over windows and doors, the Neo-French eclectic style heralded an *old house* look.

The Neo-Mediterranean house reflected a red-tiled roof, stuccoed walls, round arched windows and doors. This house was more common in California, the Southwest and Florida. Spanish architect remained popular throughout the southwest. Entire subdivisions and

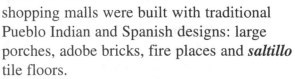

shopping malls were built with traditional Pueblo Indian and Spanish designs: large porches, adobe bricks, fire places and *saltillo* tile floors.

Deconstructionist designs were *eccentric*. Windows were placed randomly, siding was mismatched and part of the house appeared unfinished. This style was popular in some California communities.

VOCABULARY

Victorian: home interior designs reminiscent of the era of queen Victoria of England who reigned from 1837-1901
Eclectic: the best of several designs combined
Stucco: a plaster finish for outer walls
Portico: an enclosed patio or porch
Gabled: a steeply pitched and decorated entry to a home
Saltillo: a clay floor tile made in Central America
Eccentric: unusual or odd

The Neo-Victorian style home was reminiscent of late 19th century England. Its interior designs included fruit carvings and designs, comforting country scenes picturing  families enjoying leisure time together and colors of maroon, gold, cream and dark green.

American Vernacular Revival designs were classic houses that never seemed outdated. They reflected good architectural quality.

Home designs were not the only dwellings which reflected cultural changes during recent decades. Millions of Americans rent or lease apartments and condominiums.

Some are single floor buildings in quiet neighborhoods. Others are 20-story inner-city complexes with thousands of inhabitants. Large metropolitan areas like Dallas, Houston, Chicago, Detroit, New York City, Los Angeles, Atlanta or Memphis house 40 to 60 percent of their residents in apartments. These multi-family residences reflect not only changes in architectural design, but also how American life styles have adapted to population density.

Home is where people read books, watch television, listen to radio programs or play music on CD's or cassette players. Like clothing and fashions, literature and music reflected America's changing values of the era between 1960 and 2000.

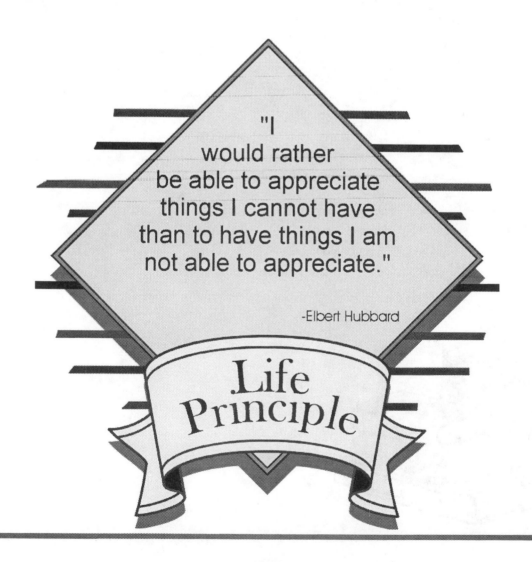

"I would rather be able to appreciate things I cannot have than to have things I am not able to appreciate."

-Elbert Hubbard

Life Principle

The Defending of America

Topic 10
Education, Music & Literature

Chapter 12

Section Two
Topics 6-10

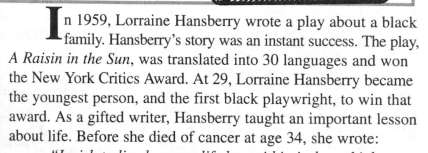

FAMILY TIES, ROOTS, AND ADVICE FROM A COWDOG

In 1959, Lorraine Hansberry wrote a play about a black family. Hansberry's story was an instant success. The play, *A Raisin in the Sun*, was translated into 30 languages and won the New York Critics Award. At 29, Lorraine Hansberry became the youngest person, and the first black playwright, to win that award. As a gifted writer, Hansberry taught an important lesson about life. Before she died of cancer at age 34, she wrote:

> "I wish to live because life has within it that which is good, that which is beautiful, and that which is love. Therefore, since I have known all of these things, I have found them to be reason enough and—I wish to live. Moreover, because this is so, I wish others to live for generations and generations and generations . . . "

In her play, three generations lived together in the ghetto, but each had his or her own dreams of finding a better life. The daughter wanted to become a doctor. The son wanted to manage his own store, and his wife wanted to move into a nice house. The son and daughter expected their mother to share the insurance money from the death of their father. However, the money was sufficient for only one dream.

The mother chose to buy a house for the family because that was her husband's dreamed. The house the mother chose to purchase was located in an all white neighborhood. A white man on the community committee offered to pay the black family (in exchange for not moving into the white community) a price he thought the family would not refuse. The family refused the offer. The son, who still wanted money for his own store, made a secret deal with the white man to accept the buy-out. On the family's moving day, the white man came to the family with the amount of money on which the son had agreed. At that moment, the son changed his heart and sent the man away.

The lasting influence of the play came from its truth about people. Family members can be confused, hard to understand, and at times, against each other. Even so, poor, hard-working people

VOCABULARY

Spellbound: very interested, mesmerized
Spectacular: visually wonderful or awe inspiring
Decline: to politely refuse
Venture capital: money obtained to start a new business
Paradoxical: contradictory statement or situation
Avant garde: leaders in a new trend, fashion or lifestyle
Inducted: brought in, accepted
Prolific: abundant
Decadent: corruption of morals, moral decay

possess pride that helps families solve problems and keep dignity.

A 1976 novel told a far-reaching story about another family whose experiences touched the nation. Alex Haley looked into his own background and found stories that led to his book, *Roots: The Saga of an American Family*. Because of stories Haley's grandmother told, Haley searched for records in the National Archives and traced his family through seven generations to the Gambian village of Juffure in Africa. Haley's writing described growing up in Africa before he was captured by Muslim traders and enslaved in America. Haley described the tragedy of losing family, followed the emotional struggle for freedom, and showed the power of human feelings that unite people into that strong bond called *family*.

Alex Haley's book was the basis of a TV miniseries in 1977. For eight straight nights, 130 million American families were **spellbound** by *Roots*—the story of a black family's experiences. Haley's story was a **spectacular** lesson in black history. The family's passage from slavery to freedom in America brought out the truth in words from the Declaration of Independence: *" . . . that all men are created equal; that they are endowed by their Creator with certain unalienable rights; that among these are life, liberty and the pursuit of happiness."*

During the 1970s, another writer was busy managing various ranches in Texas and Oklahoma. John R. Erickson grew up in Midland, Texas and graduated from the University of Texas in Austin. He spent two years at Harvard's School of Religion in the late 1960s before he became a cowboy. Erickson learned to play the five-string banjo and sing with the church choir. His religious beliefs and ranch experiences provided the foundation for stories full of humor and principles.

He wanted his children to read books full of innocent fun. He did not find many such books, so he created a cartoon cowdog named Hank who served as security guard for an imaginary ranch somewhere in West Texas. Erickson left his work as a cowboy and became a full-time writer in 1982. He submitted his books to dozens of publishing houses which **declined** to publish *Hank the Cowdog*. Erickson knew that his books would be popular, so he obtained **venture capital** and published his own books.

Plots and episodes in *Hank the Cowdog* were humorous like the tall tales of a true cowboy storyteller. The main character, Hank, created funny sayings filled with wisdom. For example, Hank told his dog friend and partner, Drover, that, *"being scared of scary things is normal."* Hank adds, *"Being afraid is the major cause of fear. If you can get that under control, you've got it licked."* Erickson said his stories were like an amusement park water slide, *"Once you're on, you can't get off, and before you know it, it's over."*

Erickson's books stirred up readers' imaginations with humor and values. Within a few years *Hank the Cowdog* books were popular in America's schools and homes from coast to coast.

America is not only a literate nation, but is also a nation that loves music. The next vignette provides information on America's wide variety of musical choices.

SOUTHERN GOSPEL, HUMOR AND EVERYTHING IN BETWEEN

The era of the 1970s and '80s was *paradoxical*. While the pop art culture was focused on rock music and *avant garde* life styles, another subculture was devoted to Gospel music, especially by southern quartets and male soloists. Southern Gospel music (also called Country Gospel) gained popularity as TV media evangelists such as Jerry Falwell, Oral Roberts, Jimmy Swaggart, Pat Robertson and Kenneth Copeland gained large audiences. Popular singers like Doug Odom, Roy Acuff, Johnny Cash, Jim Davis and Bill Gaither popularized Country Gospel. Quartets that filled music

charts with number one best sellers included the Blackwood Brothers, Weatherfords and Happy Goodmans.

The Country Song Writer's Hall of Fame *inducted* Gospel Country

song writer Albert Brumley in recognition of his *prolific* production of best sellers. During his lifetime he wrote more than 550 Gospel and Country songs. Brumley's songs were printed 15 million times in sheet music for hymnals and song books, and were recorded by popular artists such as Charley Pride, Elvis Presley, Ray Charles, The Supremes, Johnny Cash and Merle Haggard. Brumley's popular rendition of "I'll Fly Away" was inducted into the SESAC Hall of Fame in 1986 and had been recorded more than 500 times by 1986.

Another popular singer/song writer of the 1980s and 1990s was Bob Carlisle. His song, "Butterfly Kisses," racked up sales of 223,000 albums for the week before Father's Day in 1997. For the first time in history, a Christian album hit #1 on the national music charts. More than 2 million copies of the song were sold in one year. "Butterfly Kisses" was inspired by Brooke Carlisle, Bob's teenage daughter. The song is about a father's relationship with his daughter from toddler to wedding day.

Music at the opposite end of the spectrum was also popular among some teenagers in the 1990s—performers like Michael Jackson and Madonna became popular from their pop-rock vocal performances which often appealed to sensuality, promiscuity, drugs or rebellion against traditional moral values. Some Rap singers and heavy metal rock groups were so blatant in their lyrics that citizens pressured legislators to enact tough laws against songs that promoted *decadent* lifestyles such as use of illegal substances, suicide, rape and abuse or murder of children, women, teachers and police.

VOCABULARY

Consolidate: to combine small parts to create a large whole
Manipulate: to guide, direct or control
Reconstructionist: public educators who wanted to change social values
Escalated: increased
Plummeted: plunged downward
Demographics: population distributions
Disrupt: to disturb or bother
Juveniles: teenagers under 17
Mandatory: forced, not optional

A rather unusual ethnic mix occurred with music in the fall of 2000 when a large population of Asian-Americans developed an appreciation for African-American gospel music.

Humor played a significant role in America during the five decades between 1948 and 2000. People like to laugh—to feel the joy that laughter brings to the soul. Even in difficult economic and social times, humor helped America cope. Sometimes individual humorists were popular—Bob Hope, Red Skelton, Ray Stevens, Jerry Clower or Lucille Ball. Groups like Bud Abbott and Lou Castillo, Jerry Lewis and Dean Martin, The Three Stooges, and Amos and Andy made audiences "roll in the aisles." One of the most popular humorists of the 1980s and '90s was Bill Cosby. He turned everyday incidents among black families into laughable memories. Cosby taught people how to laugh even when their lives were filled with difficult and awkward circumstances.

While many enjoyed Bill Cosby's refreshing humor, some very serious changes were being made in education.

CHANGES IN EDUCATION

Major changes occurred in education during the last half of the 20th century. The most dramatic change occurred when small community schools were *consolidated* into huge school districts. Consolidation efforts were based on studies by psychologist B.F. Skinner who discovered that human behavior could be controlled and changed by *manipulating* environmental factors.

Reconstructionist educators pushed for large school buildings where students would be fed, counseled and taught all in one location. Consolidated schools led to closure of many small public schools where community values were taught. Under reconstructionism, focus evolved from learning basic skills and traditional moral values to behavior modification, group participation, introduction to career options and collaborative learning.

Unfortunately, some changes designed to improve schools did just the opposite, and the lack of emphasis on academic basics allowed thousands of students to finish high school without adequate preparation for college or the working world. Thousands of inner city youth dropped out of school.

By 1961, education nationwide was in trouble, especially among inner city schools. The 1962-63 Supreme Court rulings against prayer and Bible reading as part of public school curricula proved to be another devastating blow to students' academic achievement and decent behavior. Within a few years teen pregnancies, violence, chemical abuse and dropouts *escalated* while standardized test scores *plummeted*.

A landmark incident occurred in 1954 when National Guard troops escorted a young black girl named Linda Brown to an all white school in Topeka, Kansas. Her attendance forever changed the ethnic *demographics* of American public schools. The mid 1960s were marked by racial segregation issues. A national policy of bussing began; minority students were transported by bus from inner city schools to integrate predominately white suburban schools.

In the 1970s, government financed schools began to provide academic programs for special student population groups such as blind, deaf, crippled and mentally handicapped students. In 1973, Congress passed the Rehabilitation Act, called by many the *"civil rights act for the disabled."*

Parents also asked for and received programs to help gifted and talented children. By 1978, Congress passed the Gifted and Talented Children's Education Act which provided federal money to encourage above average students to pursue advanced educational goals.

Students of the 1970s were tested more often to determine whether educational reform efforts and bussing were actually improving academics. Test scores continued to drop while per-pupil cost rose. During the 1980s, much attention was paid to "Excellence" in the nation's schools. A book, *A Nation at Risk*, created hot legislative debates when it revealed that public school students were not learning as well as students in past years. Millions of tax dollars were appropriated for computers, teachers and books to raise test scores and reduce drop-out levels. Many states passed a "No Pass, No Play" rule for students wanting to play sports, and a "zero" tolerance for *disruptive juveniles*.

State legislatures enacted laws that brought local school-districts under tough government regulations. Average per pupil cost per year skyrocketed to more than $8000 per year. Local taxes doubled in two decades as educators attempted to raise educational standards and quality through increased funding. Teachers' unions became more outspoken in the 1970s and 1980s. The National Education Association and American Federation of Teachers asked for higher salaries and better conditions in schools. They also influenced federal and state governments to pass laws in support of union agendas. Some of the

legislation improved schools, but often it did not. By 1990, public education experienced major challenges of absenteeism, violence, drop outs, academic failure and teacher shortages. Massive reform was needed. The private and home school movements gained momentum. In 1989, 13% of America's students were enrolled in non-public school programs. By 1998, the percentage increased to above 20%. Home school and private academies enabled parents to choose the materials their children studied, and they could monitor student progress more carefully. Parents wanted to influence their children with a core set of values and beliefs. Home school students constantly scored above the national average on achievement tests. The girl who won the 1997 National Spelling Bee had been home schooled. Students whose parents could not home educate or afford private school simply dropped out of public schools. Major cities like Chicago, Detroit, New York, Houston and Los Angeles experienced drop out levels in excess of 60% for inner city ethnic students.

By 1996 the per-pupil cost of educating American public school students was among the highest in the world. In some districts the annual cost was more than $14,000 per student! Simultaneously, America also led the industrial world in juvenile rape, pregnancies, abortions, crime and drop-outs. Most states established tough juvenile behavioral policies including *mandatory* attendance at alternative schools for disruptive students.

Immigration also affected school. Some urban areas were dramatically impacted by numerous ethnic groups with limited English speaking and writing skills.

Businessmen and individuals began debating the merits of educational choice, especially for at-risk inner city minority students. By 2000, most states had initiated some form of educational choice through contracts, charters and vouchers for minority students. Arizona, California and Texas issued hundreds of charters. Minnesota and Ohio authorized educational vouchers for at-risk students to attend religious or public schools. Texas, Minnesota and the other state legislatures with privately owned contract schools provided alternative learning programs for at-risk youth. Private foundations set aside millions of dollars to scholarship at-risk youth to attend private schools in such cities as Washington, D.C., San Antonio, Texas, and Indianapolis, Indiana. Legislators and foundations did not blame public schools for all youth behavior problems and low academic performance levels. Education choices were promoted primarily as efforts to address problems resulting from dysfunctional homes. By October 2000, almost 49% of all United States marriages ended in divorce or seperation, leaving 100 million children struggling over emotional conflict associated with divided loyalties toward parents. Many school problems reflected conditions in broken families. Officials realized that school policies in operation from the 1960s-1980s simply could not adequately address changing social challenges of the '90s and beyond. America needed educational options for children from broken families.

United States Secretary of Education Bill Bennett (1985-1988) wrote *The Book of Virtues* that helped define wholesome literature which the Secretary wanted every student to learn. In 1998 he wrote *The Death of Outrage* which defined public tolerance of immoral behavior and its effect on youth and families. Both books quickly became best sellers as American's searched for ways to repair education, strengthen families and clean up media.

Radio talk shows provided a place where taxpayers could talk about education and other issues. The next lesson reveals the vast popularity of radio and TV media.

LIFE PRINCIPLE

"The way to improve our schools is not more money, but the reintroduction of moral and spiritual values."

—Rush Limbaugh

The Defending of America

Topic 11
Communication

Chapter 12

Section Three
Topics 11-15

TV COMMENTARIES AND RADIO

Every day, from coast to coast, millions of Americans tune in to *talk radio*. They hear political commentary, educational debates, celebrity interviews, sports chatter and helpful advice from such experts as psychologists, doctors, nutritionists, counselors, gardeners, attorneys and financial consultants who invite audiences to voice their opinions or ask questions. A 1993 survey concluded that almost half of all Americans frequently listened to talk radio. Several million watched TV shows that let audiences interact with *media hosts*.

The "Dean of Radio Broadcasters" since World War II has been Paul Harvey. Born in Tulsa, Oklahoma, Harvey learned to construct his own radio sets as a boy. At age 14, while many of his peers were hanging out at the soda shops looking for girls, young Paul was *pestering* the station manager of KVOO Radio for a job . The manager finally hired the eager teenager and gave him tasks such as making short commercial announcements and sweeping the office.

Harvey progressed a long way from those KVOO days. He moved to Chicago where his up-beat honesty built an audience of 23,000,000 listeners every day. He successfully created a unique blend of news, inspiration and humor. Each broadcast combined timing and the use of dramatic pauses. Listeners could count on the same chipper greeting every time Harvey began his noon broadcast: *"Hello, Americans! This is Paul Harvey. Stand by . . . for news!"*

Harvey's voice soothed Americans after tragedies, encouraged families during moral decline and consistently informed listeners of important events. Paul Harvey was a stabilizing factor in the often pessimistic messages portrayed by mainstream media. Harvey's belief in moral principles was evident in his broadcasts. On September 14,

VOCABULARY

Media hosts: the main spokespersons for radio or television programs
Lament: to complain, whine, grieve loudly
Feisty: energetic, dare-devilish
Admonish: to warn or encourage strongly
Abrasive: rough, not gentle or soft
Infuriate: to cause intense anger
Pester: to annoy, to bother

1998, while the world was in shock over President Clinton's moral chaos, Harvey asked the question, "What if the Bible had never been written?" He answered himself saying, "Even if the Bible were not divinely inspired, it would still be the best guidebook for social behavior."

Harvey wove in and out of current events, some comical, some serious, but all overlaid with his unique, chatty style. On just one program, for instance, he talked about such topics as meteors, a Presidential trip through Tennessee, misprinted college diplomas, decreasing sandwich sales at a popular fast-food chain, and a house that was built in six hours and 55 minutes. Before listeners were aware, Harvey had moved from news to commercials, promoting trucks, heat pumps, radios, garden gloves or mattresses.

One segment of Harvey's program, "The Rest of the Story," eventually evolved into a separate series. It featured true but surprise endings to seemingly ordinary tales.

Harvey was still a popular personality in 2000, but certainly not the only one. Larry King marked off a huge share of talk territory. His "Larry King Live" show was heard on radio and TV, reaching some 4,000,000 listeners. King's TV program usually hosted well know persons throughout the world.

Other radio talk shows also captured huge audiences among men and women. Millions of listeners tuned in to Dr. Laura Schlessinger. On any given day more than 60,000 callers attempted to get on the line with Schlessinger, while more than 30 million listened. Thousands more read her syndicated columns in 50 newspapers. The *feisty* talk-show hostess cut through excuses—sexual abuse, poverty, prejudice, sexual addiction and abandonment, and **admonished** callers with such **abrasive** challenges as, *"Grow up"*, *"Get over it"*, *"Quit whining"*, *"Take responsibility"*, *"You have a moral problem"* or *"Where is your character?"*

Dr. Schlessinger gave callers a consistent message—follow moral and ethical principles to stay out of trouble. In July 2000 homosexuals became **infuriated** at the talk show hostess and pressured corporate sponsors to drop financial support for TV and Radio air time.

America's most popular male talk show host during the decade of the 1990s was Rush Limbaugh, who began to dominate the national air waves in 1988 at the age of 37. Before gaining national **acclaim,** Limbaugh had a mixed career. He worked at various radio stations and for five years with the Kansas City Royals baseball club. In the mid '80s, he finally enjoyed success at a Sacramento, California radio station. *"Up until then,"* Limbaugh confessed, *"I failed at everything I did."* After gaining popularity in California, Limbaugh did everything but fail. His popularity soared to the top of radio listener charts. When Limbaugh began his radio program, only 200 such talk shows were in existence. Within a decade, more than 2,000 radio talk shows were aired over American

VOCABULARY

Acclaim: notoriety, fame
Relentless: determined, never giving up
Peril: risk, danger
Quadruple: to increase four times
Exploit: to take advantage of someone for selfish reasons
Scam-artists: dishonest people who cause financial harm to others
Solicit: to gain attention, to request help

stations. Most were patterned after the Limbaugh style.

Limbaugh's mix of conservative commentary and intellectual humor offended some listeners, but thrilled others—over 20,000,000 listeners a week. His theme was "The *relentless* pursuit of truth" with focus on moral principles, political responsibility and entrepreneurial spirit. In 1992, Rush Limbaugh published *The Way Things Ought To Be*, which reigned on top of the New York Times bestseller list for over a year. His second book, *See, I Told You So* was also a smashing success. By 1998, the Rush Limbaugh radio talk show was considered to be the most influential electronic media program in America. Callers included professional football players, homemakers, truck drivers, and prominent public figures such as congressmen and presidential cabinet members. Ted Koppel, an ABC newsman, conceded that Limbaugh was *"very smart, he does his homework. He is well-informed. And you ignore him at your peril."*

One of the most influential women in America during the 1990s was television host Oprah Winfrey. Her television program captured millions of women viewers whose lives were impacted by Oprah's comments about marriage, fashion, diet, work, positive lifestyles, recovery from abuse, celebration of free enterprise, and dozens of other topics. Oprah grew up in an environment that was a constant challenge to high and positive dreams. She was talented, pretty and intelligent, and effectively applied those characteristics to establish a successful career. Rather than lament the difficult challenges of her childhood, Oprah built a successful career on personal qualities which were

marketable—a radiant smile, down-to-earth ideas, strong beliefs, determination and a quick mind. Her television program and related commercial enterprises pushed her to the forefront of African-American millionaires and influential women. She hosted George Bush and Al Gore during the 2000 presidential race.

The 2000 presidential election was dramatically impacted by major T.V. media commentators who prematurely declared that Florida voters had given Al Gore enough electoral votes to become president. Media reporters hourly updated American viewers for two weeks after the November 7th election whle lawyers and courts determined who would be the 43rd president.

Electronic communication technology introduced the Internet super information highway. In 2000, thousands of web page locations appeared on computer screens enabling businesses and individuals to access almost any topic found in a library. Benefits and abuses quickly developed. Publishers, researchers, individuals and businesses suddenly had access to documents, reports, data, photos and literature previously unavailable. The convenience of Internet access *quadrupled* research efficiency and quality. But harmful people also quickly discovered how to *exploit* Internet users. Pedophiles, pornographers and *scam-artists* enticed web site customers. Parents and educators became alarmed at Internet abuse and *solicited* help from the U.S. Congress to "clean up" the information highway to make it safe for youth audiences.

The 1980s and 1990s were years of positive and negative changes. The next lesson is about some of the worst and best things that happened in America.

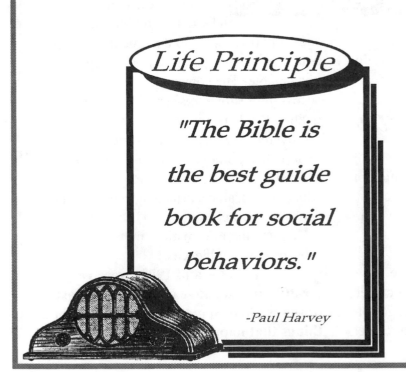

Life Principle

"The Bible is the best guide book for social behaviors."

-Paul Harvey

The Defending of America

Topic 12
Dominant Personalities & Events

Chapter 12

Section Three
Topics 11-15

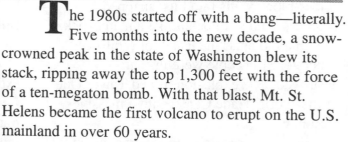

A MOUNTAIN, TERRORISTS AND GUARDIANS OF FREEDOM

The 1980s started off with a bang—literally. Five months into the new decade, a snow-crowned peak in the state of Washington blew its stack, ripping away the top 1,300 feet with the force of a ten-megaton bomb. With that blast, Mt. St. Helens became the first volcano to erupt on the U.S. mainland in over 60 years.

The furious flow of lava torched 150,000 acres of nearby forest, *annihilating* some 2,000,000 birds and animals. Mud, ice, and truck-sized boulders roared down the slopes, choking the Touttle River below and wrecking nearly 300 homes. Meanwhile, the mountain belched 400,000,000 tons of ash into the atmosphere. The ash settled in grey sheets over towns and highways all over the Pacific Northwest. Tragically, 57 people *perished* in the violent explosion.

In the middle east another kind of explosion affected America. As dawn broke on October 23, 1983 a Muslim terrorist slammed a bomb-filled truck into the U.S. Marine compound in Lebanon, killing 241 American servicemen. In October, 1985 Muslim Palestinian terrorists hijacked an Italian cruise liner and murdered a physically-disabled American passenger. Not long afterward, President Ronald Reagan ordered a breathtaking midair interception of an Egyptian jet carrying the Muslim terrorists. The jet was forced to land in Sicily, where the hijackers were arrested.

On April 5, 1986, a terrorist bomb killed two people, including an American serviceman, in a West German *discotheque*. Evidence pointed to Libya, thus U.S. President Reagan dispatched U.S. warplanes to bomb Tripoli, the capital city. After the raid, Reagan grimly commented, *"Today we have done what we had to do. If necessary, we shall do it again."*

VOCABULARY

Annihilating: destroying
Perish: to die
Discotheque: a public dance hall that serves liquor
Vaporize: to convert to smoke through extreme heat
Detonate: to set off a bomb
Perpetrator: one who disobeys the law and harms others
Disgruntled: bitter, angry
Heinous: evil
Subtle: sneaky, not easily seen
Blended families: a husband and wife who divorced and remarried different persons
Championed: supported, advocated

In the 1990s, terrorism moved to American soil. On February 26, 1993, as New Yorkers went to lunch, a yellow van quietly rolled into the basement of the World Trade Center. Unnoticed by the few people who were there, two men in the van lit long fuses and made their getaway in a red car. Minutes later, the van *vaporized* in an ear-splitting blast of more than 1,000 pounds of explosives that shredded nearby cars, blew cinder-block walls into bits, snapped a 14,000-pound steel beam like a matchstick, and cratered an 11-inch slab of reinforced concrete. Six people were instantly destroyed. The explosion turned Tower One of the World Trade Center into a massive chimney.

The terrorists were safely away at this point, hoping that the explosion had slammed the 110-story tower into its twin, taking thousands of lives. Fortunately, the loss of life was not as great as the bombers had planned but it was enough to enrage Americans.

Federal investigators identified the van license plate and traced it to four Muslim terrorists. At their court trial, Ed Smith sadly recounted how his life had changed after his pregnant wife died in the explosion. He asked, *"What type of person shows no regard for human life and would bomb the most populated buildings in the world?"* Judge Kevin Duffy sentenced each defendant to prison with no chance of parole.

Two years after the World Trade Center bombing, the viper of terrorism again bit America, this time in its mid-section. On April 19, 1995, an explosives-packed rental truck *detonated* in front of the Alfred P. Murrah Federal Building in Oklahoma City, killing 168 people—including 19 children in a daycare center. This time the *perpetrator* was not an anti-American outsider, but a *disgruntled* serviceman named Timothy McVeigh, who was caught and sentenced to death for his *heinous* crime.

At the memorial service for victims, President Clinton declared, *"There are forces that threaten our common peace, our freedom, our way of life. Let us teach our children that the God of comfort is also the God of righteousness. Those who trouble their own house will inherit the wind. Justice will prevail."* President Clinton asked Evangelist Billy Graham to lead a prayer for the victims and their families.

Since the 1970s, America experienced another kind of assault —a *subtle* and serious attack on the traditional family. Historically, the traditional family was defined as a husband and wife who were the biological parents of children in the home. By 1990, special interest groups began attacking the definition of the traditional family through three domains. (1) No-fault divorce allowed married couples to separate easily and remarry to form *blended families*. (2) Traditional marriage and stable families were threatened by unmarried couples producing children. (3) Homosexual and lesbian partners wanted official status as "married" people. Homosexuals and lesbians also wanted to form "families" by adopting children.

Two women, Phyllis Schlafly of the Eagle Forum and Beverly LaHaye of Concerned Women for America (CWA), voiced the frustration of women who felt that the traditional family unit was under increasing attack. Committed to *"fighting for the traditional Judeo-Christian values that build and strengthen families,"* LaHaye began Concerned Women for America in 1979. By 1998, CWA listed over 600,000 members. Beginning in 1972, the

Eagle Forum *championed* a pro-family agenda of lower taxes, school choice, abstinence education and pro-life policies. Ronald Reagan praised the Eagle Forum by saying, *"You've been out front on so many of the most important issues of our time. . . . Your work is an example to all those who would struggle for an America that is prosperous and free."* Psychologist James Dobson and researcher Gary Bauer were instrumental in *generating* millions of letters to Congress and President Clinton requesting that legislation be implemented nation wide to encourage traditional families.

Proponents of pornography and Satanism combined to assault America during the 1970s and '80s. Hideous attacks against women increased and grabbed national attention through the crimes of four men: Charles Manson, Jeffrey Dahmer, Ted Bundy and Steven

VOCABULARY

Generate: to start, to motivate
Repentance: to be sorry for a crime and to live a better life
Dunking: a punishment in which "sinners" were tied to a board and dunked (dipped) in water
Malicious: evil, cruel
Petty: of less importance
Brawlers: people known for getting into fights
Terminal: ending in death
Penitent: to regret; to be sorry for committing a wrong act
Unrepentant: not regretful for committing a wrong act
Forbidden: not allowed
Lethal: deadly, terminal
Note: to notice

Morin. All four men became bitter and angry over abuse and neglect during childhood. They focused their anger toward women and young boys and became involved with Satanism and pornography. Charles Manson viciously murdered actress Sharon Tate and others in California. Jeffrey Dahmer raped, mutilated, murdered and cannibalized more than a dozen young boys in Chicago. Ted Bundy became so obsessed by pornography that he stalked, raped, and murdered more than fifty women in Oregon, Washington, Utah, Colorado and Florida. Before their deaths, both Dahmer and Bundy admitted their wrongs and pleaded with civil authorities to take serious action to prohibit the sale and availability of pornography to youth.

Perhaps one of the most deadly assaults on America during the 20th century was substance abuse. Heroin, ecstacy, cocaine, alcohol and marijuana wrecked havoc on American culture. Drug related crimes dominated news reports and police files between 1990 and 2000. Syndicated crime bosses from the USA, Canada, Central and South America continued to attract youth for drug addiction creating a national crisis that screamed for relief.

The United States offers liberties unparalleled in history, such as the right to speak, worship, travel, to keep and bear arms (guns) and assemble without government interference. But that freedom is constantly challenged by special interest groups or individuals who abuse America's freedoms for personal gain at the expense of others.

After President Reagan was wounded by an assassin, the Brady Bill was passed to prohibit availability of guns to assassins, criminals and angry juveniles. It did not, however, reduce gun-related crimes. Murder by guns in the hands of juveniles and gangsters increased, thus alarm was raised among legislators and media personnel during the 1980s and '90s. Anti-gun lobbyists began a major effort to strike down the 2nd Amendment (right to keep and bear guns). The U.S. Supreme Court declared the Brady Bill unconstitutional. But the arguments against the 2nd Amendment were so forceful that movie star Charlton Heston was appointed by the National Rifle Association (NRA) to begin a major educational program to inform youth about the 2nd Amendment and gun safety. The NRA position was stated by an assistant chief of police, *"The 2nd Amendment is America's First Freedom. In the fight against crime, when your life is in danger, the 2nd Amendment is your first line of defense. . . In many cases, armed private citizens help us turn the tables on dangerous felons. . . when trouble comes, calling 911 isn't fast enough."* NRA reports indicated that personal firearms were used over two million times annually during the late 1900s for personal protection against would-be rapists, robbers and murderers.

The murders of students in Colorado, Oregon, Arkansas, Michigan and other states prompted efforts to pass laws to restrict gun ownership. But many legislators realized that the problem was not guns, but rather the presence of satanism and the absence of moral restraint and respect for life.

While responsible, law abiding citizens were protecting themselves from decadents, America's prisons were being filled with criminals who believed they would never get caught.

CRIME AND PUNISHMENT

Crime and punishment have been common in every culture. America is no exception. Laws were established for the common good of society. People who violated the laws were subject to punishment designed to cause **repentance** and/or to protect other law-abiding citizens.

Early colonists applied a variety of punishment techniques designed to reduce or discourage lawlessness. Dutch communities practiced public **dunking** for nagging, drunkenness, marital unfaithfulness, **malicious** gossip and **petty** theft. Repeat offenders and such persons as pickpockets, vandals, **brawlers**, thieves and wife beaters were placed in wooden stocks located in the city square. Often, offenders placed in wooden stocks were beaten, whipped and spit upon by citizens. Other forms of punishment were severe and sometimes **terminal**. People who raped, murdered, robbed or kidnaped were executed by public hanging or firing squad.

Imprisonment as a chief means of punishing law breakers has been practiced since colonial days. The first American prison was established by Quakers in Philadelphia in the 1690s. Prisoners were confined to solitary cells to become *"penitent, confessing their crimes before God and thereby gaining a spiritual rehabilitation."* The term *penitentiary* came from the word *penitent*—one who is repentant for his crime.

Several American prisons became places to be feared. Hardened **unrepentant** criminals were sent to such prisons as the Attica State Correctional Facility in New  York, Alcatraz Island in San Francisco Bay or the maximum security prison in Leavenworth, Kansas.

Capital punishment (execution) by electrocution was introduced in 1890 for hardened criminals, spies and malicious murderers. During the 1970s, capital punishment by electrocution was ruled unconstitutional and was *forbidden*, but execution through *lethal* injection was common in the 1990s.

Crime began to increase dramatically in the United States during the 1960s. Some historians and social scientists *noted* the rise in crime immediately after Bible reading and prayer were forbidden in public school curricula by a Supreme Court decision in 1962-63. Prisons became so overcrowded that shortly thereafter inmates were released before their time was served. Criminal behavior escalated as 70% of released convicts returned to their communities to resume life styles as law breakers. Prison reform efforts were introduced to curb criminal behavior, especially for drug-related crimes which doubled between 1985 and 1991. Reform efforts included educational courses to reduce illiteracy and to improve self discipline, TVs to "occupy time" and body building equipment to encourage "release of anger." Nevertheless, the number of violent crimes reported per 100,000 people shot up between 1963 and 1993. By 1996, the prison population had grown to more than 1.6 million inmates—the highest prison population level in the world!—14% Hispanic, 36% white, and about 50% black. Drug offenses accounted for 60% of crimes by mid 1998.

The sharp rise in the prison population alarmed politicians and preachers. Officials noticed that crime rates tended to be low in communities which taught traditional moral values in schools, homes and institutions. Chaplain services were again allowed in jails and prisons to help inmates connect with spiritual values and life principles. Consequently, prison officials began to encourage private organizations to conduct chapel services and distribute Bibles and religious materials to inmates. Several ex-convicts such as Charles Colson, William Bumphus, Bill Street Jr. and Mike Barber set up religious programs in most U.S. prisons. Chuck Colson's Prison Fellowship and Chaplain Ray's International Prison Ministry provided millions of free Bibles to prisoners. Both organizations conducted experimental programs during the late 1990s to determine how application of Judeo-Christian principles could help rehabilitate criminals in the United States, Russia, and South America.

Preservation of freedom affected everyone from voters to U.S. Presidents. The next vignettes point out the highlights of U.S. Presidents from 1950 to 2000.

AMERICA'S PRESIDENTS FROM 1950-2000

United States Senator Joseph McCarthy made headline news in 1950 at the beginning of the Cold War when he announced he had evidence that communist agents had *infiltrated* high U.S. government positions. Many of McCarthy's accusations were substantiated in 1999 when reports exposed the presence of communism throughout America during the 1950s. A popular television program of the times, *"I Led Three Lives,"* exposed the extent of the Soviet spy network within the United States. Even so, McCarthy was denounced by the media as a fanatic. However, secret government records made available to the public forty years later revealed that the Soviet Union had succeeded in establishing communist spy rings during the 1930s and '40s among America's top government leaders. Some of these included advisers to President Franklin Roosevelt: Alger Hiss and Harry D. White.

Still in shock from the McCarthy findings, voters in the 1952 presidential election chanted, *"We like Ike!"* Ike was the nickname of World War II hero General Dwight D. Eisenhower who led the D-Day invasion to liberate Europe and who replaced

General MacArthur in Korea. Ike defeated Democratic candidate Adlai Stevenson (Truman's Vice President) by promising to finish the unpopular Korean conflict and halt what he called the *"creeping paralysis"* of government expansion started by President Franklin Roosevelt's cabinet and advisors.

During his first inauguration, President Eisenhower led the nation in a prayer asking for a unified America with the ability to tell right from wrong. Eisenhower's popularity ushered him into a second term, resulting in his presiding over the prosperous decade of the 1950s. During the 1950s, America was a place of family unity and economic stability. But by 1959, many Americans became restlessness for change.

In 1960, Democrat John F. Kennedy (JFK) challenged Eisenhower's Vice President Richard M. Nixon for the Presidency. The forty-three year old Kennedy wanted to revive government spending and the U.S. role in the Cold War. The election's turning point was a televised debate in which the young, stylish Kennedy won the approval of voters. The debate gave Kennedy the slim edge he needed to win the election— however, less than 43% of the American people voted to put Kennedy in the White House. The majority of voters wanted either Nixon or minor, third-party candidates.

President Kennedy was the son of a wealthy family which made millions of dollars selling whiskey. John Kennedy's wife, Jacqueline, was an attractive socialite who invited poets and performing artists to the White House. Kennedy introduced to America the challenge, *"Ask not what*

your country can do for you, but what you can do for your country." Just three years into his presidency, Kennedy's life came to a violent end. He was assassinated by Soviet sympathizer Lee Harvey Oswald on November 22, 1963, while in Dallas, Texas. Later that day the blood-spattered First Lady Jacquelyn Kennedy stood beside Vice President Lyndon B. Johnson (LBJ) who took the presidential oath of office.

President Johnson called for continuation of Kennedy's plans. Johnson did not have Kennedy's *elegance*, but he did have thirty years of political experience. Americans saw him as the mythical "Texan"—tall, loud and *brash*.

Johnson defeated Republican challenger Barry Goldwater in the 1964 election. Goldwater's defeat was *facilitated* by media and union efforts to continue the Democratic party's Great Society and *conciliation* toward Communist Russia. The Democratic campaign portrayed Goldwater as a radical who would plunge the nation into nuclear war with the Soviet Union. The Johnson campaign showed an anti-Goldwater television ad featuring an atomic bomb exploding behind a small girl in a daisy field. Even though the ad was *outlandish*, the message led voters to assume that a republican victory would automatically lead to nuclear war with Russia. Americans, still recalling the loss of President Kennedy to a sniper's bullet, voted for "peace." Johnson was re-elected for a full four year term.

Ironically, immediately following Johnson's re-election, the Democratic President and Congress involved America heavily in the Vietnam War that lasted two decades. U.S. troops were put under United Nations policies which made U.S. troops part of an international police force that was not permitted to destroy the Communist Vietcong. The United Nations' no-win policy in the Vietnam War encouraged civil protest riots against American soldiers sent to fight in Asia. The strain proved too much for Johnson and he chose not to run for re-election in 1968. Vice President Hubert Humphrey was nominated to represent the Democratic platform. The Republicans chose battle-scarred Richard M. Nixon.

With crime rates growing, anti-war protesters clashing with police in the streets, and the Vietnam War escalating, Nixon campaigned with "law and order" as his theme and promised to bring American troops home. His basic values strategy proved brilliant. Nixon won the election over Humphrey's peace movement agenda and plans for federal government involvement in American life.

President Nixon demonstrated a mysterious personality. His cool, *aloof* manner concealed a man highly sensitive to criticism. To shield himself from political "enemies," Nixon secretly installed recording devices throughout the White House to document conspiracy movements against him. Those microphones contributed to Nixon's downfall.

During the 1972 campaign, Nixon agreed with advisors to monitor the Democrat party's political convention. The strategy back-fired. A group of Nixon's men were caught trying to install listening devices to monitor the Democratic Party strategy at the Watergate Hotel in Washington, D.C. To avoid a scandal, the President denied any knowledge of the break-in. Despite the incident, Nixon was overwhelmingly re-elected over Democrat George McGovern whose political ties to the socialistic and hippie style counterculture made Nixon's victory an easy one. American moral values were eroding severely by 1972, but the nation's voters were not ready to embrace bold-faced socialism advocated by the Democratic Party.

As celebration cheers resounded over another republican victory, echoes from the past continued to grow louder. The Watergate scandal was not dead yet. As investigations continued, evidence indicated that President Nixon was directly involved in the Watergate scheme. Mounting evidence from his own tapes verified that Nixon had known about the break-in and had attempted to cover it up. The public was outraged and the Democratic-controlled Congress wanted to put Nixon on trial. Facing *impeachment*, Richard Nixon resigned in disgrace on August 8, 1974, leaving Americans more *cynical* than ever about their federal government.

Vice President Gerald Ford assumed Nixon's duties and tried to restore public faith after the Watergate scandal. Ford pardoned Nixon, although the decision was highly unpopular. President Ford was an honest man, but two short years in office could not erase the public's memory of Watergate.

In the 1976 election, Gerald Ford lost to Democratic Georgia Governor Jimmy Carter, who ran as a blue-jean wearing peanut farmer uncorrupted by politics. Carter's biography, *Born-Again*, released weeks before the election, appealed

to Americans who were embarrassed by Watergate and skeptical of socialism.

President Carter's greatest triumph came in 1979 when he negotiated a peace treaty between warring Israel and Egypt. Success was short-lived however, as soaring inflation rates, a fuel shortage and a failed hostage rescue in Iran marred his presidential term. Americans knew Carter was a moral man, but they doubted his ability to lead the nation during the escalating Cold War with Communist Russia, China and Cuba.

In 1980, Republican nominee Ronald Reagan called for a return to traditional American values of hard work, patriotism, religion, *supply side economics* and *core* family values. He promised to lower tax rates, cut government expansion, and renew the arms race to drive the "Evil Empire" of the Soviet Union into its grave. Reagan defeated Carter in a *landslide* election. Reagan 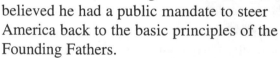 believed he had a public mandate to steer America back to the basic principles of the Founding Fathers.

Reagan's communication skills, high intelligence and moral strength equipped him to be an effective world leader. His optimistic speeches emphasizing discipline and faith were reassuring to American voters. Reagan's leadership ability carried him through two successful terms, beating out Democratic contender Walter Mondale in 1984. Democratic House Speaker Tip O'Neill said of Reagan, *"Reagan is the most popular figure in the history of the United States. No candidate we put up would have been able to beat Reagan this year."*

On January 21, 1985, Americans heard a shining example of Reagan's oratory in his second Inaugural Address:

"History is a ribbon, always unfurling; history is a journey. And as we continue our journey, we think of those who traveled before us . . . a General falls to his knees in the hard snow at Valley Forge; a

lonely President paces the darkened halls and ponders his struggle to preserve the Union; the men of the Alamo call out encouragement to each other; a settler pushes west and sings a song, and the song echoes out forever and fills the unknowing air. It is the American sound. It is hopeful, big-hearted, idealistic, daring, decent, and fair. That's our heritage, that's our song. We sing it still. For all our problems, our differences, we are together as of old. We raise our voices to the God who is the Author of this most tender music. And may He continue to hold us close as we fill the world with our sound—in unity, affection, and love."

Reagan successfully stopped the communist invasion of Granada and authorized U.S. planes to bomb military sites of Libya's Dictator Kadafi. Reagan's critics called him a radical, but his calm manner and gentle humor won respect for the Presidency. No one had to wonder where Ronald Reagan stood on issues. He was hopeful, had high moral character and surrounded himself with highly competent people. The new confidence Reagan instilled in the American Presidency carried his Vice President, George H. Bush, into office over Democrat Michael Dukakis in the election of 1988. Bush, like Reagan, emphasized patriotism (attacking Dukakis's soft stance on crime) and promised *"no new taxes."*

President Bush was a moral man, but he lacked Reagan's personality and leadership skills. Bush's popularity peaked after U.S. military forces **trounced** Iraq President Saddam Hussein in the Persian Gulf War of 1991. But the American economy labored

under a heavy war debt and big government welfare spending. By 1992, Bush had sealed his political fate by raising taxes to cover government spending and alienating conservatives with his moderate social policies.

As a result, the 1992 election produced the first Democratic president to come of age during the 1960s. Arkansas Governor Bill Clinton cut his political teeth campaigning for socialistic George McGovern in 1972. Clinton courted voters with his polished speaking style and charmed them with his tenor saxophone. He pointed to the struggling economy, emphasized a need for change, and promoted tax cuts, nationalized health care and welfare reform. He promised a relaxed lifestyle through big government programs. Clinton won the presidency despite **allegations** of sexual carelessness with women associates. His first two years in office were marked by political payoffs to special interest groups involving homosexuals, abortionists and women's rights organizations. His wife, Hillary, began an aggressive effort to nationalize American health services.

Clinton's welfare-state policies were endorsed by both the House of Representatives and the Senate, which were

controlled by the Democratic party. Congress willingly rubber-stamped the President's big government policies. By 1994, Americans were alarmed at the ultra-liberal policies of the Democratic party. Conservative Republicans won a majority in the House of Representatives and Senate by campaigning on a Contract With America—to reduce taxes, cut back on government agencies, improve education and balance the budget. House Speaker Newt Gingrich and Senate majority leader Bob Dole joined forces to put a halt to Clinton's socialistic expansionist policies.

Despite numerous scandals and socialistic policies, Clinton was re-elected in

1996. His campaign emphasized economic prosperity, balanced budget and optimism for the 21st century. A sympathetic national media focused attention on Dole's age (73) and his lack of optimism. Clinton was re-elected with less than 43% of the popular vote. He assumed his second term amid pending indictments about the Arkansas White Water scandal, Asian contributions to the Democratic National Campaign fund and confrontation with a Republican controlled House and Senate. By October of 1998, Clinton's campaign fund violations and attempted coverup of sex scandals with Monica Lewinsky, a White House intern, and many other women was so obvious that the U.S. House of Representatives and the national media began to discuss impeachment of William Clinton. His weak moral character and careless behavior as a husband dampened respect for the high office of the Presidency. The entire nation seemed to be enveloped in moral confusion as voters went to the ballot boxes in November.

The mid term elections of 1998 left the Republicans in control of the House of Representatives, the Senate and 32 Governorships. In a surprise move, House Speaker Gingrich resigned from Congress to enable new congressional leadership an opportunity to build national support for the Republican Party legislation agenda for the next century. Gingrich was replaced by Congressman Bob Livingston who promptly resigned on December 19 when the media published an account of his marital unfaithfulness. During his resignation speech to the House, Livingston urged President Clinton to do likewise as an acknowledgement of repentance for lying about his affair with Monica Lewinsky and attempting to hide evidence presented by investigators against him. President Clinton refused to resign or admit to his crimes.

Later that day, the United States House of Representatives voted to impeach President Clinton on charges of perjury and obstruction of justice. For 21 days, the U.S. Senate conducted an intensive impeachment trial to determine whether William Clinton should be removed from the office of president. The 100 senators acknowledged that Mr. Clinton had lied, interfered with trial evidence and tried to influence the testimony of a key witness, but all 45 Democrats and 5 Republicans voted to protect their own political interests rather than remove the President from his office. The President was acquitted on February 12, 1999.

After the Impeachment trial, Judge Susan W. Wright's court ruled that President Clinton was "in contempt of court for his willful failure to obey this court's discovery orders."

President Clinton was the second U.S. president to be impeached, and the first sitting president to be found in contempt of court.

The 43rd presidential race between Al Gore and George W. Bush was finally decided by the Florida Supreme Court two weeks after the election.

In the next vignette, you will meet sports figures who are heroes and examples of positive moral behavior.

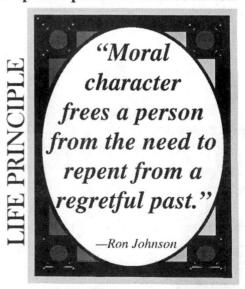

LIFE PRINCIPLE

"Moral character frees a person from the need to repent from a regretful past."

—Ron Johnson

The Defending of America

Topic 13
Sports & Recreation

Chapter 12

CHARACTER IS WORTH MORE THAN TALENT

Section Three

Topics 11-15

Sports icons come from diverse backgrounds and with vastly different personalities. Some athletes *elicit* respect; some do not. Those who impact the world are not always the ones who set records. The world applauds winners whose lifestyles inspire other people.

One of the most inspirational sports icons is Dennis Byrd, a football player for the New York Jets. One of five children of a poor Oklahoma family, Dennis grew up in the shadow of his two brothers. In Mustang, Oklahoma status was based on football. Byrd determined to impress his brothers and his town. He spent hours every day lifting weights and practicing. He made the varsity squad his senior year of high school, and that is when colleges started to show interest in Byrd's defensive line abilities.

Dennis Byrd was recruited on a full scholarship to the University of Tulsa, where he was selected for the All-American team. From there, he was recruited by the New York Jets professional football team. During college he married his high-school girlfriend and established himself as a responsible husband. His contract with the Jets allowed him to play the sport he loved while supporting a family.

During his first few seasons with the Jets, Byrd built a reputation as an all-out player but he was known as a big kid outside of football. He had a great sense of humor, loved to play pranks on people, and was generally a fun-loving, clean-living, dedicated player. His spare time was spent with his family. Byrd was a popular speaker at schools and youth groups as a role-model for kids.

Then tragedy struck in mid-game one Sunday afternoon in 1992. Byrd rushed in to tackle the quarterback and misjudged his approach. He hit the ground with his head tucked in, and his neck shattered.

VOCABULARY

Elicit: to draw out a response
Hone: to develop one's muscles or skills by practicing intensely to reach top performance
Amputate: surgical removal of arms or legs
Charisma: possessing energy and persuasiveness
Prestigious: honorable, reputable

Byrd was carried off the field with a broken spine. Emergency surgery was performed but no one believed Byrd would ever be able to use his hands or arms again except–Dennis Byrd.

Byrd's dedication, perseverance and faith over the next year was supported by  doctors, trainers and friends. Through long hours of therapy and a personal will to push beyond the limits, Byrd little by little began to gain control over his muscles. Through therapy and miracles, he was able to walk again. He had the support of his wife, daughter, teammates and fans to encourage him.

Dennis Byrd had been a hero in the eyes of fans because he was a professional football player. He became an even bigger hero when at his weakest, he refused to let circumstances hold him down. Fans honored Dennis Byrd because he overcame impossible odds to walk again. His refusal to give up became an inspiration to thousands of youth.

Other people have overcome great odds to become heros. One popular athlete was Michael Jordan, recognized as the best basketball player in the history of the sport. He did not start out as a great player, but his devotion to the game earned him a place in history before he retired in 1999.

During high school, Jordan was cut from his school team. Most teen boys would have simply quit; but for Jordan, the cut just made him practice harder. He spent every waking moment practicing shots and running drills to *hone* his skills. The next season he came back as a starter and was good enough to get a scholarship to the University of North Carolina. At UNC, Jordan was not a star player, but he got his chance to make history in the 1982 NCAA basketball championship. The score was 62-61, with 17 seconds left in the game. At the timeout, coach Dean Smith put his faith in Jordan to make the last shot, and make it he did. His perfect swish became basketball legend and the start of his reputation for being able to play with excellence under pressure.

In his first years as a professional player with the Chicago Bulls, both opponents and teammates resented Michael for his personal ego and because he outperformed other players. Michael was shunned by his own team until midway through his second season when he fractured his foot. After watching his team lose game after game, and against doctor's orders, Jordan entered the starting line up. Finally, his dedication and team effort earned respect.

Since that season, Jordan won gold as a star member of the Dream Team in the 1992 Olympics, was a key player in helping the Bulls win six NBA championships, became the world's highest paid athlete as a sponsor for McDonald's, Nike, Coca-Cola and other companies and played professional baseball and golf. Jordan recovered from the tragic murder of his father to show the world how a champion operates as a team player, practices longer and plays harder than others.

Basketball star David Robinson of the San Antonio Spurs made a name for himself, not for overcoming great hardships, but because he lived a clean life. Robinson would not even watch team cheerleaders perform because he believed that reflected disloyalty to his wife. Robinson was an example to the league of a man who was dedicated to basic family values. He attributed his success in basketball to what he believed was *"God gifting me to be a good basketball player."* Robinson kept a clean life image both on and off the court. In an interview he told reporters, *"I'm not playing for the fans or the money, but to honor God."* David Robinson's life style and basketball achievements earned him the title of Most Valuable Player (MVP).

Other athletes earned honor for their perseverance and achievements. In 1991, Gail Devers was so crippled that doctors almost **amputated** her feet. But Devers persevered through a two year bout with Graves' disease to win a Gold Medal in the 1992 Barcelona Olympic Games. She said, *"I was just hoping God would save my feet so I would be able to walk again. . . I'm a living testimony that dreams can come true."*

An outstanding Olympic athlete was Carl Lewis, nine-time Olympic Gold Medalist. During the 1996 Olympics, he came from last place to win his ninth gold medal by beating everyone on one final outstanding leap in the long jump. His distance of 27 feet 10¾ inches in the Atlanta Stadium was his best distance in four years. It seemed like a miracle to the tens of thousands of fans watching. At age 35, no one expected Lewis even to make the U.S. team, but he won the most emotional victory of his career, despite previous defeats and being 10 years older than most of his competitors.

Kerri Strug was a star in the 1996 Olympic games, but her achievements reflected more than athletic talent. Kerri's Junior High gymnastics coach had said that Kerri was not Olympic material. Her coach was very wrong: Kerri's presence on the U.S. Women's team was a testimony of hard work and determination.

Kerri was the final U.S. athlete to compete for the Women's team gymnastic gold medal. Each competitor had two attempts for each event. Kerri sprained her ankle on the first vault. She had only one last opportunity to help her team win the Gold Medal. Despite the fact she could barely walk on her ankle, Kerri shrugged off the pain and made an almost perfect final vault to ensure her team's victory. Strug's winning vault injured her foot severely, disabling her from further competition in the Olympics. That did not matter to Kerri Strug. She put her team before her personal ambitions to win an individual medal, and in doing so, became an inspiration to the world.

Emmitt Smith of the Dallas Cowboys was another athlete role model during the 1990s. His running and pass receptions earned numerous professional honors and public praise, including Most Valuable Player for most yards gained. Smith played the game of football with a sense of integrity, and off the field he earned public praise for demonstrating high moral character. His listed goals for the 1993-1994 season were stated publically:

> *"Keep Jesus Christ #1 in my life.*
> *Stay Healthy.*
> *Average 125 yards rushing/game.*
> *Lead team and league in rushing for*
>   *third year in a row.*
> *Lead league in scoring.*
> *Over 1,000 yards in rushing by eight games.*
> *Catch 70 passes.*
> *No fumbles!*
> *Be named to 1st Team All Pro.*
> *Go to the Pro Bowl for 4th year.*
> *Be named MVP of the NFL.*
> *Go to the Super Bowl and win again!*
> *(with 225 yards rushing and 3 T.D.s)*
> *Be named Super Bowl MVP.*
> *Go to Disneyland."*

Smith achieved most of those goals and in 1998 became the eighth player in NFL history to rush for 12,000 yards.

Emmitt Smith spent a lot of time speaking at schools and youth organizations to encourage young people to finish their education. During the off season, Smith attended college classes and in 1996 earned his Bachelor's degree.

In 1998, Paul Harvey called baseball the secular religion of St. Louis. Harvey's comment was in reference to the enthusiastic following of home run slugger Mark McGwire who played for the St. Louis Cardinals. In September, McGwire hit home run number 70 to break the single season home run record of 61, set by Roger Maris in 1961. Citizens of St. Louis payed $200—$1,000 per ticket to watch McGwire hit the record home runs. Sammy Sosa of Chicago also broke the old record by slugging 66 home runs during 1998.

Another inspirational and influential athlete between 1998-2000 was Tiger Woods. Woods broke nearly every record in the book as the first black golfer to win a Masters Tournament, the youngest player to win a Masters Tournament, the best scoring player in a Masters Tournament, as well as a host of other firsts. His bright smile, clean manners, and general *charisma* earned a large fan club. His performance in tournaments between 1997 and 2000 was an inspiration to the black community and to young golfers of all races. Thousands of youth became interested in golf because of Tiger Woods.

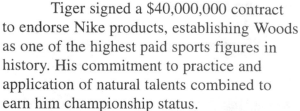

Tiger signed a $40,000,000 contract to endorse Nike products, establishing Woods as one of the highest paid sports figures in history. His commitment to practice and application of natural talents combined to earn him championship status.

One of the most refreshing athletes in the decade of 1988-1998 was Michael Chang. During that decade, Chang won more than 31 major tennis titles. In 1998, he won the French Open and thus became the youngest male to win that *prestigious* tennis title. His victory in France boosted his career earnings to almost $17,000,000. Michael Chang's life on and off the tennis court reflected self-restraint and high moral character. He was open and unapologetic about his Judeo-Christian beliefs.

Some professional sports contracts during the 1990s included character clauses that determined player's salaries. With players from almost every sport making headlines for their involvement in drugs, murder and assault, character became one of the most important qualities of professional athletes. Coaches set players' salaries on how they live in their free time as well as during games. Character clauses set new standards for sports role models.

The Summer World Olympics of 2000 were dominated by the United States who gathered 39 gold, 25 silver and 33 bronze metals. Men and women who wore the red, white and blue of the U.S.A. excelled in such events as baseball, basketball, tennis, wrestling, track and swimming.

The next lesson describes what may have been a key factor in the rise of irresponsible sports personalities during the 1980s and '90s.

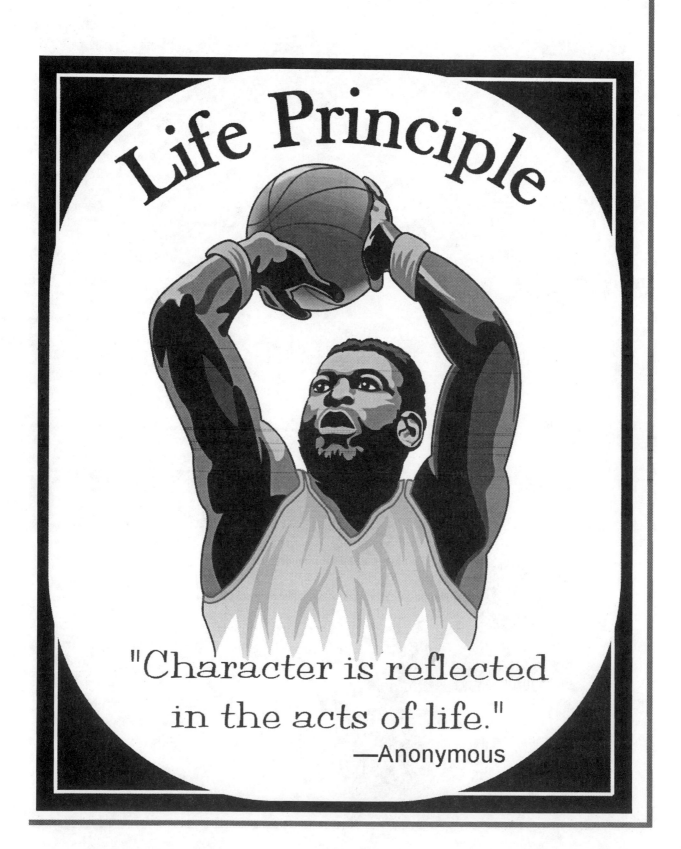

Life Principle

"Character is reflected in the acts of life."
—Anonymous

The Defending of America

Topic 14
*Family &
Home*

Chapter 12

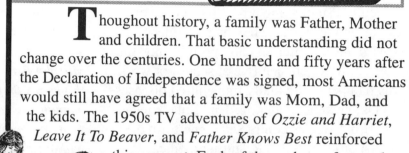

*WHAT IS A
FAMILY?*

Section Three
Topics 11-15

Throughout history, a family was Father, Mother and children. That basic understanding did not change over the centuries. One hundred and fifty years after the Declaration of Independence was signed, most Americans would still have agreed that a family was Mom, Dad, and the kids. The 1950s TV adventures of *Ozzie and Harriet*, *Leave It To Beaver*, and *Father Knows Best* reinforced this concept. Each of these shows featured a hard-working father, a *nurturing* mother, and children who always received a helping hand from parents and neighbors.

In the 1940s and '50s, the national number of divorces *fluctuated* between 250,000 and 400,000 each year. By the 1970s, the traditional family experienced dramatic changes. The national annual divorce rate rose sharply, cresting at 1,100,000 in 1979. The unfortunate tragedy of marital breakups is that thousands of children experience the negative consequences of broken homes.

Teens of divorced couples often experienced depression, poor school performance, experimentation with drugs, tobacco, alcohol and sex, had difficulty establishing lasting relationships and mistrusted adults and most authority figures.

Thousands of teens from broken homes in the 1990s were defined by such terms as the Lost Generation, Generation X, Latchkey Kids, and the "13-ers"—because they were the 13th generation since the American War for Independence.

Single-parent families increased dramatically in America between 1960 and 1990. In 1960, just over 9% of children under 18 were living with only their mothers. By 1990, the number had jumped to almost 25%. Many of these children were born to unmarried teenage mothers. Since 1950, unwed mother births skyrocketed 490%. Among black mothers in 1998, the unwed birth rate was an astonishing 68% and 19% for whites. Spin off consequences were tragic. Crime among teens of single parent

VOCABULARY

Nurture: to care for; to provide for
Fluctuate: to change back and forth
Marooned: stranded
Testament: proof of an event; a legal record of an occurrence
Epitomize: to be the ultimate example
Fallout: a strong disagreement
Analysts: professional people who analyze (study) social events
Abstinence: saving sex for marriage—not experiencing it before marriage
Endorsement: promotion, agreement with

homes rose dramatically: 94% of all juvenile crimes were committed by boys from single parent homes. Pregnancy became epidemic by 2000 as most girls from single parent homes lost their virginity by age 16. More than 800,000 became pregnant out of wedlock. Children who grew up in households of only one biological parent had difficulty establishing a positive set of core values and attitudes. They had a tendency toward anger, bitterness and promiscuity, thus their ability to concentrate at school or work was hampered. Sexually transmitted diseases (STDs) became epidemic: 1 in 2 black teens and 1 in 4 whites contracted some form of herpes or other STD. Resulting medical expenses added to family stress.

Some single parent moms criticized the welfare system for breeding dependency and rewarding unmarried births. One of the strongest critics was Star Parker, an African-American woman who gave birth to an out-of-wedlock child in 1982. *"I have been on that island where welfare women are* **marooned***,"* Parker said. *"The system makes you believe you can't do any better. You lose your self-worth being constantly told that you can't make it on your own."*

Despite four abortions, drug use, and welfare fraud, Parker changed her life, became a model citizen, married a preacher and became a loving and dedicated mother of two children. *"I believe in family and faith,"* she said. *"And I am a* **testament** *to what anyone can do if they take that first step to get off of welfare dependency."*

In 1992, Vice President Dan Quayle delivered a pro-family speech in San Francisco, California pointedly saying that *"a welfare check is not a husband. The state is not a father. Bearing babies irresponsibly is, simply, wrong."* Quayle spoke strongly against the lifestyle portrayed by television sit-com character Murphy Brown, who bore an out-of-wedlock child on the show: *"It doesn't help matters when prime-time TV has Murphy Brown—a character who supposedly* **epitomizes** *today's intelligent, highly-paid professional woman—mocking the importance of fathers by bearing a child alone and calling it just another 'life-style choice.'"*

Quayle's remarks generated a swift attack by liberals, mainly in the media, the National Organization for Women (NOW) and other feminists groups. The producer of *Murphy Brown* argued, *"If the Vice President thinks it's disgraceful for an unmarried woman to bear a child, and he believes that a woman cannot adequately raise a child without a father, then he'd better make sure abortion remains safe and legal."* That argument was countered by such groups as Focus on the Family, Concerned Women for America, Eagle Forum and Family Research Council which pointed out the high percentage of suicides and abortions among girls who participated in pre-marital sex.

After the media **fallout** settled, mainstream social **analysts** conceded that Vice President Quayle had a valid point. Writing in *Time* Magazine, Margaret Colson offered, *"What is socially and emotionally acceptable to a woman may not be so to a child purposefully brought into the world with a hole at the center of his life where a father would be."* In 1997, Congress allocated $70 million to fund sexual **abstinence** education programs in public schools, thereby establishing a national **endorsement** of saving sex for marriage as a means of reducing teen pregnancy and related personal and **familial** problems.

Congressional action was a reflection of national concern about out-of-wedlock births. Researchers such as George Barna and Josh McDowell confirmed that youth who successfully over-came negative home circumstances and avoided diseases and pregnancy through sexual abstinence most often cited religious beliefs as the basis for making critical personal decisions. Groups such as Focus on the Family, Eagle Forum and Concerned Women for America (CWA) pointed out that teenagers had a greater chance of positive development in homes where both father and mother assumed parenting responsibilities within the marriage covenant.

Research *substantiated* that a father's death did not cause as many negative consequences as a father who abandoned his children. Social scientists revealed that the influence of a deceased parent lingered in the household where pictures and positive conversations about Mother or Father could be heard. Teens from single-parent homes became successful when they identified with and came under the influence of positive male role models who helped establish a set of positive core values. Such organizations as Teen Missions, Campus Life, AWANA, Boy Scouts, Big Brothers/Sisters, and Teen Challenge established programs to help single parent at-risk youth identify with positive role models and alternatives to negative circumstances in homes.

Divorce and single-parent households were not the only major changes to the American family during recent decades. Until the 1960s, parents, children, and grandparents usually lived near one another. Aunts, uncles, and cousins often *comprised* the *extended family*, all living under the same roof or in nearby communities. By 2000, parents and adult children were likely to live on separate coasts rather than down the street. Only about one-eighth of all elderly parents in America lived with one of their sons or daughters. About 5% lived in nursing homes or similar institutions and about 10% of elderly Americans lived in retirement communities. Most senior adults lived alone in their own homes or apartments. Children seldom saw grandparents.

The most vocal opponents to the traditional family were homosexuals. In the 1990s, "gays" sought same-sex marriage licenses. Some lower state courts ruled that same-sex couples could be legally wed. More than 37 states launched efforts to outlaw same-sex marriages. Numerous states forbid such unions. In 1996, the U.S. Congress passed the Defense of Marriage Act, which did not obligate states to recognize same-sex marriages in other states.

By 2000, the modern American families were sitting on a crust of shifting values and structures. Social changes over the past 35 years had redefined the family, many times with disastrous results. Senator

VOCABULARY

Familial: having to do with family
Substantiated: proved, provided supporting evidence
Comprised: consisted of; made up of
Extended family: persons such as cousins grandparents, aunts, uncles
Trimester: 3-month section of time (often referred to in correlation with pregnancy)
Recant: to admit fault, retract statement
Age: era, time in history

Phil Gramm of Texas defended the Defense of Marriage Act by saying, *"The traditional family has stood for 5,000 years. Are we so wise today that we are ready to reject 5,000 years of recorded history? I don't think so."*

Senator Gramm's sentiments were overwhelmingly supported in the California primary election of 2000 with the adoption of Proposition 22, which stated that only marriage between a man and a woman would be recognized as legal.

While families were being defined and redefined, mothers were deciding if they would begin a family at all.

AMERICA DIVIDES OVER THE UNBORN CHILD

No issue wrenched more emotion from 20th century American families than abortion. The landmark Supreme Court case of Roe vs. Wade in 1973 legalized abortions. From that time, 40 million babies were aborted in America. By 2000 two strongly defined sides debated the abortion issue—the pro-life side (those who were *against* abortion), and pro-choice side (those who *favored* abortion).

Most pro-life proponents believed that any abortion was murder. Medical technology had advanced to allow second and third *trimester* (4-7 months) premature babies to grow into healthy children. Sonograms revealed that after only a few weeks, a fetus had small hands, feet and a head. Consequently, many Americans intensely questioned the morality of late-to-full-term abortions.

One of the most surprising people to question the morality of abortion was the woman behind the famous Roe vs. Wade case. In 1973, Norma McCorvey, known then as "Jane Roe," claimed her unwanted pregnancy was due to a gang-rape. In 1995, McCorvey, then working as a marketing director for a Dallas, Texas abortion clinic, admitted she lied about the rape. She **recanted** her position on abortion, had a religious experience, and transformed into a pro-life advocate. Her conversion to Judeo-Christian beliefs came as a result of an invitation to church by an eight-year-old girl. Interestingly, the young girl had almost been aborted by her mother.

McCorvey's change of principles was reflected in a poem she wrote:

I sit across from a playground that I visited this eve with a small child.
I know of such places where children play.
I know that I am the cause of them not being here today.
I hope, Lord, that the wonderful playground You have is well guarded with angels.
So that, when that glorious day comes; the children will not hold this sin against me.
All I did was give my baby away, so that women could tear theirs apart.
For this I will never be able to look You in the face without shame.

—*Empty Playgrounds* by Norma McCorvey

Her poem inspired the popular song *Empty Playgrounds* produced by popular music artist Phil Keaggy.

The abortion issue remained a controversial topic throughout the 1990s. Both the pro-life and pro-choice movements assumed strong and determined positions. Some extreme pro-life proponents expressed their opposition by bombing abortion clinics and shooting abortion doctors. The majority of pro-life proponents condemned these extreme measures. One of the leading pro-life advocates, Dr. James Dobson of Focus On The Family, also condemned the extreme measures, but stated, *"The most cruel moral issue of this **age** is abortion; if all the aborted babies had names printed on a wall like the Vietnam Memorial, the wall would extend 50 miles and include names of more than 30 million murdered babies."*

The National Organization for Women (NOW) and the Clinton administration argued that unborn babies were not humans and thus were not murdered when aborted. By 2000, however, the mood of the country had begun to swing back toward traditional families, moral values and religious interests, causing an increased public disapproval of abortion. Twice congress passed legislation prohibiting late term abortions, but President Clinton used his veto power to kill both bills.

Religion is a dynamic force in America. Read the next vignette to understand its impact on American families.

Life Principle

"When you put faith, hope and love together, you can be positive in a negative world."

-Zig Ziglar

The Defending of America

Topic 15
*Religion &
Celebrations*

Chapter 12

RELIGION IN
AMERICA—
THE CUTTING
EDGE

Section Three
Topics 11-15

In the 1880s, a lawyer named Robert Ingersoll announced that *"the churches are dying out all over the land."* He said this with great satisfaction, for Ingersoll was the nation's official atheistic skeptic—a man who built a second career on attempting to *debunk* Christianity.

If Ingersoll had been alive in 2000, he would have been sorely disappointed, for religion had not died in America. In fact, pollsters of the 1980s and 1990s disclosed that most Americans believed in God. Supreme Court Justice William O. Douglas wrote that *"we are a religious people whose institutions presuppose a supreme being."*

In 1980, surveys revealed that a third of America's population identified with "born-again" Christianity. In 1991, research by City University of New York showed that nearly 90% of Americans identified themselves as Christians or Jews; only 7.5% claimed no religious beliefs at all. Clearly, religion was far from dead in the United States by the 21st century.

The 1980s saw the political rise of the so-called *Religious Right*, a media term for conservative Christians. School violence, abortions, drug and alcohol abuse, divorce, pornography and political scandals caused such organizations as the Moral Majority, Eagle Forum, The Christian Coalition and the Family Research Council to express their concerns. Jerry Falwell, pastor of the 22,000-member Thomas Road Baptist Church in Lynchburg, Virginia formed the Moral Majority. Falwell stated that he wanted to *"rally together the people of this country who still believe in decency, the home, the family, morality, the free enterprise system, and all the great ideals that are the cornerstone of this nation."*

In 1988, the founder of the *700 Club* television program, Pat Robertson, made a Republican bid for the office of U.S. President. Voters did not take him seriously until he scored impressive victories in several state primary elections. Republicans did not nominate Robertson, but he poured his

VOCABULARY

Debunk: to prove as false
Rally: to gather for a cause
Decency: moral goodness
Astute: keen insight and understanding
Affair: a program or situation of importance
Prudent: to make decisions based on character
Premises: territories, areas
Inscription: writing—usually on a hard surface such as a stone tablet or plaque
Baby boomers: Americans who were born between 1946–1964
Mainstream: the majority of a certain aspect of society

energy into forming the Christian Coalition, an activist organization that described itself as pro-family and pro-life. Ralph Reed assumed the post of Executive Director. Behind the boyish grin of Reed buzzed the mind of an *astute* political strategist. With laser-like focus, he forged the Christian Coalition into a powerful grassroots movement of 1,700,000 members who became active and informed voters. Abortion and the family were not Reed's only concerns. In 1996, America was reeling in the wake of church fire bombings that targeted black congregations in the South. The Coalition offered a $25,000 reward for information leading to the arrest of anyone involved in attacking U.S. churches. In addition, the Coalition formed the "Save Our Churches Fund" which helped to restore burned churches of African-American congregations. The Christian Coalition was composed of Whites, Hispanics, African-Americans, Asian-Americans, American Indians and Middle-East Americans who were Protestant, Baptist, Roman Catholic, Greek Orthodox and Jewish in faith.

Recognition of religious influence also came from the U.S. Post Office which acknowledged the contributions of African-American Gospel singers by issuing four new commemorative stamps in July, 1998: Mahalia Jackson, Roberta Martin, Sister Rosetta Tharpe, and Clara Ward. The post office official, Le Gree Daniels said, *"They moved audiences in churches and concert halls, and helped make gospel an important part of American music and popular culture."*

Focus on the Family, founded by James C. Dobson, Ph.D., was another religious organization which influenced America in the 1980s and 1990s. Dobson's books, *Dare To Discipline* and *Love Must Be Tough*, were best sellers. Dobson, a Christian psychologist, began airing a weekly radio broadcast in 1977, addressing issues concerning the American family. By 2000, over 4,600 stations carried Dobson's syndicated radio programs in 95 countries around the world. Dobson claimed that Focus on the Family was *"dedicated to the preservation and strengthening of the home."*

In addition to his daily radio program, Dobson became involved in national social issues when several U.S. Presidents appointed him to special task forces on family topics. Focus on the Family influenced social issues nationwide. Readers and listeners applied Dobson's books to family and community *affairs.* Dobson's broadcasts often generated thousands of phone calls and letters designed to influence Congress to favor pro-family legislation.

Some liberal commentators became alarmed over conservative Christians getting involved in social and political issues. Liberals maintained that religious principles

LEGENDS OF AMERICAN MUSIC SERIES

Gospel Singers

should be a private matter with no bearing on government, schools or society. A number of liberal editorialists used their media columns to oppose politically-active Christians. Robert H. Meneilly, writing for the *New York Times*, said, *"The religious right confronts us with a threat far greater than the old threat of Communism."* Another *Times* writer commented, *"The Christian Coalition is one of the most dangerous forces on the American scene today."*

Respected Commentator Cal Thomas argued that Judeo-Christian voters were a balance to secular humanists. William Federer, an astute historian, responded to columnist Meneilly by quoting John Witherspoon in a speech delivered in 1776, *"If your cause is just, if your principles are pure, and if your conduct is **prudent**, you need not fear the multitude of opposing hosts . . . he is the best friend to American liberty, who is most sincere and active in promoting true and undefiled religion, and who sets himself with the greatest firmness to bear down profanity and immorality of every kind."*

One of the most volatile church-state issues in the last three decades of the 20th century was school prayer. The American Civil Liberties Union (ACLU) repeatedly defended the 1962 Supreme Court decision that banned prayer in public schools. Some ACLU proponents insisted that schools and government buildings should remove all traces of religion from their **premises**, including nativity scenes, religious **inscriptions**, even the words *In God We Trust* from American coins.

The ACLU historically opposed any public display of Judeo-Christian beliefs and symbols on government property, including schools. Long time ACLU Director Roger Baldwin (1920-1955) openly embraced atheistic communism and called for total elimination of Judeo-Christian influence in American culture.

Christian activists believed that teachers, students and officials had the Constitutional right to hold Bible studies and religious rallies on public grounds. Recent Supreme Court decisions established that public school students were permitted to read the Bible, pray and discuss religious issues as long as such student led activities did not disrupt the educational process. The American Center for Law and Justice (ACLJ) actively defended Christians and Jews who were prohibited by school officials from practicing Judeo-Christian beliefs at public schools.

While Judeo-Christian principles were being challenged, the so-called *New Age Movement* offered Americans a spiritual smorgasbord, including witchcraft, crystal healing, astral projection and other non-traditional options. Hinduism and Buddhism, two major Eastern world religions, experienced some growth in the 1990s. Islam followers more than doubled in America from 1980-1990. In some regions, Islam was the fastest growing religion.

Louis Farrakhan, a black Nation of Islam leader, grabbed America's attention in the 1980s with his controversial anti-white remarks. Branding Judaism a *"gutter religion"* and saying that the *"time of doom"* had arrived for whites, Farrakhan attracted disenchanted inner-city blacks. Some black followers defended Farrakhan's racist remarks because he also advocated personal responsibility, self reliance and unity among blacks. However, his "hate speeches" regarding whites and Jews alarmed many Americans—both black and white.

On October 16, 1995, hundreds of thousands of black men converged in Washington, D.C. for Farrakhan's *Million Man March*. The march did not attract a million men and it sharply divided the black community. Some black Christian leaders would not endorse the march, while the Jewish Anti-Defamation League accused Farrakhan of being racist, sexist and anti-Christian. In September 2000 Farrakhan called on muslims to make the United States a muslim nation.

Throughout the 20th century Christianity remained the dominant faith in America. A 1993 study showed the following breakdown:

Christian	86.5%
Jewish	2.4%
Non-religious	8.7%
Muslim	1.8%
Buddhist	0.4%
Hindu	0.2%
Baha'i	0.02%

In the early 1990s, some of the old mainline denominations, such as Methodists and Presbyterians, became painfully aware that they had been losing members for two decades. While some had migrated into non-traditional, non-denominational conduct vast numbers were returning to *that old-time religion*—with a new twist.

Realizing that **baby boomers** and their children were often absent from church pews, some pastors began addressing family issues while spicing up their worship services with multimedia and upbeat music. Willow Creek Community Church in South Barrington, Illinois attracted more than 14,000 people every Sunday. Texas Pastors John Hagee of San Antonio, and Tony Evans of Oakcliff, offered Biblical guidance for building strong families, while hammering the homosexual community and evolutionists as enemies of American families. Other issue-oriented preachers who attracted audiences that numbered in the thousands included Charles Stanley at Atlanta's First Baptist Church,

James Kennedy of Coral Ridge Presbyterian Church, and Dr. E.V. Hill and Robert Schuller from Los Angeles.

A quieter and more reserved method of promoting Biblical principles was introduced by Bill Gothard through the Institute In Basic Life Principles (IBLP). Gothard conducted week long seminars for youth and adults who wanted to learn practical applications of Bible principles to everyday life circumstances: how to overcome anger, bitterness, rejection, abuse, divorce and addiction. Gothard offered practical Biblical guidelines for handling finances, maintaining marriages and building positive relationships. The IBLP attracted crowds ranging from a few thousand to 27,000. More than 2,500,000 people had attended Gothard's IBLP seminars by the dawn of the 21st century.

Another religious movement that drew large crowds among all ethnic groups in the '90s was the Promise Keepers. Launched in 1991 by Colorado University football coach Bill McCartney, Promise Keepers sponsored huge rallies throughout the nation to strengthen religious and family commitments of men. The first rally, held at the University of Colorado, drew 4,200 attendees. By 1998, Promise Keepers had attracted more than 2,000,000 men to stadium rallies through a high-energy blend of *Praise Music*—music composed specifically for worshiping and praising God—testimonies and no-nonsense preaching that focused on commitment to marriage vows and positive treatment of wives and children based on Biblical structure of the family.

Women also attended seminars on "Godly" living—how to be wives and mothers based on Biblical premises. More than 53,000 women attended an Atlanta, Georgia conference to hear T.D. Jakes, an African-American counselor and seminar speaker, discuss ways to build strong families. His book, *The Lady, Her Lover, and Her Lord* was a best seller in 1998.

Religious TV programs increased dramatically during the 1980s and '90s. Paul Crouch started the Trinity Broadcasting Network (TBN) in 1973 with one station in southern California. By 2000, more than 700 television stations worldwide were broadcasting TBN programs featuring application of Biblical principles to such varied topics as medical problems, marriage conflicts, family relationships. expressions of joy and man's quest to know God.

One of the most popular means of conveying the role of religion was *Jesus,* a video produced by Campus Crusade for Christ International. By January, 1999, the film had been seen by more than 1,623,129,222 viewers in 222 countries. The film depicted the life of Jesus and His message of love and forgiveness.

The Christian Broadcasting Network (CBN) was another religious television network which appealed to millions of viewers. Lawyer—turned evangelist—Pat Robertson began CBN with one station in 1962. By 1999, the main CBN program, called the "700 Club", was seen daily by more than 1,000,000 viewers. The show format consisted of a mixture of information, interviews and inspiration on topics ranging from sports, law enforcement, parenting, debt, music, voting and marriage.

What will be the future of religion in America? Followers of Robert Ingersoll and Roger Baldwin might contend that science and education will eventually disprove belief in a supreme, supernatural Being. But most Americans believed otherwise at the dawning of the 21st century. *Mainstream* America still embraced the national motto, "In God We Trust."

Senator John Glenn looked out of the *Discovery* space ship window as it orbited Earth in November 1998 and said, "to look at the window . . . as I did that first day . . . to look out at this kind of creation and not believe in God is to me impossible."

Religion is part of what made America. It is etched into our coins, written into our Pledge of Allegiance, and belted out in such national songs as "God Bless America" and "My Country, 'Tis of Thee." Americans even have a National Day of Prayer. While some citizens railed against religion, they could not deny the force it has exerted in shaping *The People, Places and Principles of America*.

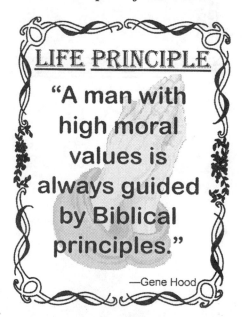

LIFE PRINCIPLE

"A man with high moral values is always guided by Biblical principles."

—Gene Hood

Congratulations! You have successfully completed *The People, Places and Principles of America*. You have a better understanding of your American heritage and now greater responsibility rests on you. The future of the United States may well be determined by your decisions as you reach adulthood, become a voter and contribute to the American dream. Practice your citizenship carefully, for your children will live under the people and principles you endorse.

—Ronald E. Johnson, Publisher

The People, Places and Principles of America

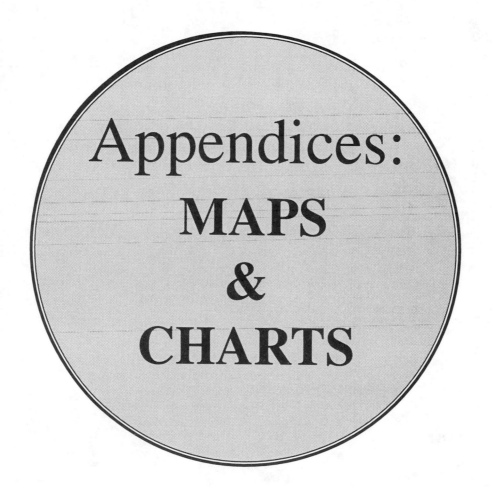

Appendices:
MAPS
&
CHARTS

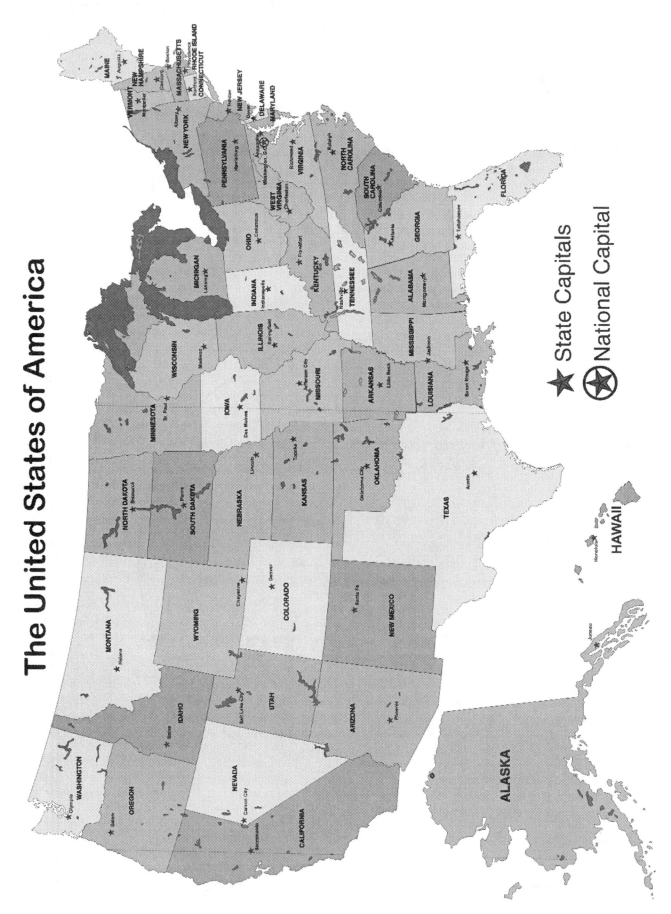

The United States of America

★ State Capitals
⊛ National Capital

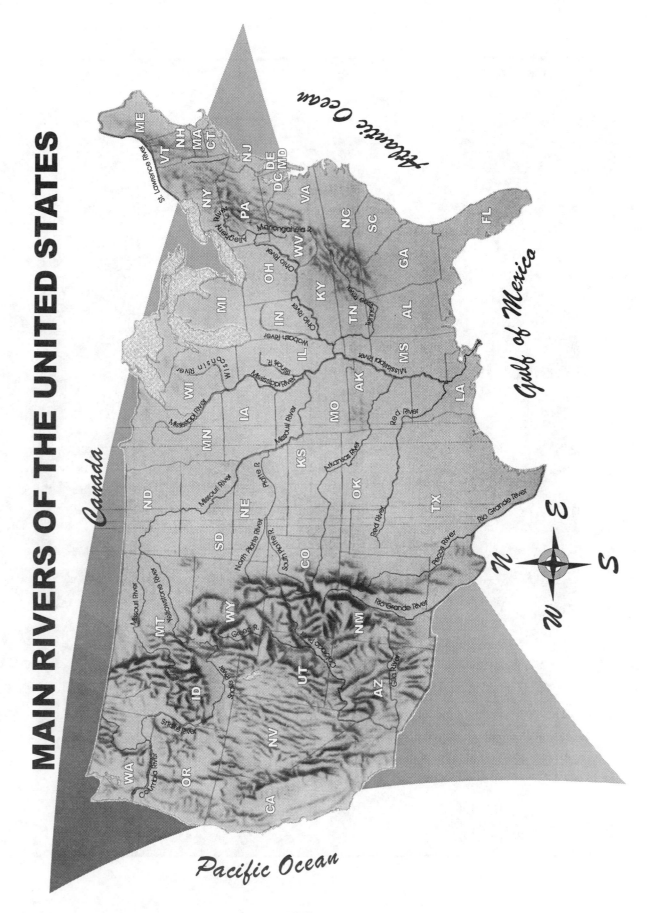

MAIN RIVERS OF THE UNITED STATES

Territorial Growth of the United States

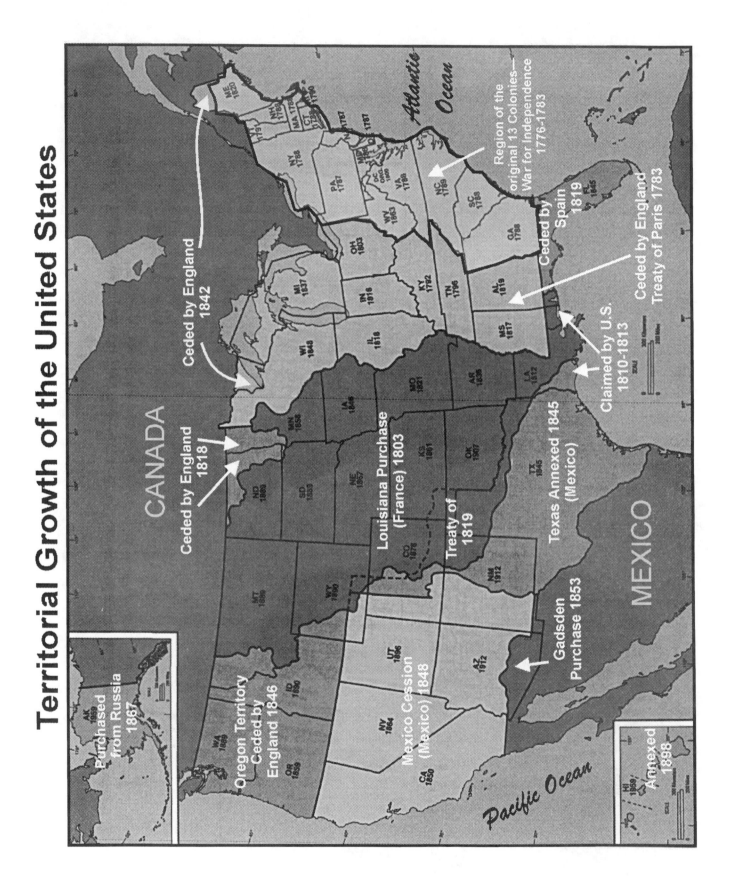

STATES OF THE UNITED STATES

★ ★

States (Abbr.)	Admitted to Union	State Capitals
Alabama (AL)	1819	Montgomery
Alaska (AK)	1959	Juneau
Arizona (AZ)	1912	Phoenix
Arkansas (AR)	1836	Little Rock
California (CA)	1850	Sacramento
Colorado (CO)	1876	Denver
Connecticut (CT)	1788	Hartford
Delaware (DE)	1787	Dover
Florida (FL)	1845	Tallahassee
Georgia (GA)	1788	Atlanta
Hawaii (HI)	1959	Honolulu
Idaho (ID)	1890	Boise
Illinois (IL)	1818	Springfield
Indiana (IN)	1816	Indianapolis
Iowa (IA)	1846	Des Monies
Kansas (KS)	1861	Topeka
Kentucky (KY)	1792	Frankfort
Louisiana (LA)	1812	Baton Rouge
Maine (ME)	1820	Augusta
Maryland (MD)	1788	Annapolis
Massachusetts (MA)	1788	Boston
Michigan (MI)	1837	Lansing
Minnesota (MN)	1858	St. Paul
Mississippi (MS)	1817	Jackson
Missouri (MO)	1821	Jefferson City

States (Abbr.)	Admitted to Union	State Capitals
Montana (MT)	1889	Helena
Nebraska (NE)	1867	Lincoln
Nevada (NV)	1864	Carson City
New Hampshire (NH)	1788	Concord
New Jersey (NJ)	1787	Trenton
New Mexico (NM)	1912	Santa Fe
New York (NY)	1788	Albany
North Carolina (NC)	1789	Raleigh
North Dakota (ND)	1889	Bismarck
Ohio (OH)	1803	Columbus
Oklahoma (OK)	1907	Oklahoma City
Oregon (OR)	1859	Salem
Pennsylvania (PA)	1787	Harrisburg
Rhode Island (RI)	1790	Providence
South Carolina (SC)	1788	Columbia
South Dakota (SD)	1889	Pierre
Tennessee (TN)	1796	Nashville
Texas (TX)	1845	Austin
Utah (UT)	1896	Salt Lake City
Vermont (VT)	1791	Montpelier
Virginia (VA)	1788	Richmond
Washington (WA)	1889	Olympia
West Virginia (WV)	1863	Charleston
Wisconsin (WI)	1848	Madison
Wyoming (WY)	1890	Cheyenne
District of Columbia (DC)	1790	National Capital

UNITED STATES PRESIDENTS
1789-2000

George Washington
1732-1799
Born in Virginia
No political party
President: 1789-1797

John Adams
1735-1826
Born in Massachusetts
Federalist
President: 1797-1801

Thomas Jefferson
1743-1826
Born in Virginia
Democratic-Republican
President: 1801-1809

James Madison
1751-1836
Born in Virginia
Democratic-Republican
President: 1809-1817

James Monroe
1757-1831
Born in Virginia
Democratic-Republican
President: 1817-1825

John Quincy Adams
1767-1848
Born in Massachusetts
Democratic-Republican
President: 1825-1829

Andrew Jackson
1767-1845
Born in South Carolina
Democrat
President: 1829-1837

Martin Van Buren
1782-1862
Born in New York
Democrat
President: 1837-1841

William Henry Harrison
1773-1841
Born in Virginia
Whig
President: Mar. 4-Apr. 4, 1841

John Tyler
1790-1862
Born in Virginia
Whig
President: 1841-1845

James J. Polk
1795-1849
Born in North Carolina
Democrat
President: 1845-1849

Zachary Taylor
1784-1850
Born in Virginia
Whig
President: 1849-1850

Millard Fillmore
1800-1875
Born in New York
Whig
President: 1850-1853

Franklin Pierce
1804-1869
Born in New Hampshire
Democrat
President: 1853-1857

James Buchanan
1791-1868
Born in Pennsylvania
Democrat
President: 1857-1861

Abraham Lincoln
1809-1865
Born in Kentucky
Republican
President: 1861-1865

Andrew Johnson
1808-1875
Born in North Carolina
Democrat
President: 1865-1869

Ulysses S. Grant
1822-1885
Born in Ohio
Republican
President: 1869-1877

Rutherford B. Hayes
1822-1893
Born in Ohio
Republican
President: 1877-1881

James A. Garfield
1831-1881
Born in Ohio
Republican
President: March 4-Sept. 19, 1881

Chester A. Arthur
1829-1886
Born in Vermont
Republican
President: 1881-1885

Grover Cleveland
1837-1908
Born in New Jersey
Democrat
President: 1885-1889

Benjamin Harrison
1833-1901
Born in Ohio
Republican
President: 1889-1893

Grover Cleveland
1837-1908
Born in New Jersey
Democrat
President: 1893-1897

William McKinley
1843-1901
Born in Ohio
Republican
President: 1897-1901

Theodore Roosevelt
1858-1919
Born in New York
Republican
President: 1901-1909

William Howard Taft
1857-1930
Born in Ohio
Republican
President: 1909-1913

Woodrow Wilson
1856-1924
Born in Virginia
Democrat
President: 1913-1921

UNITED STATES PRESIDENTS
1789-2000

Warren G. Harding
1865-1923
Born in Ohio
Republican
President: 1921-1923

Calvin Coolidge
1872-1933
Born in Vermont
Republican
President: 1923-1929

Herbert Hoover
1874-1964
Born in Iowa
Republican
President: 1929-1933

Franklin D. Roosevelt
1882-1945
Born in New York
Democrat
President: 1933-1945

Harry S. Truman
1884-1972
Born in Missouri
Democrat
President: 1945-1953

Dwight D. Eisenhower
1890-1969
Born in Texas
Republican
President: 1953-1961

John F. Kennedy
1917-1963
Born in Massachusetts
Democrat
President: 1961-1963

Lyndon B. Johnson
1908-1973
Born in Texas
Democrat
President: 1963-1969

Richard M. Nixon
1913-1994
Born in California
Republican
President: 1969-1974

Gerald R. Ford
1913-
Born in Nebraska
Republican
President: 1974-1977

James E. Carter, Jr.
1924-
Born in Georgia
Democrat
President: 1977-1981

Ronald W. Reagan
1911-
Born in Illinois
Republican
President: 1981-1989

George H. Bush
1924-
Born in Massachusetts
Republican
President: 1989-1993

William J. Clinton
1946-
Born in Arkansas
Democrat
President: 1993-2000

INDEX

U

V

W

XYZ